WALKS OF
THE PACIFIC
NORTHWEST

WALKS OF THE PACIFIC NORTHWEST

GARY FERGUSON

Illustrated by Kent Humphreys
Research Coordinated by Jane Ferguson

PRENTICE
HALL
PRESS

New York   London   Toronto   Sydney   Tokyo   Singapore

PRENTICE HALL PRESS
15 Columbus Circle
New York, NY 10023

Copyright © 1991 by Gary Ferguson

PRENTICE HALL PRESS and colophon are registered trademarks
of Simon & Schuster, Inc.

Library of Congress Cataloging in Publication Data

Ferguson, Gary, 1956–
Walks of the Pacific Northwest / Gary Ferguson : illustrated by
Kent Humphreys ; research coordinated by Jane Ferguson.
        p.   cm.
ISBN 0-13-945080-7
1. Walking—Northwest, Pacific—Guide-books.   2. Hiking—
Northwest, Pacific—Guide-books.   3. Northwest, Pacific—
Description and travel—1981–   —Guide-books.   I. Ferguson, Jane.
II. Title.
GV199.42.N69F47   1991
917.95—dc20   90-46213
                                                                CIP

Designed by Irving Perkins Associates

Manufactured in the United States of America

10 9 8 7 6 5 4 3 2

First Edition

To Ken, Bernie, Janice, Steve, John,
Cheryl, Joan, Chuck, and Brady.

And to Stanley, Idaho—the best town
this kid ever had.

Contents

THE COAST 81

THE MOUNTAINS 143

Washington

Oregon

Idaho

THE DESERT 219

Introduction

If I were allowed just one last, grand dance across the great natural areas of the world, certainly some of my first steps would be through the 250,000 square miles of mountains, forests, coast, and desert that mark the American Northwest. Within this vast landscape is a staggering range of ecosystems, broad and deep enough to please the most discriminating nature lover. In western Washington you'll find the largest mountain glacier system in the continental United States, while within a day's drive to the southeast is the deepest major river gorge on the North American continent, patiently slicing its way through the dry, tawny hills of Idaho. Here it's possible to watch the sun rise across one of the largest volcanic plateaus in the world, and by the afternoon be wrapped in a cool fern garden at the feet of a thousand-year-old forest of western red cedar and Douglas-fir. In May you can walk across snow twenty feet deep in the Cascades, and then head east a short distance into a braid of parched desert canyons, quiet but for the sound of hot winds hissing past their smooth, varnished walls. And there is still more: rain forests, sand dunes, estuaries, and alpine meadows; coastal blowholes and volcanic blow downs; waterfalls, marshes, and deep glacial lakes.

Political and economic motives aside, it seems there has always been a sense of grand possibility about the Northwest, of wild secrets waiting to be uncovered. When Captain James Cook arrived off the coast of Vancouver Island in the spring of 1778, he came as an explorer, geographer, and scientist, bent on ultimately unraveling one of the most exciting puzzles in the civilized world—the whereabouts of the fabled Northwest Passage. Just twenty-seven years later Lewis and Clark set out on their great overland journey to the Pacific. It was another trek of grand discoveries—one that would again catch the spirit of a nation.

It wasn't long before others made the decision to see the lands of the Northwest for themselves. By the time John Fremont began his trailblazing expeditions in the 1840s, interest in the Northwest was already reaching a swell. While bad economic conditions and a series of flood-related disasters helped give many people a push toward greener pastures, there were many others who just plain liked the whole idea of heading west. Wealthy entrepreneur Nathaniel Wyeth, who helped popularize the route that would later become the Oregon Trail, expressed the feelings brewing inside of thousands of easterners itching to head for Oregon. "I cannot divest myself of the opinion," he wrote, "that I shall compete better with my fellow men in new and untried paths than in those which require only patience and attention."

Of course it didn't hurt to have a good publicity department, and in that the Northwest never seemed to be lacking. In 1839, Horace Greeley ("Go west young man!") hired writer Thomas Farnham to make a trip to the Willamette Valley and share his experiences with those readers who might be interested in making a similar journey. "To conclude," Farnham says in the last paragraph of his *Wagon Train Journal,* "few portions of the globe are so capable of being rendered the happy abode of an industrious and civilized community. . . . No portion of the world beyond the tropics can be found that will yield so readily with moderate labor, to the wants of man."

Say no more. Between 1840 and 1860, more than 50,000 people made their way along that long, dusty trail from the Missouri River into the Oregon Territory.

Sadly, the fevered pace at which the Northwest was settled, going in eighty years from an uncharted wilderness to a rather vigorous economic center, has not been without cost to the wild spirit of the land. Until very recently, conservation has not been a legacy of the Northwest. Minerals were pulled from the mines of Idaho with utter abandon. The air and water were badly poisoned by smelting operations and tailings piles—many of which remain serious problems to the health of residents to this day. And while logging may well be the economic lifeblood of western Oregon and Washington, the logging companies' insistence on cutting and burning under shorter and shorter rotation periods has turned millions of acres of rich forest into little more than tree farms. (There have been periods over the past forty years where some species, such as Sitka spruce, were harvested at a rate more than ten times their annual growth rate.) This is hardly just an aesthetic problem. The truth is that homogeneous forests are far less stable than are those cut by means of selective harvesting.

Fortunately, all is not lost. The sheer vastness of this region, combined with a changing philosophy of resource management, has left literally thousands of square miles of rich, unfettered landscapes open to anyone who would merely set his or her feet to walking. This book is meant to be a celebration of those places—a guide to reconnecting with the calm and the beauty, the rhythm and the rhyme that come from this good land.

To that end you'll find the walks that follow are not so much concerned with destinations as they are with journeys; indeed, the turnaround points for many are rather arbitrary. These small slices of trail were chosen not so much because they led to the biggest, tallest, or best of any one thing, but rather because they served as quiet, yet engaging introductions to the secrets that seem to shimmer beneath these coasts, mountains, deserts, and forests. Do note that all of the distances listed for the walks are round-trip mileages; the vast majority can easily be lengthened.

Thomas Huxley once said that to a person unfamiliar with natural history, "his country or seaside stroll is a walk through a gallery filled with wonderful works of art, nine-tenths of which have their faces to the wall." And yet real familiarity with the natural world—the kind that feeds not only the head but also the heart—is to a great extent based simply on your own personal relationship with nature, on what Thoreau once described as being "conscious of a friendliness in her." This book is meant to take you to places where such friendships come easy—where the land is alive, and the ground rolls gently underfoot.

THE FOREST

To a great many lovers of the out-of-doors, the term "Northwest" is another word for trees—vast sweeps of western hemlock and Douglas-fir huddled against the shoulders of a quiet trail, gentle flows of red alder running like dappled gray rivers down the moist lowland valleys to the sea, hushed groves of western red cedar spiked by the soft flutter of maple leaves. Filling in as background for these daydreams are lush cloaks of shrubs and flowers: huckleberries, ocean-sprays, rhododendrons, currants, and blackberries; trilliums, violets, buttercups, pipsissewas, and false lily-of-the-valleys. There can be no doubt that for the most part, our fantasies of the Northwest tend to be rich and fertile ones, reflections of the fact that in certain portions of this region can be found what are arguably the most beautiful, most diverse coniferous forests in the world.

Besides the obvious beauty of such places, perhaps there's some kind of reassurance to be found in a land that can sprout trees like winter wheat, a land that provides its wild inhabitants with such feasts of berries and insects and seeds. Much of this great gush of life is, as you might have guessed, thanks to the influence of the sea. The Pacific Ocean moderates temperatures, and delivers oodles of moisture in the form of rain, snow, and fog. These conditions allow life in these great coniferous forests to run with total abandon, to achieve what is surely the ultimate expression of the forest primeval. Six of the dozen most-common conifers in a Northwest coastal forest live for 500 years—a rate of longevity almost unheard of anywhere else. Even the shortest-lived species—the grand fir—can hang on for an impressive 300 years.

Once you move away from the coast, past the rugged wall of the Cascade Range that grabs so much moisture from the skies— once you lose the temperature-moderating effects of the ocean, the complexion of the Northwest forests changes dramatically. We have then the stately ponderosa pine parks in Oregon's Wallowa Mountains, mountain meadows in central Idaho framed by dark huddles of subalpine fir. To many, it's these more loosely woven forests that are the real highlights of the Northwest. Indeed, the silhouette of even one lone curl-leaf mahogany hanging from the steep brown slope of a high desert canyon can reach out and grab you every bit as much as can the trunk of a mammoth western red cedar rising through the gray soup of a coastal fog.

As you walk through the forests that follow, you may enjoy examining the different "layers" you'll find growing there. In much the same way that different life zones run up a mountain, offering birds and animals different niches to live in, so do the different canopy layers of a forest offer very different places for the residents to feed, nest, and even conduct their courtship rituals. In some cases this specialization becomes a rather fine art. For example, in the coastal forests of Oregon and Washington, the territories of the black-capped chickadee and chestnut-backed chickadee overlap. To settle the matter, the two birds have developed a rather sporting arrangement wherein the black-capped feeds in the lower portions of the tree, and the chestnut-backed takes to the top. This is a fine example of how nature is far less a cutthroat struggle between species than it is an attempt to actually minimize such struggles by evolving into specific, noncompetitive niches.

Something else you'll notice on these forest walks is that the tune these plants must dance to is largely called by the blend of sunlight and moisture. A south-facing slope in Idaho's Pioneer Mountains will dry out much faster than will its north-facing counterpart, giving rise to a much different composition and density of plants. A young hemlock may slowly work its way up into the most shaded tree canopy, while its neighbor, the Douglas-fir, won't be able to reproduce until there's enough of an opening in the tree canopy to let sunlight through. Such patterns are important clues to what's really going on in a forest: precious toeholds from which you can begin to see the real genius of natural design.

Washington

LAKE TERRELL
WILDLIFE AREA

Distance: 0.8 mile
Location: From Interstate 5 north of Bellingham, take the Ferndale exit, and head west for 4.5 miles to Lake Terrell Road. Turn
right. In 0.4 mile you'll see a small parking area at the south edge
of Lake Terrell. Park here, and begin your walk on a dirt road that
runs along the lake shore.

Sandwiched between a grid of country farm roads, Lake Terrell isn't
exactly a source of dramatic inspiration. Yet anyone who loves
waterfowl—the quack of harlequin ducks or the white flash of whistling swans—will find this to be one of the more charming, and often
uncrowded nooks in all of northwest Washington. In fact, Lake
Terrell currently plays host to every species of duck found in this
portion of the state.

In the fall Lake Terrell is the first stopover point for thousands
of waterfowl heading south out of British Columbia along the Pacific
Flyway. Although the hunting that is allowed during this time of year
on about half of the reserve may dissuade some from visiting then, an
autumn visit can actually be delightful. On any given day, 5,000
birds may drop out of the sky into this pocket of wood and wetland,
turning it into an absolute spectacle of migration. As you'll see along

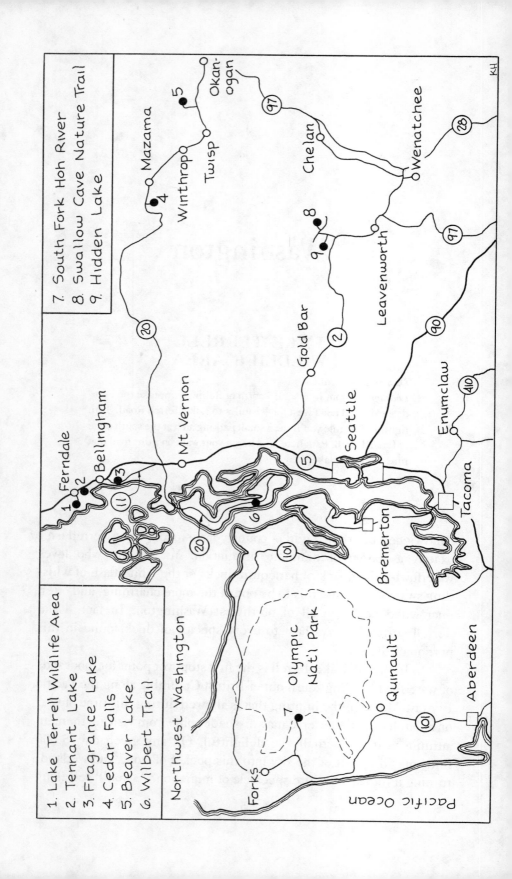

7. South Fork Hoh River
8. Swallow Cave Nature Trail
9. Hidden Lake

1. Lake Terrell Wildlife Area
2. Tennant Lake
3. Fragrance Lake
4. Cedar Falls
5. Beaver Lake
6. Wilbert Trail

Northwest Washington

Pacific Ocean

Okanogan
Mazama
Twisp
Winthrop
Chelan
Wenatchee
Leavenworth
Gold Bar
Mt Vernon
Bellingham
Ferndale
Seattle
Bremerton
Tacoma
Enumclaw
Olympic Nat'l Park
Quinault
Forks
Aberdeen

97
28
97
90
410
2
5
20
20
101
101

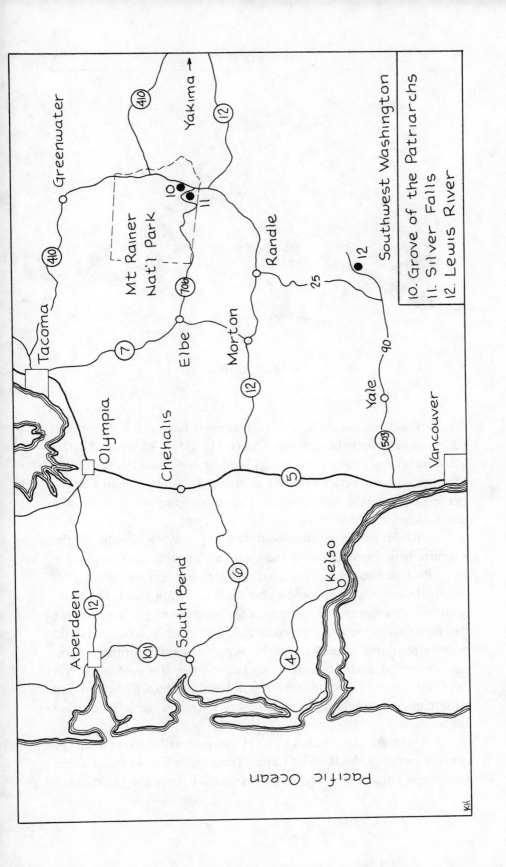

Southwest Washington

10. Grove of the Patriarchs
11. Silver Falls
12. Lewis River

Raccoon

the back side of the walk, refuge managers have planted corn and barley to help fuel these hungry fliers. (In 1989, 4.5 tons of barley alone was planted over sixty acres.) Late each evening, well after the October sun has set, thousands of mallards, pintails, and Canada geese can be heard waddling into the surrounding fields to begin a night of unfettered feasting.

While winter, spring, and summer may lack some of the magnitude of the migration parade, they are nonetheless fine times to visit. Blue herons are fishing, and northern harriers are sailing over the fields and wetlands looking for mice or young birds. Raccoons scour the shoreline for frogs, grebes fast-step across the water trying like mad to become airborne, coots dive for dinner, and beavers build ever-better dams. (Speaking of beavers, not long ago refuge managers removed a dam here that was causing flooding problems. Not only did the incensed rodents rebuild a three-foot high, ten-foot wide dam in a single night, but this time they wove a thorny rose bush into it!)

Our walk begins along a level dirt pathway skirting a narrow corridor between the shore of Lake Terrell and a fine weave of alder, vine maple, blackberry, and pine. The small islands you see sticking out of the water were built expressly to create waterfowl nesting sites out of easy reach of hungry weasels and coyotes. Indeed, nesting is a time of extreme danger for most waterfowl, as it means leaving the safety of open water. Canada geese will sometimes take to high stumps for protection, while mallards have even been known to nest in trees. Vulnerable western grebe chicks spend the first couple weeks of their lives on their parents' backs, riding in a special pouch located between the wing and back feathers. In this way one parent can fish while the youngsters bob around contentedly on the other one's back, far from the hungry jaws of a weasel or the talons of a northern harrier.

Stay along the lake shore for 0.45 mile, at which point you'll reach the paved entry road that leads to the refuge headquarters. Turn left here, and begin a quiet trek past a fine patchwork of vine maples, alders, and blackberries on the left. (For a longer walk, take a right at the pavement and follow the road past the refuge headquarters and onto a dirt road that winds back to yet another Lake Terrell inlet.) You'll notice that in places here the blackberries form extremely dense thickets—a wall of fearsome thorns and barbs that only birds and small mammals manage to penetrate. Besides providing birds and other careful pickers with delicious fruit, man has long used the berries, roots, and leaves of the blackberry to stop diarrhea. And to this day some herbalists prescribe chewing the leaves of the plant as a treatment for bleeding gums.

Yellow-rumped Warbler

All too soon—at 0.8 mile, to be exact—you'll find yourself back at your car. On most days, once around this loop is simply not enough. Head down the path yet again and see all you missed the first time: that little marsh wren scurrying around a huddle of cattails, the fresh tracks of a black-tailed deer in the trailside mud, the trumpeter swan floating on the far side of the lake like a tiny puff of cloud.

TENNANT LAKE

Distance: 0.5 mile
Location: From Interstate 5 north of Bellingham, take exit 262, and head west for 0.5 mile to Hovander Road. Turn left (south). In 0.2 mile turn right onto Nielson Avenue, and follow this for 0.75 mile to the Tennant Lake Interpretive Center parking area. Our walk begins near the interpretive center, beside the large wooden observation tower.

Like Lake Terrell Wildlife Management Area just to the west, Tennant Lake is a bird-lover's dream. Besides an excellent wetland habitat, however, here you'll also have the added delights of an herb garden with plants you can actually touch, as well as a fine interpretive center (open Wednesday through Sunday).

The very beginning of this walk is framed by a fine patch of cattails. Certainly one of the most easily recognized of all wetland plants, for centuries the cattail has had tremendous significance for people around the world. As a food source it is almost unparalleled. The roots can be roasted, the pollen used for flour, the flowers eaten like corn on the cob, and the young shoots eaten raw. Not that this has been just a pantry plant, mind you. The fuzzy down that covers the spikes in the fall was often collected by Northwest mountain men and stuffed into their shoes as an insulator against the cold. Native Americans, on the other hand, used the down as a chafeless diaper wrapping (rather as we use baby powder today), while many cultures

Lesser Scaup

around the world have long found it to be a perfect stuffing for pillows. Native American women also used the leaves to weave mats that would serve as flooring in lodges or sweat houses.

While cattails are particularly good at producing seeds (a quarter of a million seeds on a single spike is not unusual), they also are very adept at creating new plants by sending shoots up from horizontal stems. As you walk past these cattail marshes, keep your eyes open for dome-shaped structures made of mud and various plants. These are the homes of muskrats, who absolutely love the fleshy underwater stems of cattails. This is also a perfect place to see both marsh wrens and red-winged blackbirds.

The stroll along this boardwalk, while short, is nothing less than delightful—a watercolor of wigeons, shovelers, scaups, and teals bobbing on Tennant Lake, and, at least on a clear day, Mount Baker rising thick and white in the eastern sky. On many days the scene is capped off by a red-tailed hawk scanning the surrounding fields for mice, or, just as often, a northern harrier patrolling a patch of reeds for unsuspecting young birds. Whether you know much about how ecosystems work or not, if you sit and watch for a while you can almost feel the interconnectedness that exists between species on this preserve—the interplay of plant and bird, the dance of predator and prey.

Trying to get a handle on which bird is which in a rich wetland like this can be an overwhelming task. One thing you can do to make it easier is to think in terms of habitats. When it comes to feeding, most of the birds here have certain places where they like to look for food. The marsh wren, for example, spends its time hunting insects in thick, low marsh vegetation. In fact, it's the only wren to be found in such places. Northern shovelers, on the other hand, float in shallow places, straining water through their broad shovellike bills. Ruddy ducks are deep water divers; you'll need your binoculars to recognize them bobbing out in the middle of the lake. Both great blue and green herons wade in shallow water or stand on the edge of a bank, ever on the lookout for a fish to gobble. Indeed, the creatures who live here are not in a flurry of competition with each other for the same food source. Instead, they've evolved as specialists, each species capitalizing on what's available in a particular niche of the environment.

In 0.1 mile the boardwalk will split. If you stay to the left, very soon you'll come to a fine observation platform—the perfect place from which to survey this rich braid of marsh and open water environments.

FRAGRANCE LAKE

Distance: 0.9 mile
Location: Larrabee State Park. From Interstate 5 south of Bellingham, Washington, take exit 250, following the signs for Washington State Highway 11. In about 8 miles you'll reach Fragrance Lake Road, on your left. Turn here, and follow the road upward for 2.2 miles to the Fragrance Lake Trailhead.

With the scents of cedar, salt air, and wild rose drifting up the lush hillsides that flank Samish Bay, Fragrance Lake lives up to its name. Established in 1915, this is Washington's very first state park, and a fine preserve it is. The short 0.9 mile loop around this lake is a perfect

12

trek for slow goers—those who can appreciate rubbing noses lei-surely with sword ferns, cedars, broadleaf maples, and firs, as well as with fine seasonal eruptions of trilliums, bleeding hearts, currants, columbines, skunk cabbages, and calypso orchids.

From the parking area it's a quick 0.2-mile descent to the junction with the trail that loops around the lake. Stay right here, and at 0.3 mile pass a beautiful patch of salal growing thick and leathery along the right side of the trail. If you've not seen this common plant in the wild before, you may at least recognize its leaf from a delivery made to you by your local florist. The rich, hearty salal leaf is often used in commercial flower arrangements, tending to hold up well long after it's been cut. For people who lived in this region long ago, however, salal had a distinctly more pragmatic value. They ate the fruits and used the chewed or pounded salal leaves to treat painful burns or skin abrasions. Some Indian tribes also made a tea from the leaves, claiming that it relieved sore throats and coughs.

As you make your way along the lake shore, keep your eyes open for a belted kingfisher, which sometimes can be seen perched on shoreline branches or stumps, carefully scanning the water below for a fish dinner. Kingfishers can be recognized by a white belt around

Belted Kingfisher

the neck and a tassled tuft of head feathers that looks much the way some people's hair does when they get out of bed in the morning. It's a thrilling sight to see one of these solitary birds suddenly drop off its waterside perch and splash into the water, flying back out a second later with a small fish in its beak. The belted kingfisher's species name, *alcyon*, is a reference to the myth of Alcyone. One day beautiful Alcyone was told that her seafaring husband had been killed in a shipwreck. Consumed by despair, Alcyone jumped into the ocean to end it all, but instead she was changed into a kingfisher.

As you round the back side of the lake, you may notice the moist ground spattered with a large-leaved plant that sports greenish spikes surrounded by a tall yellow bract open on one side. This is the skunk cabbage, and if you happen to be close enough to smell the flowers you'll understand where it got its name. While this odor may not be perfume for our noses, it's more than a little appealing to flies, who happen to be the primary pollinators of the plant. (Generally, the flowers bloom too early to be pollinated by bees.) Like salal, the leaves of skunk cabbage were often used to treat cuts and skin abrasions. The roots, however, were the main source of medicine, being used for everything from bronchial infections to venereal disease, asthma to contraception.

At a point along the last quarter of your circle around Fragrance Lake, you'll find the path suddenly framed on the right by beautiful, sheer sandstone cliffs rising fifty to sixty feet through the lush forest canopy. Fragrance Lake lies in a tilted trough called a plunging syncline. When glaciers poured through this ravine during the last ice age, they scooped out the softest rock, and thereby formed the basin for the lake. The ice also ground away at the walls of the ravine, leaving the cliffs of scoured, fairly erosion-resistant sandstone you see today. Glaciers form, incidentally, not necessarily under conditions of bitter cold, but after an extended period in which more snow falls in the cold season than melts in the warm. After many years these heavy layers of snow compact into glacial ice—a solid substance, but one which has certain properties not altogether unlike some liquids.

CEDAR FALLS

Distance: 4 miles
Location: Okanogan National Forest. From the town of Winthrop, head west on Washington State Road 20. Go 0.5 mile past mile marker 176 and turn left (south) onto Forest Road 200. Follow this for 1 mile, where it will dead-end at the trailhead.

Being influenced to some degree by the rain shadow effect (the process whereby mountains block the advance of moisture), the Cedar Falls Trail is wrapped in a wonderful blend of dry and wet—of thin veils of timber that allow nice views, as well as of hushed pockets of cedar that cradle a refreshing braid of streams and rivulets. This walk is the perfect antidote for road-weary travelers who find themselves struck with the sudden urge to chuck the camper and see what this country looks like from the inside out.

Our trek begins in a fairly open weave of ponderosa pine, Douglas-fir, willow, and snowbrush. This latter plant, which has thick, finely toothed evergreen leaves, takes its name from its habit of growing in areas of heavy snow, sometimes hanging off of steep mountain slopes in great green tangles. The weight of the snow pack on the branches eventually leaves snowbrush with a permanent curve. Because of its tendency to grow into dense, almost impenetrable thickets, the plant is a favorite hiding place for deer.

Before long, over your left shoulder, a nice view will open up of the Methow Valley, framed in the back by Goat Peak. The name Methow, first assigned to the river that runs from the high crest of the Cascades down to the Columbia, was taken from the name of an Indian tribe that once lived on a beautiful wedge of land bordered by Lake Chelan and the Columbia. These people's rather more colorful name for the river was *buttlemuleemauch*, which is generally thought to have meant "salmon falls river."

These view spots will slowly fade into more dense stands of conifers, their bottom branches pruned off by the trees themselves because they no longer have access to the sun. It's pretty obvious from the great number of conifers growing throughout the West that there are several advantages to the evergreen way of life. First, they don't have to expend energy every year to create new leaves, and when growing seasons are short and nutrients sparse, that can be a real advantage. Second, when favorable conditions for growth do occur—as they often do outside of what we consider to be the standard growing season—these trees can really make the most of them. Finally, conifers are well suited to the dry summers that mark so much of the West, including the coast; not only can they store more water than hardwoods, but the waxy coating on their needles helps them conserve it better, too. This isn't to suggest that hardwoods don't do well in certain niches. But their requirement of moderate summer temperatures and regular moisture isn't easy to find here. If a hardwood tries climbing the mountains to get more precipitation it will find conditions too cold; if it goes down slope to warm up, conditions are too dry. It's no wonder, then, that in the Northwest the volume of conifer wood compared to hardwood has been estimated at a thousand to one.

By 0.75 mile the trailside textures have grown even more interesting. There are the soft drooping branches of western red cedar and bracken fern, and the furrowed cinnamon bark of ponderosa pine. There are shaggy braids of lichen dripping from the branches of the conifers and soft green maple leaves rustling in the wind; the frothy white blooms of ocean-spray, and the smooth green leaves of pipsissewa.

Cedar Falls is waiting for you at the 2-mile mark. This is a fine little double waterfall, a fifteen-foot dive split by a tongue of rock, and then another plunge of a dozen or so feet right below that. In fact, if you sit down on the large rock between these two plunges you can enjoy the delightful experience of stereo waterfalls. There are some beautiful cedars cradling this stream channel, as well as maple, black cottonwood, and a giant old Douglas-fir—one that probably got down to growing in this secret little spot about the time the Pilgrims first stepped off the Mayflower.

BEAVER LAKE

Distance: 2.5 miles

Location: Okanogan National Forest. From the town of Twisp, Washington, head east on Washington State Highway 20 for approximately 12.5 miles. Just west of the Loup Loup Summit, turn north onto Forest Road 42. Follow this for 3.8 miles, and turn left onto Forest Road 100. Stay on Forest Road 100 for 3.6 miles to the trailhead. (Note: This trailhead is easy to miss; watch closely for a small sign on the right side of your vehicle marking trail number 356.)

The longer you poke around the rugged peaks that divide the Okanogan and Methow river valleys, the more the place seems to pull you in. There's plenty of natural beauty here: mountains clad in yarrow, syringa, paintbrush, balsamroot, and sagebrush, and framed on either side by bottomlands that each spring fill with blankets of apple blossoms. There's also some rather fanciful history to be found here, as suggested by such names as Happy Hill, Fuzzy Canyon, and Graveyard Flat. To me the most intriguing of these old names is Loup Loup, a name you already encountered on a highway summit leading to this walk.

Loup is French for wolf, and it was the name first given to a nearby stream by French Canadian fur trappers. Why it ended up Loup Loup instead of just Loup, though, is anyone's guess. I personally picture a trapper running out of the woods with his pants around his knees yelling "Loup! Loup!" as he bolts by his astonished friends. At any rate, the name was later tacked onto a silver mining town a short distance east of here. The town boomed during the 1890s, but then collapsed into oblivion as the price of silver took a nosedive.

Just north of the old town of Loup Loup is the site of another mining town named Ruby. Ruby was a mecca for seamy adventures of all kinds, which led one writer to call it "the Babylon of Washington Territory." In the late 1800s one of Ruby's leading citizens was found to have made a tidy enterprise of rustling his neighbors' cattle and then selling the meat in his downtown butcher shop. One night the local cattlemen rode into town carrying a long rope with the butcher's name on it, but fortunately some of the butcher's drinking

17

buddies managed to stop the execution by promising a trial. The cattlemen placed the butcher under heavy guard; alas, the guards got drunk and the butcher hightailed it for the hills. (It's easy to see why part-time Methow Valley resident Owen Wister pulled several of the characters for his book *The Virginian* right out of these mountains.)

This area was logged not too long ago, and the first part of our walk passes through a fairly homogeneous forest of young lodgepole pines with a few hemlocks and white pines, the forest lightly sprinkled with buffalo berry, strawberry, and whortleberry. On the left at about 0.2 mile you can see a giant tamarack and Douglas-fir that somehow escaped the loggers. The latter tree is surrounded by splendid mats of kinnikinnick. Kinnikinnick was a very popular ingredient in the smoking blends of Native Americans across the continent (in the West it was often mixed with the bark of red-osier dogwood), while herbalists all over the world swore by the plant as a diuretic. The rather strange-sounding common name actually originated among the Algonquian Indians of the East, and was carried here by French Canadian fur trappers. It means nothing more than "smoking mixture."

At 0.6 mile is a split in the trail; stay left. As you continue to climb, at 1 mile you'll be afforded a fine view of the Cascade Range rising off to the west. Most of the moisture that drifts west off of the Pacific is snagged by these mountains. The peaks you're walking in now wring out most of what's left, leaving the country immediately to the east high and dry. Besides rainshadowing, as it's called, there are two other factors that will influence the amount of moisture in any given place. The first of these is elevation. The higher you go, the cooler it gets. Cooler temperatures not only tend to bring additional precipitation but they also reduce the rate at which that moisture is lost through evaporation. In a similar vein, the kinds of plants you see growing on south slopes under the full slap of the sun will often greatly differ from the kinds of plants on shadier, cooler north faces.

You'll reach Beaver Lake at 1.25 miles. This is a delightful little water pocket, rimmed by a rather nice weave of spruce, fir, pine, and alder. If you look at a national forest map you'll note that there are actually many landforms in this area with the name "beaver" attached to them—an indication that this was once prime fur trapping country. For a time the local Indians called Concully Valley east of here Sklow Outiman, which means "money hole." The name was adopted because trappers could drop into the valley, nab a beaver, and then use it as currency at nearby Fort Okanogan.

WILBERT TRAIL

Distance: 1.2 miles

Location: South Whidbey State Park. From the junction of Washington State Highway 20 and State Highway 525 on Whidbey Island, head south on State Highway 525 for 4.5 miles and turn right (west) onto Smugglers Cove Road. Our trailhead is 4 miles down this road, on the left; the main entrance to South Whidbey State Park is 0.4 mile further, on the right. (Coming from the south, the turnoff to Smugglers Cove is about 17 miles north of the Ferry Dock.)

> *Hear the voice of the Bard!*
> *Who Present, past, and Future sees,*
> *Whose ears have heard*
> *The Holy Word*
> *That walked among the ancient trees.*

> —WILLIAM BLAKE

With the recent controversy over the survival of the spotted owl, there are few people in America who haven't become at least casually familiar with the "old-growth forests" of the Pacific Northwest. Truly, these are environments like none other on earth. Beyond their almost haunting beauty, to amble among trees that are 300, 500, or even 1,000 years old is to become much more closely connected with the idea of forever than you've likely ever been. Wedged between the feet of these giants lies a window into what seems to be a different reality altogether—an unfolding of time that's so far outside of our typical day-to-day experiences as to spin us into a fine state of intoxication.

A Pacific Northwest old-growth forest requires about 200 years to develop; most, like this one, are more in the neighborhood of 300 to 500 years old. As you'll see when you walk the Wilbert Trail,

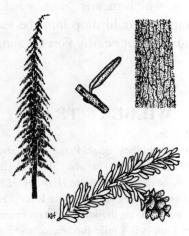

Western Hemlock

the number of plants growing on the floor of such forests depends on how much light makes it past the layers of needles that tower high overhead. In some places the canopy is so thick that the ground is nearly bare. When a big tree does fall, however, it's almost as though a starting gun has been fired: In the years that follow a variety of shrubs and wildflowers can be seen jockeying for a place in the sun. Likewise, a young hemlock that may have been waiting patiently in deep shade for twenty years will really take off when the forest canopy finally opens.

Before you begin, notice the sign beside the highway that marks this as a "Classic U Forest." For many years the state of Washington has sold the timber from its forested lands and used the profits to support the University of Washington. The "U" stands for "university." This tract of land was slated for just such a harvest when a group of local people, headed by a retired engineer named Harry Wilbert, began a vigorous effort to save it. Happily, the group was successful. The forest is currently slated to be brought under the protection of South Whidbey State Park sometime around 1992.

As you make your way around this loop, take a close look at the leaves of some of the plants that seem to be thriving in the more shaded areas. You'll notice that many sport fairly good-sized leaves with few or no hairs on them, giving them a smooth luster. This is no accident; both size and hairlessness help these plants maximize their ability to conduct photosynthesis under low-light conditions.

A few yards into the walk you'll see a faint trail taking off to the left. Stay right. A short distance past this junction is another fork, the right one leading to a fantastic old western red cedar thought to be about 500 years old. It's a rather humbling thought to consider that when this tree was a young seedling, Leonardo da Vinci was just putting the finishing touches on the Mona Lisa! Most of the other trees you'll see along the trail—many of the Douglas-firs—range in age from 200 to 300 years.

Headed down the main trail again, you'll be meandering through a fine mix of Douglas-firs and western hemlocks, with some splendid groves of red alders visible through the forest on your left. Notice how the large conifers of the forest have few or no branches along the lower portions of their trunks. Trees that grow close together often "self-prune." They do this because so little sun comes in that these lower branches can hardly earn their keep when it comes to producing more energy than they consume. Very large conifers may not have a single branch growing along the first hundred feet of their trunks.

Coltsfoot

Take a right at the T intersection at 0.2 mile, where you'll see some nice tufts of Oregon grape and red huckleberry. Shortly after this junction is a large Douglas-fir that has fallen and is now serving as a "nurse log" to several small hemlocks. In very moist forests you can sometimes spot trees that have quite distinct arches at the base of their trunks—often large enough for a person to easily crawl through. What probably caused this is for many years the tree straddled a nurse log like this one. When the nurse log finally decomposed—a process that may have taken centuries—the tree on top was left with an arched base, planted in the ground like a bowlegged cowboy.

Continue past a wet area stitched with a weave of skunk cabbage, deer fern, and mosses—a kind of inner fairyland guarded by the ancient trees. At 0.85 mile you'll reach an intersection with a service road. Turn right here, and follow the road for 100 yards or so past beautiful thickets of salmonberry and patches of horsetail to the Smugglers Cove Highway. If you're here in early spring, scan the side of the highway for signs of coltsfoot blooms. These silky, purplish-white flowers are among the first to bloom in the spring, sometimes opening up before the plant has even had a chance to unfurl its leaves.

SOUTH FORK HOH RIVER

Distance: 3.6 miles
Location: Olympic National Park and the Washington State Department of Natural Resources. From the town of Forks, Washington, head south on U.S. Highway 101, and turn right left (east) on a road that takes off at mile marker 176. (This turn is about a half-mile south of a bridge crossing the Hoh River.) In 6 miles, turn left onto State Road H1000. Follow this road 10.5 miles to the trailhead, passing the South Fork Hoh Campground at 7.8 miles.

The great gulps of moisture that roll eastward from the Pacific to the shoulders of Mount Olympus, dropping 140 inches of precipitation a year along the South Fork of the Hoh River, have given rise to a

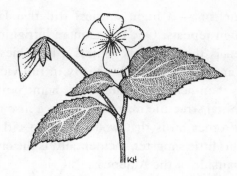

Yellow Violet

startling world of green giants. This is without question the greatest untrammeled rain forest to be found anywhere in the continental United States, and certainly the most accessible. There are portions of this walk that will leave you feeling like you're passing through one big ooze of chloroplast. It is Longfellow's "forest primeval," William Henry Hudson's "green mansions," and George Meredith's "enchanted woods" all rolled up into one. Of all the forest walks you will ever take, you will never forget the Hoh.

Our walk begins in a wash of sword and deer ferns, salmonberry, oxalis, and trailing yellow violets—all growing at the feet of conifers and broadleaf maples that are absolutely dripping with thick curtains of clubmoss. The first conifer here to greet you will be the Sitka spruce. Growing from the Alaskan Coast Ranges southward to the coast of California's Mendocino County, the Sitka attains tremendous stature here on the west side of the Olympic Peninsula. Indeed, the second largest Sitka spruce in the entire world is found along the Lower Hoh River. It is not at all unusual to run across Sitkas 200 feet high and ten feet in diameter, some of which likely have been growing for 800 years. One can hardly help but be a little giddy at rubbing elbows with trees that were up and at it when Marco Polo was setting sail for China.

As you settle into this walk, keep your ears and eyes open for a host of beautiful birds, including hairy woodpeckers, dark-eyed juncos, rufous hummingbirds, and winter wrens. If you do spot winter wrens here, it will probably be as they flit through shrubs and dense undergrowth searching for insects. But it's more likely that

23

you'll hear their song—a high, musical trill that lasts for several seconds, and then repeats. One of the more intriguing behaviors of the winter wren is that the male builds a large nestlike structure complete with an entrance portal, usually in full view of any passerby. The birds then nest somewhere else. Some ornithologists suspect that this initial structure may actually be a ruse meant to throw off animals and other birds that would prey on either the eggs or young birds. This little songster, incidentally, is the only wren whose range extends outside of the Americas.

Continue past hemlocks, spruces, and an occasional broadleaf maple, as well as blue huckleberry, buttercup, foamflower, skunk cabbage, and vanilla leaf, the latter plant easily identified by its three wavy-edged leaves that look something like the wings of a butterfly. True to its common name, the dried leaves of the plant do have an odor somewhat reminiscent of vanilla. At 1.2 miles you'll pass a lovely stream, its cool, sweet cargo bound for the South Fork of the Hoh, but not before passing dozens of rocks covered with tiny gardens of moss and oxalis. Oxalis, the plant that looks like a shamrock, is also known as wood sorrel. Many people believe another variety of wood sorrel to have been the original Irish shamrock, the plant Saint Patrick used to explain the concept of the Christian

Sitka Spruce

Trinity to the Celts. For several centuries, soldiers fastened sprigs of wood sorrel to their helmets or swords for protection against witches and other magicians—a practice that, at least when standing in this fantastic Druidscape of a rain forest, doesn't seem that silly at all.

At 1.5 miles, roughly a mile after entering Olympic National Park, you'll come to Big Flat, a fine open area studded with several beautiful broadleaf maples. This park is kept clear for the most part by the ferocious appetites of Roosevelt elk, which waste no time in nipping any young trees that try to get a start here. Olympic National Park contains one of the best herds of Roosevelt elk in America, consisting of several thousand animals. For a time, there was a strong push to name this preserve not Olympic, but Elk National Park. You'll have the best chance of seeing these regal animals if you're here in winter, since during the warm months they migrate up into the higher reaches of the Olympic Mountains.

Just before leaving this first park area, on your left you'll see a good example of what biologists refer to as a tree "colonnade." Colonnades are formed when several trees begin growing on top of a single fallen "nurse" log. Eventually the nurse log rots away, and what is left is a long line of trees, the entire row looking very much like it was planted there. Sixty yards or so past this first open area is another opening, this one flanked on the left by a lovely stand of red alders. Red alders are often confused with birch trees, as they have a mottled white trunk like the birch, covered with crusty plates of lichen. (The only red coloring these trees can claim is their inner bark.) Red alder is like aspen in the fact that it does extremely well reclaiming burned, insect-killed, or logged-over areas. Alas, its days are numbered: If no further disturbance of the area occurs, spruce, hemlock, and cedar will overtake it.

From this grove continue for about 150 yards, past a fine alder park that frames the right side of the trail. At a point where the trail comes fairly close to the South Fork of the Hoh River (a massive Douglas-fir snag will be visible directly ahead of you), leave the path and make your way to the bank of the river. This is a lovely, serene place—a wonderful spot to nap, picnic, or simply watch the summer light playing off the ripples of the river. Keep your eyes open for belted kingfishers, which do quite nicely dining on the smaller fish that live in this cool, clear waterway.

SWALLOW CAVE NATURE TRAIL

Distance: 1.3 miles
Location: Wenatchee National Forest. From the town of Leavenworth, head west on U.S. Highway 2 for approximately 14
miles, and turn right (east) onto Washington State Road 207. In
3.7 miles, near the east end of Lake Wenatchee, turn right onto
County Road 22. Proceed 1.2 miles after this junction, turn left
(north) onto Forest Road 62 and follow this for just over 3 miles,
to a point where it crosses the Chiwawa River. Just after this river
crossing is a small pull-off area on the right side of the road. This
is our trailhead.

Perhaps the only negative thing about this delightful little jaunt to
the sunny banks of the Chiwawa River is that parts of the trail are
open to ORVs (off-road vehicles)—an unfortunate fact that suggests
the most appropriate time for a stroll here is either in the off season, or
at least in the peace and quiet of early morning. (One thing about
ORVs: You don't see many people taking off on one in the first light
of dawn to look for sapsuckers.) In the early portion of the walk I had
to work my way around several trees that had fallen across the trail,
but after thirty yards or so the path gained a clear, sunny bench, and
remained easy to navigate all the way to the river. At various points
along this walk you'll see paths and small roadways taking off to your
left; keep bearing to your right at each of these.

After scrambling out onto the open bench you'll find the path
lined with a loose collection of grand fir, as well as lupine, bracken
fern, Oregon grape, wild rose, kinnikinnick, and wild blackberry.
Below you on the right is a fine view of a floodplain stitched through
with cottonwood, red alder, snowbrush, and willow, backed in the
distance by a nice curtain of mixed conifers. As the name Swallow
Cave Nature Trail would suggest, you will see swallows flitting above
the wet areas along the walk, nabbing insects with the greatest of
ease. As for the cave promised in the walk name, however, either it
never existed at all, or those who know aren't talking.

Of all the plants you'll see on this walk, perhaps none is more
pleasing to the eye than the stately ponderosa pine, which grows in
relative abundance just 0.3 mile into the walk. Easy ways to identify

this large, "ponderous" pine are by its long needles, which grow three to a bundle, and by its scaly, cinnamon-colored bark. While ponderosa seeds were not as cherished by local Indian peoples as those of other pines, they did on occasion grind them into fine meal, as well as peel away the thick bark to get at the sweet cambium layer that lies just underneath. If people haven't exactly relished the seeds, there are plenty of other creatures who do, including squirrels, quail, and chipmunks. Several varieties of ponderosa can be found throughout the West; put them all together, and you have the most widely distributed pine on the continent.

To the right of the path at 0.3 mile you may notice a large, leaning ponderosa with a tremendous collection of gnarly knots and boils growing on its main trunk. This is the result of dwarf mistletoe, a disfiguring, ultimately fatal parasite that seems especially prone to attacking trees that have set up shop in very dry, or otherwise harsh, environments. Indeed, that's often just where ponderosas will be found, where few other trees, save an occasional Douglas-fir or lodgepole pine, could be expected to survive. The plants that you'll see growing here—rose, Idaho fescue, bluebunch wheatgrass, and Oregon grape—are frequent companions of the mighty ponderosa throughout most of its range.

At 0.65 mile you'll reach the beautiful Chiwawa River. The name Chiwawa, incidentally, is a shorthand version of an Indian word

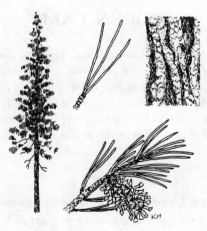

Ponderosa Pine

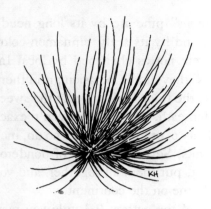

Idaho Fescue

that means "lost canyon next to the mountains." The river rises far to the northwest in the shining high country of Glacier Peak Wilderness, and takes its first fast steps not too far east of the cold, icy shoulders of Clark, Richardson, and Butterfly glaciers. From where you now stand the Chiwawa continues to run generally southward, joining forces first with the Wenatchee River and then with the Columbia, the latter being the route that all the mountain waters of this region take to their final rendezvous with the Pacific.

HIDDEN LAKE

Distance: 1.1 miles
Location: Wenatchee National Forest. From the town of Leavenworth, head west on U.S. Highway 2 for approximately 14 miles, and turn right (east) onto Washington State Road 207. In about 4 miles, turn left (west) onto Forest Road 6607, which runs along the south side of Lake Wenatchee. Our trail takes off from the very end of Forest Road 6607, at Glacier View Campground.

The trail to Hidden Lake is one of those delightful forest pathways that seem to surround you in beauty from start to finish. Though the trail is an uphill affair for most of its 0.5 mile route, you'll never be but

28

a step or two away from either an engaging quilt of vegetation, or a cool, deep view of Lake Wenatchee shimmering through the spruce-fir forest far below. In the early morning or evening hours you can also count on a nice medley of bird song, including some rather sweet-sounding numbers by mountain chickadees, red-breasted nut-hatches, cedar waxwings, evening grosbeaks, rufous-sided towhees, dark-eyed juncos, and downy woodpeckers, as well as some more raucous offerings by gray and Steller's jays, Clark's nutcrackers, and pileated and hairy woodpeckers. If you arrive at Hidden Lake at dusk, you can expect to see some rather impressive acrobatics by swallows and brown bats.

Our path begins in a thick mix of grand fir, queen's cup, Oregon grape, twisted-stalk, trillium, false Solomon's seal, pyrola, bracken fern, and devil's club. Devil's club, which is actually a relative of Asian ginseng, is most appropriately named, as anyone who's had the misfortune to come in contact with the nasty barbs and spines that line its stems and leaf veins can attest. (The Latin name of the plant, *Oplopanax horridus*, means "horrible weapon"!) Nevertheless, this was an important plant to many of the native peoples of Washington, who used it for everything from a treatment for diabetes to a means of preventing head lice. Devil's club also had a fair reputation as a personal power plant for shamans of the region, who would regularly either adorn their lodges with the plant, or sometimes use it as a primary building material in order to keep evil spirits at bay. Despite the formidable, no-nonsense appearance of devil's club, deer and elk absolutely relish the plant; in fact, if you want to see either of these animals, one of the best ways to do it is to perch yourself some morning or evening in the bottom of a valley or shaded ravine, where devil's club is most often found.

At 0.4 mile you'll run across some fine ponderosa pines—a tree we usually associate with much drier conditions than those found along the shores of Lake Wenatchee. Actually, while this stately giant does do well growing in areas with as little as thirteen or fourteen inches of precipitation per year, you can also find it growing happily in regions with more than twice that much moisture, which certainly is the case here. (When you do see ponderosas growing in the upper limits of their range, you can bet that they'll have set up shop on generally sunny, well-drained soils.) One of the reasons this area is so

Common Loon

special when it comes to plant life is because it is sandwiched between two very different precipitation zones, and freely borrows residents from both. While Lake Wenatchee typically gets about forty inches of moisture a year, Leavenworth, to the east, gets twenty-four; Steven's Pass, just to the west, may get eighty!

Just about the time you've had enough upward motion for one day, the trail flattens out on the spine of a small ridge. Behind and well below you are the sparkling waters of Lake Wenatchee, while directly in front, framing the rich green waters of Hidden Lake, is a striking ponderosa park land spiked with lupine, pipsissewa, and star flower. On the other side of the lake is a lacy mix of cedar and fir, the latter tree rising in dizzy leaps and bounds up the sheer cliffs that rise along the south side of the lake, finally crowning out at 6,000-foot-high Nason Ridge.

If you're lucky, you just may spot a loon barely suspended in the quiet waters of Hidden Lake. I say "barely suspended" because the bones of loons are much more solid and weighty than those of other birds. In much the same way that a diver will wear a weight belt to match himself to the relative gravity of water, the loon's more massive bones allow it to make deep dives with relative ease. Of all the sounds that still float through the American outback, from the bugle of an elk to the call of a Canada goose, perhaps none can prickle the skin like the wild, haunting laugh of the loon.

GROVE OF THE PATRIARCHS

Distance:　1.25 miles
Location:　Mount Rainier National Park. From Enumclaw, Washington (east of Tacoma), follow Washington State Highway 410 for about 42 miles, to a junction with Washington State Highway 123, on the east side of the park. From this junction, follow State Highway 123 south for about 11 miles to the Stevens Canyon Road. Turn right (west) here, and go past the national park entrance station about 0.1 mile to a large parking area on the right (north) side of the road. Our walk takes off from here, heading north.

It stretches the imagination to think that when some of the trees you'll meet on this walk first poked their green heads above the soil, Viking raider Leif Erickson was about to stumble onto "Vinland"— his name for the North American continent. By the time King John's arm was being twisted into signing the Magna Carta, or eighteen years later, when Ferdinand and Isabella were presiding over the horrors of the Spanish Inquisition, some of the Douglas-firs and western red cedars along this path had already seen 200 years pass through the dark green valley of the Ohanapecosh River. And by the time Captain George Vancouver "discovered" mighty Mount Rainier in the spring of 1792, or when Lewis and Clark made note of it on their return trip up the Columbia River, these trees were splendid, herculean giants. Today this forest is among the most magnificent old-growth areas in the entire Northwest—a haunting destination that will steal the breath of even the most jaded outdoor traveler.

The two largest trees you'll be seeing here are Douglas-fir and western red cedar, thirty of which measure more than twenty-five feet in circumference; one red cedar—a staggering thirty-five feet around—is the largest tree in the entire park. You'll also see plenty of

31

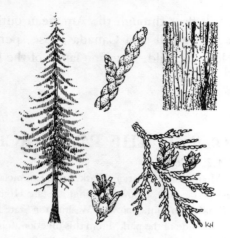

Western Redcedar

hemlocks throughout this walk, though they reach nowhere near the proportions of the Douglas-fir and red cedar. (Red cedar is also sometimes called "canoe cedar," as coastal Indians used the tree for the construction of canoes. Indeed, the art of canoe building has never reached a higher level than in the cedar vessels constructed by the coastal tribes of Washington and British Columbia. Voyaging canoes sometimes were sixty-five feet long, bore three masts, and could carry between thirty and forty people.)

On your way to the Grove of the Patriarchs you'll pass a wonderful variety of plants, most of which will show up on other walks you do in the area. On the ground beside the trail look for twisted-stalk, bunchberry, salmonberry, devil's club, trillium, vanilla leaf, star flower, foamflower, and queen's cup. You'll recognize this latter plant by its two or three smooth green leaves, six inches to eight inches long. Following the arrival in May or June of one white, six-petaled flower about an inch across, queen's cup produces a hard, oval-shaped berry of the most beautiful deep blue.

Rounding out the common flora are tufts of strawberry leaves, graceful vine, and broadleaf maples, and the large, soft leaves of thimbleberry, once used to make a tea for treating anemia. There are also some wonderful clusters of ferns here, their soft fronds lending a delicate touch to a world ruled by giants. Ferns reproduce not by seeds but by tiny spores. Hundreds of thousands—in some species even millions—of these spores are produced each season. Spores are held in tiny spore cases, many of which are heaped together into tiny dots known as sori. These sori, or "fruit dots," appear as dark-colored spots on the underside of fertile leaflets. It's usually dry when fern spores are released into the forest, because such conditions help them disperse over a wider range. Those that land in the right setting and at the right temperature will soon begin developing into a small plant called a prothallus. This prothallus has both male and female organs present; once sperm is released and united with an egg, the egg begins developing into what will become a new fern.

During the Renaissance, a belief known as the Doctrine of Signatures became a steering philosophy of medicine and remained so for centuries to come. In essence, this doctrine said that plants bear certain signs, or signatures, meant to instruct man as to their medical use. In the case of ferns, because the spores—the "seeds" of the plant—were so tiny, it was long believed that those who carried or ate them would also be made invisible.

Two of several ferns you'll be passing on this walk are sword fern and wood fern. Both of these were used by Northwest Indians to treat skin injuries; the roots of the wood fern were mashed and put on cuts, while spore cases were collected from the underside of sword fern fronds and placed on burns.

At 0.4 mile you'll come to a fork in the trail. Stay to the right, and cross a bridge over a fork of the Ohanapecosh River to a lovely

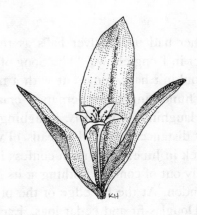

Queen's Cup

grove of red alder. Soon you'll be gliding by splendid standing old growth and mammoth fallen trunks, their root systems sticking into the air like some kind of wild modern art. At 0.5 is a small loop trail, where you'll bear to the right through the heart of the Grove of the Patriarchs.

If you find this particular cathedral too busy for your tastes, then return to the trail junction at 0.4 mile—the one you came to right before crossing the bridge over the Ohanapecosh River. This other trail will carry you northward on a path that meanders along the west bank of the Ohanapecosh. While you won't find the trees to be as large along this path as they were on the island, there is certainly no shortage of grand, hushed old growth to sink into on a summer afternoon.

SILVER FALLS

Distance: 1.4 miles
Location: Mount Rainier National Park. From Enumclaw (east of Tacoma), follow Washington State Highway 410 for about 42 miles, to its junction with Washington State Highway 123, on the east side of the park. From this junction, follow Washington State Highway 123 south for about 11 miles to the Stevens Canyon Road. Turn right (west) here, and go past the national park entrance station about 0.1 mile to a parking area on the right. Our walk takes off across the road and about fifty yards to the west.

If Minnehaha's father had used Silver Falls as the inspiration for naming his daughter in Longfellow's "The Song of Hiawatha," you can bet that she wouldn't have come out with a name that means "laughing water." Thundering water, perhaps—crazy, hysterical water maybe, but not laughing. (Curiously, Laughingwater Creek enters the river a short distance below Silver Falls.) I visited this place during the third week in June, and I must confess I've rarely seen a cascade so splendidly out of control, frothing at its banks with complete and utter abandon. At the far edge of the plunge pool was a large collection of Douglas-fir and cedar logs. Each one had been pounded and pummeled by the Ohanapecosh River until it was free of every inch of bark and branches, much the way rough rocks tossed into a gem tumbler come out looking smooth and polished.

These late spring and early summer torrents of water serve as a firm reminder that Mount Rainier is a place with no shortage of moisture. The highest seasonal snowfall in the world was recorded west of here, at Paradise, during the winter of 1971–72: a staggering ninety-four feet. (The average annual snowfall is about half that, which still makes it a very snowy place.) With this amount of white stuff in the high country, you can't help but have significant runoff in the spring; in those years when the warm weather comes in too fast, some of these streams run down the mountain like runaway freight trains.

This path tends to be more open than the one leading to the Grove of the Patriarchs (see page 31), allowing shrubs like huckleberry to flourish. Also here are wood and deer ferns, pipsissewa, Oregon grape, bunchberry, and devil's club. Though it may not look it, devil's club, which brandishes spines on its stems and thorns beneath its big leaves, is actually a cousin of the Asian ginseng.

Before you reach the boom and rumble of the cascades that precede Silver Falls, turn up your ears for the sound of bird song. The

Olive-sided Flycatcher

35

Beargrass

various canopies present in a mixed conifer forest are like life zones, each vertical band providing food and shelter for different kinds of birds, each bird with specific eating and nesting habits. In the low shrub layer of the forest will be found song sparrows, rufous-sided towhees, brown creepers, and Wilson's warblers, all of which find their food and shelter close to the ground. Up high, on the other hand, feeding on insects found in and around the tree canopy, are birds like the olive-sided flycatcher and western tanager. (Note that it's primarily the birds living in the protection of high canopies that wear vivid colors like those of the western tanager; birds nesting close to the ground are more plain, having a greater need to blend in with their surroundings.)

By 0.5 mile you'll see a small side trail taking off to the left that will give you a good view of the riotous cascades that serve as an introduction to the grand plunge of Silver Falls. Returning to the main trail, continue along the river for another 0.2 mile, at which point you'll see a pathway taking off to your left that leads to a marvelous view of Silver Falls. Along the way look for salal, evergreen huckleberry, western red cedar, and Oregon grape, as well as shiny tufts of bear grass. Because bear grass tends to bloom only every several years, during some visits you may see nothing but low, shaggy mats of grass (tasty looking, but unpalatable to most big game), while in other years it can seem that every plant is topped by a three-foot-tall flower stalk, each one waving a beautiful cluster of white blooms.

LEWIS RIVER

Distance: 5 miles

Location: Gifford Pinchot National Forest. From Interstate 5 north of Vancouver, Washington, take Exit 21 and head east on Washington State Highway 503. At the town of Yale, continue east on Forest Road 90 for about 40 miles to Lower Falls Campground. Our walk takes off from the northeast corner of this camping area.

If you ever find yourself overwhelmed by the rate at which the natural areas of the Northwest are being lost to industry and development, if your own good fight for wild places suddenly seems to be turning heavy and sour, then come to Lewis River. This is a healing place. It is Washington at its very best—a splendid, unfettered watercourse, dancing like a prima ballerina through hushed woodlands pleated with ferns and flowers. If, like Izaak Walton, you are a person who loves "any discourse with rivers," then I can promise that your walk along the Lewis will be one of the finest conversations you'll ever have.

Starting from the cold bellies of glaciers lying on the western side of Mount Adams, the Lewis actually traverses a tremendous number of beautiful places, bringing bright flushes of life to its banks all the way to the western edge of the Gifford Pinchot National Forest. A mere fifty years ago, the "natural" feeling of the area extended well past even that. The 1941 WPA guide to Washington paints the lower Lewis River Valley as an idyllic place. Around Merwin Reservoir, for instance, it boasts that "first-growth timber still crowns the hillsides," and that the surrounding area "abounds with duck, pheasant, bear and deer." Further east yet, toward Woodland, "strawberries, raspberries, youngberries and cranberries grow in generous quantities." (Youngberries, in case you're wondering, were a cross between a trailing blackberry and a southern dewberry.) "The fields yield heavy crops of peas, garden vegetables and alfalfa. Dairy farms and poultry ranches where many turkey are raised, also thrive on the countryside."

From the trailhead parking area at Lower Falls Campground, head upstream on trail number 31. This path is appealing from the very beginning, cradled along its early reaches by vanilla leaf, three-leaved anemone, pipsissewa, bunchberry, and the small greenish flowers of broad-leaved twayblades. The flower of this latter plant has a small coiled mechanism with a sticky ball of pollen attached. A visiting insect triggers the coil, which then shoots the pollen onto its body, to be carried to other twayblade flowers for fertilization. There are actually three kinds of twayblades in western North America, and Washington contains them all. One easily recognized feature is the pair of opposite leaves that grow about halfway up the stem.

Before long the path has climbed onto a bench that sits high above the river. While there are times when the water is lost from sight, it's never lost from sound; the hiss and rumble of one set of rapids never quite fades out before another one chimes in to take its place. One reason for this is the formation of the riverbed, which in places consists of flat slabs of volcanic rock stacked on top of each other like fallen dominos. By 0.4 mile you can look down from your elevated position on the trail into a beautiful, shaded floodplain thick with carpets of sword ferns. Overhead lie scattered groves of Pacific silver fir and Douglas-fir, as well as an occasional alder, hemlock, and western red cedar.

The rather sorry-looking bridge visible on the right about 0.2 mile after this lowland garden is known as Old Sheep Bridge, and it was used primarily by sheep ranchers and miners to access the east side of the Lewis River. In 1968, however, a mud slide roared down the valley north of here, damming the Lewis River. When the dam finally broke the Lewis came through here like a runaway train, taking the bridge ramps with it. Since mining and grazing activity had pretty well subsided by then the bridge was never rebuilt; the Forest Service is, however, considering constructing a pedestrian crossing here.

If by now the whole place has started to massage you into a fine state of lethargy, just past the old bridge is a delightful stopping point. Here a lovely little stream comes laughing out of an alder-covered hillside, and then suddenly plunges with a fine hiss over a fifteen-foot precipice lying just to the right of the trail. Bedstraw and yellow monkeyflower are plentiful here, as are the beautiful blooms of Siberian miner's lettuce—a plant that bears five notched white petals with red lines running down them.

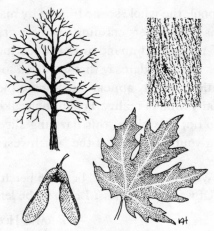

Broadleaf Maple

Also growing along this stretch of trail are a few nice broadleaf maples. The beautiful twelve-inch-long, deeply lobed leaves of this tree have shaded many a western Washington neighborhood from the sizzle of summer. In spring, about the time that the leaves are 80 percent grown, the broadleaf maple sends out delicate clusters of drooping, bright yellow flowers. Though these flowers soon fade, color returns to the tree again in the fall, when its leaves glow with shimmers of yellow and orange. During the heyday of fur trapping in the Northwest, the men of the Hudson's Bay Company were especially fond of gun stocks carved from this tree.

After yet another warm-up waterfall on Copper Creek at 1.5 miles, you'll come to Middle Falls—a splendid, Niagaralike cascade split by a smooth tongue of rock. Those who have little time or energy can turn around here, though I promise you that the additional mile to the Upper Falls is worth every single step. The trail climbs sharply just past Middle Falls but then quickly levels out again, offering much the same kind of walk that you've had up until this point. Added to the scene, however, are an abundance of springs flowing out of the rock, in one case creating a high, vertical wall draped with an exquisite array of tiny ferns and brilliant green tufts of moss, each with clear, cool water dripping off the tips.

As for the Upper Falls of the Lewis, they are indescribably beautiful. The river literally thunders over high cliffs into a large emerald plunge pool, the whole scene framed by mammoth trunks of red cedar. This is wild water, crashing out of a grand, green forest with the kind of unfettered abandon that does much to shock the human heart back to life. I daresay that were you to see this scene in a painting, it would probably appear much more the work of wishful thinking than of any kind of reality. For all the walking you have ever done or are yet to do, this place, this dazzling slice of wild, will lie long and lovely in your memories of the Northwest.

> What would the world be, once bereft
> Of wet and wildness? Let them be left. . . .
>
> —GERALD HOPKINS

Oregon

HEAD OF JACK CREEK

Distance: 0.4 miles
Location: Deschutes National Forest. From the intersection of U.S. Highway 20 and Oregon State Highway 22, head east on U.S. Highway 20 for 13.8 miles, and then turn left (north) onto Forest Road 12. (Coming from the east, Forest Road 12 would be about 11 miles west of Sisters.) Continue north for 4.5 miles, and pick up Forest Road 1230, which continues to the north a short distance and then turns west. Go 0.6 mile from this last intersection and make another left onto Forest Road 1232, and follow it for 1.3 miles to Forest Road 400. Our trailhead is located 0.5 mile down Forest Road 400, on the left side of the road.

When I visited Head of Jack Creek, it seemed like an orphan—a neglected, forgotten paradise in the midst of clearcuts and hunting camps and pickups speeding down dusty roads. The trail itself is in places hard to follow, and at times the interpretive brochures for the walk are missing from the trailhead altogether. Yet within this tiny enclave is one of the most verdant, restful places you could ever set foot in; a rich wonderland of springwater and conifers, moss and flowers. In the end what matters most is you simply get the chance to soak in the beauty of this area; orphaned or not, there's no nicer place for miles around.

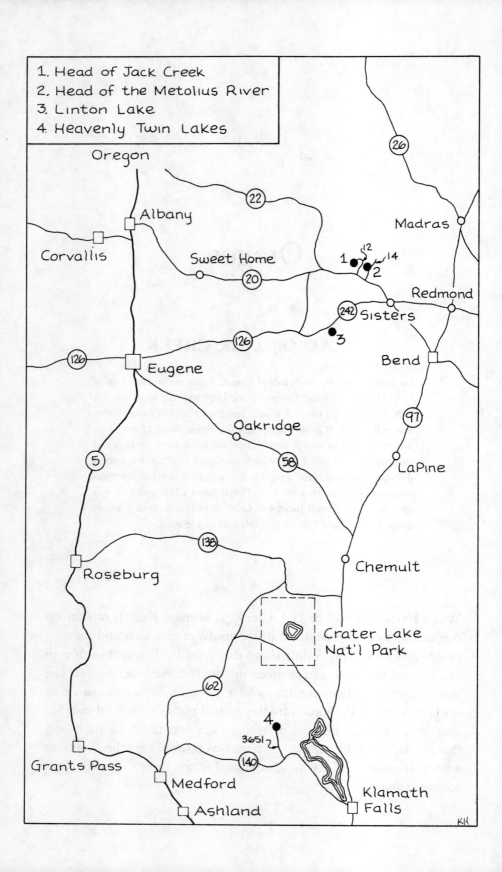

1. Head of Jack Creek
2. Head of the Metolius River
3. Linton Lake
4. Heavenly Twin Lakes

Oregon

Albany

Corvallis

Sweet Home

22

Madras

1 12 14
2

Redmond

242 Sisters

20

126

3

Bend

126 Eugene

97

Oakridge

58

LaPine

5

138

Roseburg

Chemult

Crater Lake
Nat'l Park

62

4

3651

140

Grants Pass

Medford

Ashland

Klamath
Falls

26

KH

Much of the magic to be found here is due to a splendid gush of springwater that's managed to find its way to ground level through cracks in the underlying volcanic rock. (Just east of here, the Metolius River and Wizard Falls have equally charmed beginnings.) The difference that a little springwater can make is striking. Just a few steps from the information shelter you'll pass out of a somewhat parched-looking ponderosa pine forest into a lush huddle of hemlock, Pacific yew, vine maple, monkeyflower, moss, and lady fern. You first join Jack Creek just a few yards below one of the main springs, and then follow it downstream for about 0.1 mile before crossing.

Notice the downed timber lying in the stream near this crossing. While resource managers used to think that such downfall "choked" streams, and that it was best removed, they now realize that besides being good for erosion control, the pools and eddies they create form perfect habitats for trout. Throughout the West right now, the same work crews who once had the job of removing fallen trees from our waterways are now going around putting them back in again! "Nature," as Aristotle tried to tell us 2,300 years ago, "does nothing uselessly."

Oregon Junco

Shortly after crossing the stream, another spring-fed fork of Jack Creek will join you on your left. Along this bank are beautiful bouquets of queen's cup, twinflower, thimbleberry, monkeyflower, false mitrewort, and pipsissewa. For all the confusion that common names of plants sometimes cause, they often give good clues to identification. Thimbleberry does in fact grow berries that resemble a thimble, while twinflower sports its sweet-smelling, trumpet-shaped pink flowers in pairs. And if you use a little imagination, the bloom of the monkeyflower can look rather like a monkey's face. Knowing the language behind a plant's scientific name is also helpful. The genus name for the beautiful little evergreen pipsissewa is *Chimaphila*, which is derived from two Greek words that mean "winter-loving." False mitrewort's genus name of *Tiarella*, from a Greek word for a turban once worn in Persia, refers to the shape of the flower's pistil.

This stretch of trail is also a fine place to catch sight or sound of several different species of woodland birds. Even if you don't actually see the beautiful red-breasted sapsucker during your visit, you can spot its handiwork in the form of nesting holes in dead snags. Oregon juncos are also plentiful here, as are mountain chickadees, Steller's jays, and brown creepers, the latter bird named for its habit

Brown Creeper

of patiently spiraling up tree trunks in a search for insects. Saw-whet owls, which in daylight are one of the more approachable of the owls, are also no strangers to this forest.

The path continues to wind through a beautiful garden of ground plants, as well as over a rather beefy assortment of hemlock roots lining the spring channel. Finally, at 0.3 mile, it climbs to a drier, much more open bench. On the way down to Jack Creek you'll pass several fine clusters of elderberry. While blue elderberries are commonly used to make wine and jelly, the bark, roots, and leaves of both red- and blue-berried plants are generally considered toxic. Elderberry plants have hollow stems that through the ages have been used to make everything from pipes to flutes to taps for maple trees.

HEAD OF THE METOLIUS RIVER

Distance: 0.4 mile
Location: Deschutes National Forest. From the intersection of U.S. Highway 20 and Oregon State Road 22, head east on U.S. Highway 20 16.6 miles to a signed turnoff heading north along Forest Road 14, toward the Metolius River and Camp Sherman. (Coming from the east, Forest Road 14 is approximately 9 miles from the town of Sisters.) Follow this road 4.3 miles to the parking area and trailhead, on the left.

There was a time, so geologists say, that the waters of the Metolius ran not on the earth but beneath it, in the dark, volcanic passageways that course through the feet of the great Cascades. And then, in an event that could have come out of the book of Genesis, the Green Ridge fault began to shift and grind, pinching the underground waters upward until they burst forth as a full-fledged river—one that would ultimately give rise to a magnificent bounty of life and beauty both in its waters and along its banks. What's more, another, smaller spring system about 9 miles downstream from here feeds the Wizard

Falls Fish Hatchery. The waters there pour from the earth at a year-round temperature of fifty degrees, which is perfect for the hatching and rearing of fish. In fact, in a single year up to 5 million eggs of six different fish species may be hatched at Wizard Falls.

Because the easy paved trail to the head of the Metolius River can at times be rather thick with people, you may want to take this walk either well off season, or else on some shining summer morning not long after sunrise. But no matter when you decide to go, do be sure to make the trip. Even though two other tributaries of the Deschutes River are also born from underground springs (Spring and Fall rivers), you'll never find another as stunning as this one. To see the cold, clear waters of a large, fully formed river pouring out from a crack in the earth seems to speak to some kind of deeply ingrained mythology of plenty. The view immediately downstream, which includes a pine-clad parkland, and behind that, the majestic, snow-capped Mount Jefferson, hardly hurts the effect.

The name Metolius first appeared as "Mpto-ly-as" in a mid-nineteenth-century Pacific Railroad survey report. While there's some disagreement as to the exact meaning of the word, most scholars agree that it refers to a light-colored salmon, which, unfortunately, is no longer found here. From the point where you now stand the Metolius runs northward through ponderosa pine forests, makes a wide curve through a spectacular 1,500-foot canyon, and finally ends its showy dance by doing a quiet disappearing act into the slack waters of Lake Billy Chinook. All in all, few rivers pack more scenic punch per mile than this one.

Bitterbrush

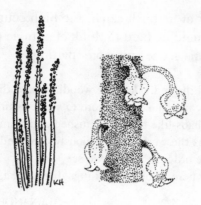

Pinedrops

The trail to the headwaters of the Metolius begins in a fine ponderosa forest, the understory spattered with tufts of manzanita and bitterbrush. Writing in his mammoth volume, *A Natural History of Western Trees*, Donald Culross Peattie describes the look and the location of the ponderosa well. "Its shade is never too thin and never too dense," he explains. "Its boles and boughs frame many of the grandest views, of snowcapped cones, Indian-faced cliffs, nostalgic mesas, and all that brings the world to the West's wide door."

More than a few of the ponderosas you see around you here sprang from the efforts of chipmunks and squirrels who were either absent-minded or over-prepared, having left large caches of ponderosa pine cones buried throughout the forest. Like other trees, this pine tends to have a much higher sprouting rate when helped by busy paws than it has when simply scattered loosely on the surface of the ground. The smallest trees you see here are not as young as you might think. A ten-year-old ponderosa may be only a foot or two high, having put a lot of its energies during the early years into establishing a good root system. Not until they reach the age of fifteen or twenty will these trees start putting on height and mass at a faster rate; that growth will continue for 120 or 130 more years, and then slow to a crawl.

The end of this trail is reached much too soon—after only 0.2 mile of easy walking. Standing here staring at the first brilliant steps of a river just out of its birth canal, the high country flashing in the background, it would be hard to think of a single thing that could be added to make this scene any more inviting.

> Here hills and vales, the woodland and the plain,
> Here earth and water seem to strive again,
> Not chaos-like together crushed and bruised,
> But, as the world, harmoniously confused:
> Where order in variety we see,
> And where, though all things differ, all agree.

> —ALEXANDER POPE

LINTON LAKE

Distance: 3.6 miles
Location: Willamette National Forest. From the town of Eugene, Oregon, head east on Oregon State Highway 126, continuing past Blue River and McKenzie Bridge. Near mile marker 55, turn right onto State Highway 242. Our trailhead is 10.5 miles from this junction, on the right (south) side of the road.

Rather than being set in the scoured rock and alpine meadow lands that mark some of the Three Sisters Wilderness, Linton Lake is largely a creature of the forest—ridges covered with thick timber, and the shore itself washed in a rich green tapestry of both coniferous and deciduous trees. But for the thunder of Linton Falls, which makes a glorious run down a 1,200-foot-high ridge behind the lake, the feeling here is more subdued than stark. Loose groups of brown creepers, white-breasted nuthatches, mountain chickadees, and ruby-crowned and golden-crowned kinglets flutter through the forest in a patient search for insects. On forest edges, blue grouse quietly tend their nests, well concealed by a rock or tree stump. Pacific tree frogs make their way to the shallows of Linton Lake to breed in the spring, and then gingerly hop off to spend the rest of the summer feeding in nearby shrubs and on fallen logs.

Three Sisters Wilderness has actually been a protected area for some time, having been established as a Primitive Area back in

White-breasted Nuthatch

1937. These 242,000 acres contain a fabulous medley of Cascade environments, from thick forests like this one of Douglas-fir, white pine, hemlock, and Engelmann spruce, to cool alpine meadows stitched with swamp laurels, elephant-heads, shooting stars, blue-bells, and heather.

While the plants that define the various ecosystems of Three Sisters have been fairly easy to decipher, the geological story of the rock beneath them has been another matter. Geologists now feel that there was a sinking of the Central Cascade volcanoes roughly three million years ago; the land was then flooded with thick rivers of lava. North Sister was the first to be built on top of these deep volcanic slabs, later followed by Middle and South Sister. Perhaps the most striking evidence of the extent of volcanic activity that has occurred in this area can be had just west of here, along the vast outpourings of basalt and andesite that line the McKenzie Pass road. You'll also be crossing some fairly recent outflow along this trail. The volcanic rock crossed at about a mile into the walk is part of a westward-running flow of lava from Collier Cone that dammed Linton Creek. The land behind the dam then flooded to form Linton Lake. (If you wonder why you can't see any water flowing out of the lake, it's because Linton Creek is running beneath these lava flows.)

Mountain Chickadee

Walking through these lush forested corridors, huckleberry and rhododendron blooming by your side, it's hard to imagine that this was a land born of such blistering fire. You will get a much better feel for this fact if you walk along the Yapoah flow, just east of McKenzie Pass, on the north side of the highway past a thin line of trees. Here the basalt is thought to be only about 500 years old. Looking at it, you could easily imagine that it erupted just last year!

The first slice of the trail to Linton Lake is lined with nice mats of strawberry, bracken fern, queen's cup, beargrass, star flower, three-leaved anemone, pipsissewa, huckleberry, pyrola, and wild ginger. Wild ginger sports pairs of heart-shaped, veined leaves one to four inches across, growing from a trailing root stem. The brown to greenish, three-petaled flowers bloom early in the spring, but are often hidden by the leaves. Early blooming means that bees and butterflies are not around for pollination; thus, like the skunk cabbage, the flowers of wild ginger have a fetid odor, which proves quite effective for attracting flies. This plant was long used by Indians and settlers alike to relieve indigestion and stimulate the appetite. A decoction of ginger root was used by Native American women in tribes across the country for contraceptive purposes. Though this is not the same ginger plant that's raised commercially for cooking purposes, the root can be used in much the same way.

At a junction at 0.9 mile, turn right, climbing a hill that will take you atop the lava flow mentioned earlier. You'll cross this relatively flat area for about 0.3 mile and then begin a short descent, reaching the quiet shores of Linton Lake at about 1.6 miles. You'll have to continue along the north edge for about 0.2 mile, though, before reaching the main body of water. For those of you who like to fish, there are some very big trout in here, most of them wise enough to not yield easily to a fisherman's hook.

HEAVENLY TWIN LAKES

Distance: 6.1 miles

Location: Winema National Forest. From Klamath Falls, head west on Oregon State Highway 140. At about mile marker 41 you'll come to Forest Road 3651 taking off on the right (north), toward Cold Springs trailhead and campground. Our walk leaves from the trailhead/campground area, which is just over 10 miles north of Highway 140.

As far as I can tell, the person who named the natural features along this lovely slice of the Winema National Forest must have been on some kind of cosmic vision quest, most of which seems to have been a rather pleasant affair. The place we're bound for, for example, bears the rather striking title of "Heavenly Twin Lakes." Appropriately, it lies just a short distance north of Imagination Peak. If you go north about 5 miles you'll end up even farther out in the universe, this time at the feet of Venus and Jupiter peaks. Evidently some kind of battle with temptation arose during the planet-hopping phase of the trip, though, because right next to Venus and Jupiter peaks are Lucifer Mountain and Devils Peak. (Whoever did the naming along this ridge farther north must have been on a somewhat more down-to-earth journey: There the mountains are called Maude, Ethel, and Ruth.)

A walk across this gentle forested plateau is perhaps best described not as a hike but as a meditation. Who knows in what universe your own mind will end up by the time you reach Heavenly Twin Lakes? It's one of the best places in the entire area to work on Thoreau's notion of sauntering, to feel like Rudyard Kipling's cat, out "walking by his wild lone." In addition to a nice trailside mat of bleeding heart, twinflower, pipsissewa, whortleberry, and trillium,

51

much of the forest itself is composed of lodgepole pine, mountain hemlock, Engelmann spruce, and white pine. Since you'll be spending the next 6 miles with these chaps, perhaps we should get to know a little bit more about at least a couple of them.

Engelmann spruce, which grows rather sporadically throughout this forest, is a dark tree—one that lends a feel of rich texture to the timber of the mountains. It's the Engelmanns you'll often see huddled around the lakes of the high country, their straight spires poking into a thin blue sky. The Engelmann's seedlings are an important factor in its survival. They can grow in the shade of their parents, patiently waiting there for their own chance in the sun when the older generation finally succumbs to age. Thus, barring fire, harvest, or avalanche, a forest made up of Engelmann spruce will likely remain that way. The wood of this tree is strong and straight, and it has long been harvested for use in making telephone poles.

The mountain hemlock, on the other hand, is one of the more graceful-looking trees you'll find in the forest, its slender branches curving slightly downward in a gentle arc. Like its cousin the western hemlock, the needles of this tree are short, only one-half to one inch long. Unlike the western hemlock, however, these needles spread on all sides of the twig instead of in two rows. Also, the cones of the mountain hemlock may be two or even three inches long, whereas the western hemlock rarely produces cones much more than an inch long. As it climbs higher and higher up into the mountains, where the

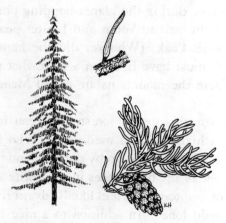

Englemann Spruce

climate is increasingly harsh, this tree becomes shorter and shorter. What was growing a hundred feet tall down in the moist lowland valleys, will at timberline be little more than a prostrate shrub.

You'll intersect the Sky Lakes Trail at 2.75 miles, where you'll bear to the right. A short distance later will be another intersection, this one with the Isherwood Trail; once again, bear to the right. (If you want to add a couple of extra lakes to your trip with only about another 1.3 miles of walking, you can go left on the Isherwood Trail, which eventually loops around the north side of Heavenly Twin Lakes. At the next intersection you take a right, following Heavenly Twin along its east shore until you meet up once again with the route for this walk.)

Very soon after this last trail junction you'll see the small round basin of south Heavenly Twin Lake on your right, which is followed soon thereafter by the north, and much larger, Heavenly Twin. Besides the comings and goings of waterfowl, this is a good place to watch for osprey. At this time these beautiful birds are not nesting along the lake shore, but a few do come fishing here from nesting areas 6 to 8 miles away. Unlike other birds of prey, the osprey eats nothing but fish; watching one hang high over a lake and then plunge straight down to grab a trout with its talons is an extraordinary sight. Because pollutants tend to accumulate in the tissue of fish, osprey are hit hard when toxic chemicals enter the water system. The birds were declining rapidly when DDT was still being used, for example, because the poison was altering the composition of their egg shells, causing them to break prematurely.

Sitting on the shore of this beautiful lake on a silvery autumn evening, a wedge of geese flying overhead bound for Klamath Lake, you can begin to feel a kind of sweet timelessness that so often rises from the heart of wild places. In certain moments you can almost feel akin to those French soldiers who were assigned the task of fanning out into the wilderness of the New World. Nineteenth-century historian Francis Parkman captures the feeling of that other time:

> A boundless vision grows upon us; an untamed continent;
> vast wastes of forest verdure; mountains silent in
> primeval sleep; river, lake and glimmering pool;
> wilderness oceans mingling with the sky.

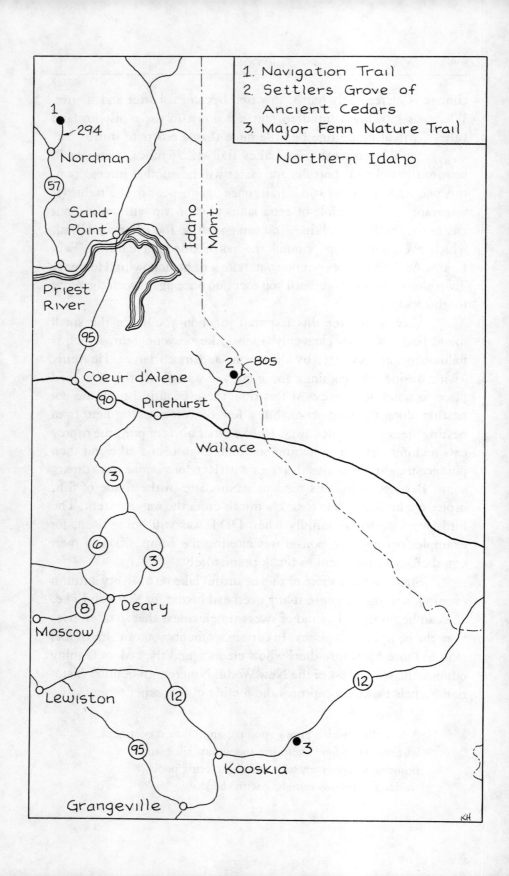

1. Navigation Trail
2. Settlers Grove of
   Ancient Cedars
3. Major Fenn Nature Trail

Northern Idaho

1
294
Nordman
57
Sand-
Point
Idaho   Mont.
Priest
River
95
Coeur d'Alene
90
Pinehurst
Wallace
2   805
3
6
3
8   Deary
Moscow
12
Lewiston   12
95
Kooskia
Grangeville

KH

Idaho

NAVIGATION TRAIL

Distance: 5.1 miles
Location: Kanisku National Forest (within the Idaho Panhandle
National Forests). From the town of Priest River, Idaho, head
north on State Road 57 for approximately 38 miles, to the village
of Nordman. Turn right here (east) onto Forest Road 1339, and
follow it for 12 miles to Beaver Creek Campground. Once inside
the campground complex, follow the signs to the trailhead.

Upper Priest Lake, nestled in the arms of the Selkirk Mountains in
the northwest corner of Idaho's Panhandle, is like a vision from the
past. Walking among these quiet groves of hemlock and cedar and
river birch, a lone canoe paddle flashing on the waters of the lake, you
can almost get a sense of what the Panhandle country was like before
waves of white men began to roll across the land: before the British
pushed into the lake country looking for furs, before the Jesuits and
the Methodists began arm wrestling each other for control of Indian
souls (Priest Lake takes its name from this era), before the first of
what would turn into $4 billion worth of precious metal was pulled
from these mountains, before timber companies took over the lion's
share of the great Panhandle forests, acquiring great stands of old-
growth timber at $1.25 to $2.50 an acre.

 While the trek from Beaver Creek Campground to Upper
Priest Lake is longer than many in this book, it's really just a gentle

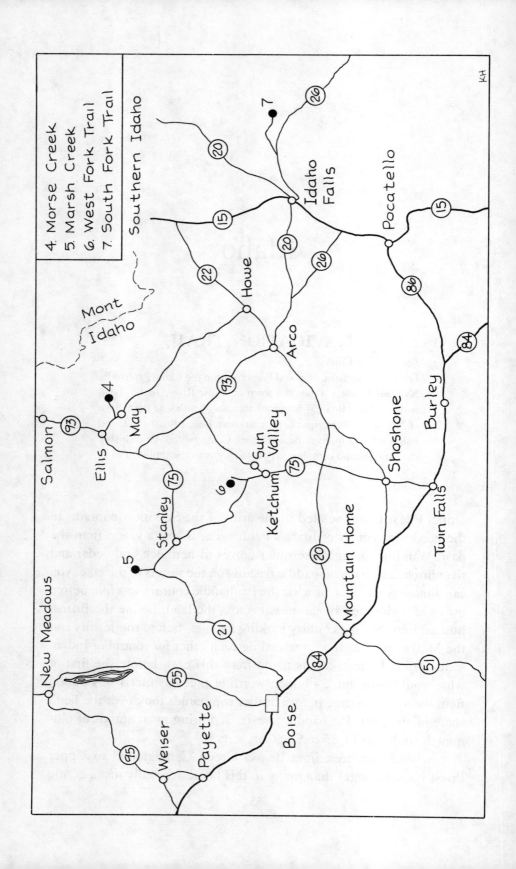

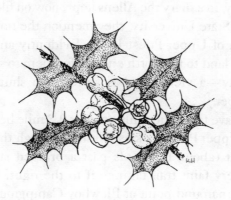

Oregon Grape

woodland stroll, easily managed by a wide variety of age groups.
(One note of caution, though. Because the trail does cross some wet,
muddy cedar and black cottonwood bottoms, wear something on your
feet that you don't mind getting wet.) The first stretch of pathway is
through a fine middle-aged forest; on its edge can be found beargrass, pipsissewa, yellow violets, trillium, and bunchberry, as well as
the hollylike evergreen leaves of Oregon grape. Oregon grape, one of
the most important of all medicinal plants, is one that you'll come
across time and time again during your forays into the woods of the
Northwest. The presence of certain alkaloids in the roots of Oregon
grape gives the plant a number of unique medicinal qualities. The
presence of berberine, which is a muscle stimulant, made it popular
as a drug to use during childbirth for easing the passage of the
placenta. (Interestingly, berberine is also what produces the beautiful yellow dye extracted from Oregon grape and used to color
clothing.) Indians and settlers alike used Oregon grape as a diuretic
and antiseptic, while a tea from the roots was for years a standard
treatment for venereal disease.

At about 2.3 miles into the walk, you'll see a small cabin off to
the left of the trail. This was built sometime between 1910 and 1920
by a man named Alva Allen, who lived in Spokane and worked for the
railroad. Alva and his wife Myrtle christened this humble little abode
the "Allen A Dale," and spent many fine times here wrapped in the
thick weave of wilderness that ran out from their door in all direc-

tions. Curiously, in a diary the Allens kept, now on file in the archives at Washington State University, they mention the fine view they had from the cabin of Upper Priest Lake. Evidently an earlier fire had opened up the land to the north enough for them to see the waters of the lake clearly—a view that has since been shut off by a thick curtain of timber.

You'll have to wait roughly another 0.2 mile before you can see the waters of Upper Priest Lake sparkling through the forest. Shortly after this point (about 100 yards past a bridged stream crossing), you'll find a very faint trail taking off to the right. This short path leads to our turnaround point at Plowboy Campground, a dispersed camping area with a splendid slice of shoreline. From this point you'll be able to glean spectacular views of the lake basin, framed to the east and north by the dramatic green and grey folds of the Selkirk Mountains. Though they've been used and abused in years past, the Selkirks are still a magnificent mountain range—a mix of glacial valleys, abrupt ridgelines and thick, wet forests of cedar, hemlock, and Douglas-fir. (About 10 miles to the east and slightly north of Plowboy Campground is Long Canyon, where you can still find some magnificent groves of 500-year-old western red cedars.)

The Selkirks are also home for the only known group of woodland caribou in the United States—a small herd that makes regular runs in and out of British Columbia. These members of the deer family spend January through May on the high, sparsely forested ridges of the Selkirks, where the snow is compacted enough to allow the animals easy travel. (Snow walking is also made easier by the caribou's large feet, their hooves spreading some six inches across.) Here in the high country they subsist primarily on arboreal lichen, that greenish-gray, mosslike plant you may have seen hanging from the branches of conifers. The catch is that arboreal lichen tends to grow only on trees that are at least a century old. Intense clear-cutting has sharply reduced these important feeding grounds; in addition, the roads constructed during logging operations have resulted in greater access to the herd by hunters, who frequently mistake them for deer or elk. There is currently a strong effort to increase the Selkirk herd of woodland caribou, primarily by augmenting the herd with transplants from British Columbia. (There's some concern that the Selkirk herd is having reproduction problems due to heavy inbreeding.) This truly is a grand struggle, a heroic attempt to restore an animal population that in this region has long been skating on the brink of oblivion.

SETTLERS GROVE OF ANCIENT CEDARS

Distance: 2 miles

Location: Coeur d'Alene National Forest (within the Idaho Panhandle National Forests). From the town of Wallace, Idaho, head north on Sixth Street, toward Dobson Pass. Follow this road for approximately 16.5 miles, and turn right just after crossing the Coeur d'Alene River. Make another right in 1.7 miles onto Forest Road 9, and take this eastward for just under 3 miles, where you'll turn left onto Forest Road 152. About 1.3 miles after this last turn the road will fork; stay to the left, turning onto Forest Road 805. Settlers Grove of Ancient Cedars is about 6 miles down Forest Road 805.

The Settlers Grove of Ancient Cedars does not just show up as some kind of unexpected gift from the highway gods as you fly down the exit ramp looking for a bathroom. Reaching this place requires a rather long, twisted journey over narrow roads; those relatively few who end up here had every intention of doing so. On the other hand, the journey itself is in many ways as fine as the destination. There are a couple of tantalizing views of the beautiful Coeur d'Alene River along the way, as well as a lovely drive along the bottom of Pritchard Creek. The last 6 miles of forest road have more picnic sites and camping spots than you could shake a cedar at, most fronted by the delightful gurgle and froth of the West Fork of Eagle Creek.

Once on the trail itself, these woods seem to gently pull you in, twisting in a lazy meander back and forth over Eagle Creek.

Red-breasted Nuthatch

Cedars and Douglas-fir of fairly moderate size slowly but surely give way to bigger and bigger trees, until by about 0.25 mile you realize you're in a land of utter giants. If you care to exercise your imagination a bit, try to think what it would be like if this grove of creek-bottom cedars were not an anomaly but a normal, everyday swath of forest—if the loggers and road builders and miners had not yet come, if this kind of forest could still be found cloaking river and stream bottoms across much of the Pacific Northwest. What a thought! True, such daydreaming may just be a shameless romanticizing of the past. But when you're steeped in the shade of trees this big, some of which were already a century old when Joan of Arc was raising the siege of Orleans—then such fantasies seem to flow very easily indeed.

At about 0.5 mile, just downstream from the fourth bridge crossing the West Fork of Eagle Creek, you'll see a large downed log—one of several that line much of this trail. The small hemlocks, Douglas-fir, and patches of moss growing out of the top of this fallen giant are good examples of why such downed trees are often referred to as "nurse logs." Bacteria present in the wood of the dead log take nitrogen from the air and convert it to a form that can be used by these new plants, a process referred to as nitrogen fixation. What's more, trees that actually fall into streams, like the jumble of toppled conifers you saw near the second bridge crossing, may be responsible for *most* of the organic nutrients found in the stream system: They hold back debris long enough for it to be biologically broken down.

But that's only the beginning of how valuable these fallen giants can be. The limbs and root tangles serve as perches, feeding sites, and nesting areas for winter wrens, thrushes, juncos, woodpeckers, western flycatchers, chestnut-backed chickadees, and red-breasted nuthatches. Blue grouse dance for a mate on the tops of these fallen trees, and squirrels use them as feeding tables from which they can keep a close eye on the surrounding terrain. There are literally dozens and dozens of birds, mammals, and invertebrates that use such downed timber every day. Such trees are hardly "wasted," as some people would have you believe, simply because they never make it to the lumber mill.

At 0.7 mile is yet another stream crossing, this one marked by a lovely downstream vista of timbered islands and braided channels. On either side of the bridge keep your eyes open for violets, trilliums, wild gingers, and western goldthreads. Our turnaround for this walk is completely arbitrary. From a short distance past this last bridge a faint trail continues to climb along the West Fork of Eagle Creek, topping out in just under 4 miles at an old forest road that heads north to Bloom Peak—a 5,800-foot-high promontory sitting smack-dab on the forested ridge that divides Idaho from Montana.

MAJOR FENN NATURE TRAIL

Distance: 1 mile
Location: From U.S. Highway 12 along the Lochsa River, turn into the Major Fenn Picnic Area, located 0.2 mile west of mile marker 108. To reach the nature trail, cross a small bridge over a flood channel, and turn left. Numbered posts correspond to a plant identification guide, copies of which you should find near the parking area.

When you find out that the Major Fenn area contains a large "coastal disjunct plant population," your first instinct may be to run off and phone the exterminator. But what this scientific jargon really means is that as you walk this short trail you'll be passing fifteen plants that aren't supposed to be here at all, but rather 400 miles to the west, along the coasts of Oregon and Washington. As if that alone weren't enough reason to come here, you'll also find identified an entire garden of wild plants common to much of northern Idaho; in fact, walking this trail is a perfect preview of what you'll see on other hikes in the region. The Clearwater National Forest and the Clearwater Valley Garden Club have done a splendid job on the plant identification guide found at the trailhead—a brochure that's keyed to fifteen stops, each offering a nice mix of both natural and cultural history. Perhaps the only fly in the ointment is that this area does lie awfully close to the highway; fortunately, the noise can be avoided simply by planning your visit for early in the morning.

Since the Clearwater Valley Garden Club has made sure you'll get your fill of plant information, let's talk a little bit about the cultural history of the area. First and foremost, perhaps, is Major Fenn, whose name graces not only this trail and picnic area, but a mountain peak in the Selway Crags. The Major's parents were among the first families to settle in central Idaho during the 1860s. They had a son named Frank who, along with six other children, attended Idaho's first public school in a town along the Salmon River by the name of Florence—a town, incidentally, that by the summer of 1862 was producing $50,000 worth of gold a day! Frank left the boomtown life for the adventure of the military, graduating from the Naval Academy

KH

River Otter

and carving out a distinguished military record in the Spanish-American War. He eventually returned to Idaho County, however, and wore the hat of every profession from lawyer to teacher to newspaper publisher. Fenn finally landed a position as the first supervisor of the Clearwater National Forest—indeed, one of the first forest supervisors in the entire state of Idaho.

Of course there were other people living in these rugged mountain folds long before white men started writing their history across the land. Archaeological finds indicate that people were roaming this region 12,000 years ago; gathering seeds and berries, taking mussels and fish from the rivers, and hunting the great wooly mammoth with spears. As the centuries went by they became more and more proficient at gathering food, especially the salmon, which they found could be caught in healthy numbers using special fishing platforms that leaned out over the Lochsa, Clearwater, and Selway Rivers.

A somewhat drastic, but exciting change happened during the 1700s to the people we know historically as the Nez Percé, spurred by the arrival of the horse. Not only did these people put the horse to work expanding their hunting grounds to the buffalo country of Montana (often traveling the Lolo Trail, which lies just to the north of where you now stand), but they also bred horses—most notably the beautiful Appaloosa.

The political system of the Nez Percé was not a ruler-based form of government, but a loose network of family bands who the elders advised, but did not command. This system, which greatly honored the autonomy of the individual and the family unit, made the idea of blanket treaties utterly ludicrous. Even though certain elders did sign such agreements with the American government, the treaties meant virtually nothing to those who refused to do so. When treaty makers tried to talk Chief Joseph into selling Nez Percé lands he told them rather matter-of-factly that such a request was ridiculous: "The earth is too sacred to be valued by or sold for silver and gold."

The number of cultural tales running up and down the Lochsa would fill volumes. (Lochsa, incidentally, is a Flathead Indian word meaning "rough water.") An old rifle found in the hills might be that of a lone hunter who died from a bad fall on the Lolo

Trail, while an ax-hewn log high on a river bank could be a piece of a raft used by hunters trying to escape the cold slap of winter. An overgrown, unmarked grave is perhaps that of dance-hall girl Moose Creek Molly. And the same patch of ground you settle into on a cold fall night might just be the same one used by Lewis and Clark on their epic journey to the Pacific Ocean in 1805. Sometimes it seems that more than any other forest in Idaho, on the Clearwater the old days and ways are still wonderfully fresh and alive.

Besides the plants described in the Major Fenn Plant Identification Brochure, would-be botanists might also want to keep an eye out for heal-all, yarrow, mullein, twinflower, twisted-stalk, queen's cup, and on the final stretch of trail along the flood channel, tall weaves of orchard grass and the soft white blooms of dogwood. Should, heaven forbid, you not find one of the trail brochures waiting for you, the following is a list of each plant and the post that marks it. After you come off the trail, call or stop by a Clearwater National Forest ranger station for a copy.

1. sword fern
2. serviceberry
3. Pacific yew
4. Douglas hawthorn
5. kinnikinnick
6. bear grass
7. Oregon grape
8. black cottonwood
9. red-osier dogwood
10. snowberry
11. horsetail
12. ocean-spray
13. syringa
14. paper birch
15. cascara

MORSE CREEK

Distance: 4.3 miles

Location: Challis National Forest. From U.S. Highway 93 at the tiny town of Ellis, turn southeast along the north side of the Pahsimeroi River, following a road that leads through the village of May. Follow this for 10.7 miles to Forest Road 094 (a small landing strip is at the southeast corner of this intersection). Follow Forest Road 094 east for just under 7 miles to the Morse Creek Campground. Our trail takes off on a narrow road to the left just before you cross a bridge leading into the campground. (Note: Much of Forest Road 094 is narrow and one-lane, not suitable for large vehicles or those pulling trailers.)

Long before you actually reach the trailhead for the Morse Creek walk you'll find yourself immersed in some of the most classic stretches of sage-covered basin and range scenery to be found anywhere in the Northwest. The lonely Pahsimeroi Valley sprawls for miles and miles between the timbered flanks of the Lemhi and Lost River ranges, the vastness either completely overwhelming you, or dazzling you with such a scouring brightness that the whole scene shimmers on in your mind long after you've gone. Most visitors to Idaho never end up anywhere close to this area, opting instead for the Pioneer or Sawtooth Mountains, or the big lakes and thick green forests of the Panhandle. But those willing to spend a little extra energy to access these more remote southeastern regions will find no shortage of reward.

Before you leave the Pahsimeroi Valley to make your way up into the cool timber of the Lemhi Range, look carefully across the sage flats for pronghorn, which are as plentiful here as in any other part of the state. If ever there was an animal built for this wide open country, this is it. If you can get a look at the face of a pronghorn through field glasses, you'll notice that its eyes stick out from the side of its skull, giving it an astonishing degree of peripheral vision. Add to that the fact that pronghorn can see small movements miles away— perhaps the equivalent of eight-power binoculars—and you get the idea that no one sneaks up on these guys.

Even if you did get fairly close to a pronghorn, considering that they've been clocked over short distances doing seventy miles per hour (making them by far the fastest animal on the continent), it's not likely that you'd get close for long. Baby pronghorns can outrun a man when they're just four days old! Finally, pronghorn are able to

Pronghorn

Balsamroot

subsist on very scant range vegetation, and can go without water for extremely long periods of time. Thus while the wide, windswept sage flats of the Pahsimeroi may look inhospitable to us, to the fleet-footed pronghorn, perhaps no environment in all the world could be any better.

Our walk begins on the north side of Morse Creek, along a broad green line of aspen, alder, and cottonwood, as well as thimbleberry, red-osier dogwood, and wild rose. In addition to being beautiful to look at when in bloom, wild roses have had a long history of use throughout the world. They were hung on cradleboards by Idaho's Nez Percé Indians to keep evil spirits away from babies. The fruit, or "hips," were collected by the ton in Great Britain during World War II to make a vitamin-rich syrup, since at the time citrus could not be imported. (Three rosehips have the same vitamin C content as a large orange.) The Greeks associated the rose with Aphrodite, the goddess of love, and Egyptian rulers literally slept on beds stuffed with rose petals. Christianity later adapted the rose for its own purposes, blessing it as associated with the Virgin Mary. Early peoples of this region often used the wild rose plant medicinally, treating everything from nosebleeds to sore eyes to diarrhea.

As the road climbs onto drier ground high above the stream

corridor, the vegetation begins to change. Sage does well here, as does rabbitbrush, broom snakeweed, and balsamroot—the latter plant casting lovely yellow blooms across the hillsides from mid-May through early July. In many ways this walk passes through an ecological bridge that exists between the alpine peaks ahead, and the high, hot desert down below. One minute you'll be beside an awesome slide of bare and broken talus, with tiny pikas running between the boulders; and the next beside a pocket meadow thick with grasses and wildflowers. There are beautiful Douglas-firs and Engelmann spruces here, as well as curl-leaf cercocarpus (sometimes called "mountain mahogany") and small huddles of black willow and chokecherry.

Shortly after passing a magnificent talus slope at 2 miles in, the canyon will begin to narrow. In another 0.2 mile you'll reach our turnaround at the point where Cold Creek comes in from a deep ravine to the north. In the summer this makes a wonderful lunch stop, as most of the immediate area is bathed in the cool shade of spruce, fir, and aspen. Were you to walk another 3 miles up the trail (doing some serious climbing along the way), you'd find yourself on the spectacular Lemhi Divide. Strung together by 10,000- and 11,000-foot peaks, this craggy backbone of the Lemhi Range is pure alpine. It's a place of lingering snows and fast-stepping streams and tiny pocket lakes—a crisp, soaring landscape, a world away from the Pahsimeroi and Lemhi valleys far below.

MARSH CREEK

Distance: 2.6 miles
Location: Challis National Forest, Frank Church–River of No
Return Wilderness. From the town of Stanley, head west on
Idaho State Highway 21. Go 0.5 mile past mile marker 113 and
turn right. Immediately after making this turn bear to the left,
following Forest Road 83. Our trailhead is at the end of Forest
Road 83, 1.5 miles from where you turned off the highway.

By the time Marsh Creek enters the Frank Church–River of No
Return Wilderness, miles from the calm waters laced with beaver
ponds that mark its headwaters, it has considerably picked up its
pace. For the next 5 miles it will dance down a rugged canyon framed
by steep slopes covered in ragged cloaks of pine and talus, eventually
joining Bear Valley Creek. Together these two watercourses will
thunder northward, forming the wild beginnings of the famed Middle Fork of the Salmon River.

To lovers of wild rivers, the various forks of the Salmon are a
kind of Xanadu—a fantasy place so magnificent, so completely free-
flying that you almost hold your breath for fear they will dissolve
before your eyes. Indeed, the Salmon is the longest river in the lower
forty-eight that's contained within the boundaries of a single state. It
drains a phenomenal 14,000 square miles of land, and much of that is
as grand and untamed as the twentieth-century traveler could ever
hope to find.

The Shoshone chief Cameahwait warned the Lewis and Clark
expedition not to follow the Lemhi to the Columbia—that it would
first join a fearsome watercourse called "the river of no return." (It
was too filled with rapids to make upstream travel practical.) After
reaching the point where the Lemhi joined the main Salmon, Clark
headed down about 50 miles of the watercourse to see for himself.
"The mountains are close and there is a perpendicular cliff on each
side . . . [the river] continues for a great distance and . . . the water
runs with great violence from one rock to the other on each side

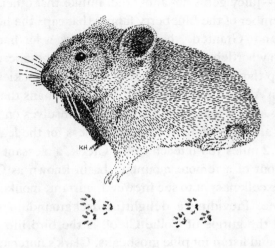

Pika

foaming and roaring through rocks in every direction, so as to render the passage of anything impossible." Although the trek along the Clearwater drainage to the north was gruesome, and the Lolo Trail was filled with seemingly endless snow and mud and steep saddles, the decision Clark made not to attempt passage on the Salmon undoubtedly saved the expedition from disaster.

A short distance into our walk you'll pass a large talus slope on the left. This is a perfect place to look for pikas—busy little creatures that appear to be half-rabbit and half-guinea pig. They find a perfect home in these great jumbles of rock. Even if you don't see pikas here, more than likely you'll hear their shrill "Eeek! eeek!" ringing down the mountainside. Lacking that, look carefully around the talus for small piles of grasses and leaves spread out across some sunlit slab of rock. These are the pika's harvests, set out to cure and then be stored underground as winter rations. (Pikas do not hibernate.) A more industrious farmer you'll never see.

The path moves through lodgepole pine, spruce, and fir to a fine elevated perch above Marsh Creek at 0.9 mile. Along this stretch look for fireweed, strawberry, and yarrow, as well as a thick understory of whortleberry. Though tiny, the berries of this latter plant are

71

quite tasty—juicy gems not altogether unlike that other, much more familiar member of the blueberry family that caps the heath balds of New England. Granted, you'd have to work a lot harder to fill a bucket with whortleberries than you would with blueberries, but that doesn't stop thousands of outdoors-lovers in the Rockies from heading out each August to do just that. Nor are humans the only fans of these plants. Bears make regular pigs of themselves on the whortleberry crop, and deer and elk have a fondness for the leaves.

In 1.2 miles you'll reach Collie Creek, a pleasant little stream that pours out of a remote mountain basin known as Collie Lake. This is an excellent spot to see fireweed, currant, monkeyflower, and rue anemone. Providing a delightful background to the flush of flowers and the gurgle of Collie Creek is the bird life to be found here. Look and listen for pine grosbeaks, Clark's nutcrackers, mountain chickadees, golden-crowned kinglets, white-breasted nuthatches, evening grosbeaks, and hairy woodpeckers.

WEST FORK TRAIL

Distance: 2 miles

Location: Sawtooth National Recreation Area. Travel north out of Ketchum on Idaho State Road 75 for approximately 7 miles, and turn right onto a road that runs along the east side of Sawtooth National Recreation Area Headquarters. (This road is located 0.3 mile north of mile marker 136.) Follow this for 5.4 miles to the trailhead parking lot. Two trails take off from here; ours runs west, descending to cross the West Fork of the Big Wood River.

The walk up the West Fork (actually the West Fork of the North Fork of the Big Wood River) is not really spectacular, though there are some rather impressive views of the craggy scarps that make up the southern edge of the Boulder Mountains. But more than having great

72

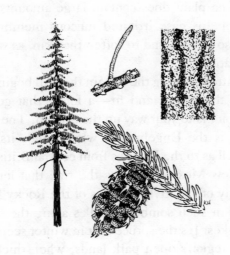

Douglas-fir

views, this walk is a gentle meander through a mature spruce-fir forest—a loosely woven cathedral of conifers spiked here and there by sunlit meadows of grass, wildflowers, and currants.

The path begins with a gentle descent to the West Fork, which it then crosses on a set of fallen logs. This is a good place to look for strawberry, rue anemone, milk vetch, monkeyflower, yarrow, sticky geranium, and, in the more open areas, paintbrush and mullein. The two-foot- to six-foot-tall spikes of mullein, with their fuzzy leaves and tightly packed clusters of yellow flowers, is one of the easiest of all plants to identify. Step up for a closer look at the hairy leaves of this plant and you'll understand why it's also sometimes known as "flannel flower" or even "bunny's ears." For centuries people living in cold climates have packed mullein leaves into the bottoms of their shoes in order to keep their feet warm. In Roman times the stems were often dipped in fat and used as torches, while no witch of the Middle Ages worth her cauldron would be caught without mullein as an ingredient for love potions.

Mullein also has a fairly impressive list of medical attributes. Northwest pioneers found out from various Indian peoples of the region that smoking the leaves of the mullein would relieve coughs and asthma. (The plant does contain large amounts of mucilage, a substance that helps ease irritated mucous membranes.) Mullein extracts have also been found to soften the skin, as well as to relieve minor skin irritations.

Shortly after crossing the stream the trail begins a fairly gentle ascent through the spruce and fir—a forest that gets increasingly impressive as you make your way up the canyon. The primary spruce you'll see here is the Engelmann, which lends its beauty to the Cascades, as well as to the Rockies from central British Columbia all the way into New Mexico. This is the tree that lends such a rich luster to so many of the idyllic scenes of the Rocky Mountains; the one that stands in such somber huddles along the shores of quiet, mid-elevation lakes. It's the spruce that in winter seems to punctuate so many of the region's open park lands, when thick quilts of new snow hang from its dark, supple branches. (Engelmann spruce takes on a decidedly different look along many highways, where it has been used to fashion a great many of the nation's telephone poles.)

Unlike the seedlings of many conifers, Engelmann seedlings can live and grow, albeit slowly, in the shade of their parents. When older trees weakened by age or disease start falling over, the young-sters suddenly find themselves in streams of sunlight, where they can really kick into high gear.

Though there are subalpine firs here, the second most-common conifer that will be keeping you company along this walk is the Douglas-fir. Except for the two sequoias found farther to the west, this mammoth tree is the largest in North America. It was to the Douglas-fir that the lumber industry turned at the end of the nineteenth century when the great stands of eastern white pine played out. When it came time to replace the masts of the great historic ship *Constitution* ("Old Ironsides"), no eastern white pine of sufficient size could be found for the task. In the end, it was Douglas-fir that filled the bill. Identifying Douglas-fir (which, by the way, is not a true fir at all) is relatively easy. Just take a close look at one of the cones. Between the scales lie soft, three-pointed bracts—the Douglas-fir is the only tree to bear bracts in these tridentlike shapes.

When botanist David Douglas first strode ashore near the Columbia River in 1825 and began measuring the species that would one day take his name, he was hardly unimpressed with the size of these giants. One fallen specimen measured 227 feet long and was 48 feet around! While the Douglas-firs along this trail are hardly that big, several are thought to be at least 400 years old. That means when these trees were seeing their first splashes of sunlight, a math professor named Galileo was running around the town of Pisa, speculating on the nature of gravity. By the time these trees had twenty-five years under their roots, that same math teacher was standing in front of the Inquisition, about to be ordered by the Roman Catholic Church to stop his scientific work altogether.

In about a mile the trail will have rejoined the stream again, directly across from a number of beetle-killed trees, as well as a fine avalanche slope where young spruce and fir are already racing to reclaim the land. There's good access here through the open forest and past the currant bushes to the banks of the West Fork. This is in every sense a delightful stream, one with waters that can carry your troubles right out of this forest and on to the Snake River, far to the south.

SOUTH FORK TRAIL

Distance: 3.8 miles

Location: Targhee National Forest. From the town of Idaho Falls, head east on U.S. Highway 26. About 10 miles out of town, turn left (north) onto Heise Road, following the signs for Heise Hot Springs. (This turn is 0.3 mile past mile marker 352.) Follow this road north for 2 miles, and turn right (east) for 1.4 miles. Turn right again here, and pass by Heise Hot Springs resort. At a point 2.5 miles from this last junction you'll turn right once again onto Forest Road 206 (also known as the Snake River Road). Follow Forest Road 206 for 13.3 miles (it makes a jaunt to the right at 8.1 miles), and then bear right at a Y intersection, following the signs for Black Canyon. Our trailhead is 1.8 miles from this Y intersection, on the right side of the road.

Because reaching this trailhead requires navigating a rather long and twisted line of dirt road, it's not a jaunt for those in a hurry. On the other hand, a particularly beautiful stretch of the Snake River will accompany you for many of those miles, offering plenty of splendid places to pull off and soak up the roll of mountain water, the honk of Canada geese, and the gentle flutter of aspen, willow, and cottonwood. In fact, if you're not in a hurry, you may find that the drive to South Fork Trail is one of the more engaging aspects of this entire trip.

This is one of the last places where the Snake, fresh out of Wyoming, can be considered a river of the high country. Though it has so far kept close company with some of the most beautiful mountains in the West, a half-dozen or so miles downstream it will begin to settle into a long, haunting mosaic of high desert—a swath of sand and sage and basalt that will frame these banks all the way to the Snake's confluence with the Columbia.

The Northern Shoshone Indians, who once occupied much of southern and eastern Idaho, western Wyoming, and northeastern Utah, have a wonderful myth to explain the origin of the Snake River. One day Coyote, that clever trickster of so many American Indian legends, was out walking in the Yellowstone country, when he came upon an old woman (Mother Earth) with a giant basket of water filled

Coyote

with beautiful big fish (Yellowstone Lake). "I'm so hungry," he told the woman. "Won't you cook some of those fish for me?" The woman agreed, but before she set off to fix him his dinner, she warned him not to touch her basket of fish. Of course Coyote couldn't behave himself, and before long he'd managed to knock the entire container over, sending water and fish sprawling all over the place.

Coyote ran ahead of the water as fast as he could, trying to stop it by piling rocks in its path. But when he did, the water simply broke through his makeshift dam—first creating upper, and then lower Yellowstone Falls, and eventually the entire Yellowstone River.

Next Coyote ran to another channel of spreading water and tried to stop it the same way. Time after time he piled up rocks in the path of the water to stop it, but each time the torrent broke through, creating what we know today as Idaho Falls, American Falls, Twin Falls, and even Hells Canyon. And it's because of these great waterfalls Coyote created, over which no fish can pass, that salmon are no longer found along the upper regions of the Snake River. Interestingly, many geologists believe that there were times when Yellowstone Lake did in fact drain into the Pacific via the Snake River, instead of into the Gulf of Mexico by way of the Missouri and Mississippi, as it does today.

A rather less-complicated explanation of how the Snake River came into being concerns Paul Bunyon. One night, after drinking nine kegs of rum, Paul went tottering off into the dark night, weaving the crazy meanders of the Snake River channel along the way.

Our trail begins with a crossing of Black Canyon Creek, and then starts a fairly steep, 0.3-mile climb to a saddle separating the parking area from the Snake River Valley. On both sides of this saddle you'll see places where people have "cut switchbacks," a common habit in mountainous areas that quickly leads to serious erosion problems. Since most of the topsoil has already been washed away, it will be years before plants can stabilize these deep troughs.

When you reach the top of the saddle, you'll have a striking view of the Snake River below—a lush tapestry of willow-lined channels that are often thick with various kinds of songbirds and waterfowl. A bird that's especially easy to see here in early summer is the Canada goose, that grand symbol of wildness that tugs at our hearts with each long, honking flight line we see streaking south across the autumn skies. Once the flock arrives in an appropriate breeding area, such as these quiet river channels along the Snake, the female Canada goose will direct the search for a good nest site, the male following close behind. When a suitable place is found, the female spends the next several hours hollowing out a shallow depression in the earth and lining the perimeter with grasses, twigs, etc. (In some areas Canada geese nest on tall stumps, or in specially constructed elevated breeding boxes.)

The female goose typically lays one egg per day until the entire clutch of four to six eggs is complete. Whenever she leaves the nest to feed, she first covers it with leaves, feathers, or twigs. The hatch takes twenty-eight days. Once the kids are up and about, which takes only a few days, the defense of the nesting territory, with its concomitant loud, raucous honking and intense posturing by the male, comes to an end.

If you're here in midsummer you'll find Canada geese more difficult to spot. This is when the adults are going through a molt that renders them unable to fly for several weeks, a period when they stay very secluded, dashing for cover whenever they detect the slightest threat. About the time the molt ends the young geese become able to fly, and at that point the family comes together with other families in open feeding grounds.

Canada geese mate for life, and return from their wintering areas to the same breeding grounds year after year. The internal map that leads these birds back and forth across thousands of miles is imparted by the parents to the offspring in just a single migration.

The path descends through a blend of serviceberry, bitterbrush, sage, larkspur, juniper, and arrowleaf balsamroot, framed by high, rugged cliffs and parapets that have been chiseled out of volcanic rock. Once you've completed the short descent, the path will take you eastward on a lazy meander through a mix of deciduous and coniferous trees underlain with whortleberry, wallflower, and Oregon grape, the gush and whisper of the Snake River always by your side. In 1.1 miles you'll cross a small cattle guard; 0.2 mile later you'll reach our turnaround, which is at a point where the trail opens up into a flat, open parkland studded with junipers and cottonwoods. Immediately across from this park is a sizable river island—a perfect place, at least in early summer, to see the comings and goings of Canada geese.

THE COAST

I always leave this primitive beach reluctantly. The music of the ocean front seems to establish a rhythm in man. For hours and even days afterward I can almost hear the booming of the tides on the headlands and the sound of the wind in the giant spruce.

—WILLIAM O. DOUGLAS,
at Olympic National Park

It seems there is almost no ill feeling, no worry or wave of hopelessness that the coast of Oregon and Washington cannot ease. Here are long curls of sand to walk down on bright blue days, and furious, wind-driven waves that rip to shreds the dullness we've accumulated in the trenches of the city. Here are shimmering tide pools with all the strangeness of Alice's looking glass, and estuaries that each autumn shudder with the rise and fall of beating wings. It seems the coast is the one ecosystem we can never fully know, no matter how long we spend with it—that place where minds lose their moorings, drift out, and are lost to the visions of the earth.

Perhaps what is ultimately so surprising about the coastal environment is how many different habitats are squeezed into such a narrow ribbon of land. There is the sand dune world—foredunes capped with soft lines of sea rocket and silky beach pea, and wet deflation plains fringed each morning with the fresh tracks of raccoon. On the Olympic coast there are gray beaches guarded by black, almost haunting sea stacks. On the leading edges of the great sand spits you'll find the playgrounds of whales and harbor seals, while on the trailing edges is safe winter harbor for black brants, arctic loons, buffleheads, goldeneyes, scaups, teals, pintails, and Canada geese.

83

In the tidal pools the habitats are even more compressed. Suddenly life is perched along narrow bands that represent the most delicate balance of elements imaginable; for many kinds of creatures, to move even a few yards closer or farther from the sea would mean certain disaster. (Because of this precarious existence, it's extremely important that you put any tide pool rocks you may have moved back exactly where you found them. Never disturb eggs of any kind.)

The edge of the sea is perhaps the most astonishing of the Northwest environments—for its beauty, its richness, its strangeness. Whether you dive into these mysteries with books at hand and binoculars blazing, or come for nothing but an ocean sunset; whether you spend weeks prowling this maze of hidden coves and pocket beaches, or just stand beside Highway 101 for five minutes letting the rhythms of the waves roll across your shoulders, the Northwest coast will make your world a little broader, a little brighter than it was before.

Washington

ROSARIO BEACH

Distance: 0.7 mile
Location: Deception Pass State Park. From Interstate 5, head west on Oregon State Highway 20 for 16 miles. Turn right (north) following the signs for Rosario Beach. The trailhead is 1.2 miles down this road, adjacent to a picnic area. Our walk takes off from the west side of the turnaround loop, descending a small bluff onto a rocky beach filled with driftwood. (The main pathway—not ours—goes south, toward the large story totem near the picnic area.)

Rosario, named for the patroness of the Spanish exploring ship *San Carlos*, is a wonderful mix of rough, rocky headlands and shimmering tidal pools. If you'd like to explore the tidal pools, be sure to plan your visit for low tide; the Deception Pass State Park office can advise you on when low tides will be. Even if your timing is off, though, a trip here is still worthwhile. A longer, somewhat more rugged trail takes off to the east from near the picnic grounds toward Bowman Bay and Lighthouse Point, passing a fine weave of paintbrush, broomrape, camas lily, stonecrop, kinnikinnick, and rice-root along the way.

Upon first reaching the beach, make your way south past the large piles of driftwood to the smooth black tiers of basalt that are riddled with various-sized pockets of seawater. If you've never visited

85

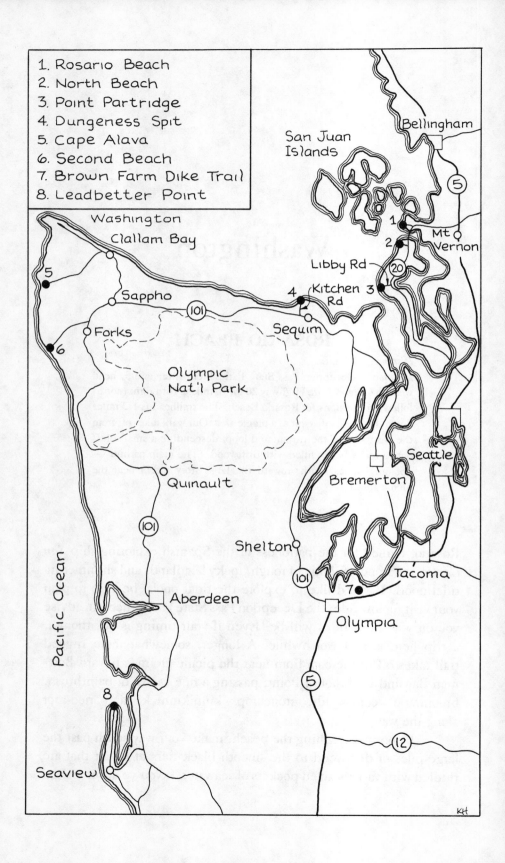

1. Rosario Beach
2. North Beach
3. Point Partridge
4. Dungeness Spit
5. Cape Alava
6. Second Beach
7. Brown Farm Dike Trail
8. Leadbetter Point

San Juan Islands

Bellingham

Mt Vernon

Washington

Clallam Bay

Libby Rd

Kitchen Rd

Sappho

Sequim

Forks

Olympic Nat'l Park

Quinault

Shelton

Bremerton

Seattle

Tacoma

Olympia

Aberdeen

Pacific Ocean

Seaview

KH

a tide pool area like this before, some of the first creatures you may want to take a closer look at are the barnacles that lie plastered to the rocks. Barnacles feed only when submerged in water, extending small, feathery appendages known as cirri to collect algae, microscopic animals, and the tiny eggs of other creatures.

Because barnacles always "eat in," they expend no energy trying to find food. Their problem is not one of travel, but rather of how to stay put—how, in other words, to keep from being ripped from their moorings by the strong slap of ocean waves. To achieve this, barnacles secrete an incredibly strong adhesive from glands located near their front pair of antennae. (This cement is so powerful that corporate chemists spent years studying it in order to come up with their own formulas for super industrial adhesives.) For a long time people didn't know what to think of this strange little critter with the calcium plates. Was it plant or was it animal? At one point it was even suggested that barnacles were neither—that they in fact grew from sea bird feathers that had dropped onto the rocks.

One clue to remember if you are looking for specific forms of sea life is that most creatures here are picky about how much time, if any, they spend either out of water or exposed to sunlight. An acorn barnacle or an eroded periwinkle can feed, rid itself of waste, and perform necessary respiration functions during relatively brief ocean dousings. Other plants and animals, such as bull kelp, starfish, and mussels require much greater exposure to the ocean, and thus will be found further down, in what are called, from highest to lowest, the middle littoral, lower littoral, and sublittoral zones. While setting up shop in such tight, specific zones might seem like a precarious way to live, in some ways it's not altogether different from terrestrial animals. A great many birds, mammals, reptiles, and insects live in life zones of their own: ones bracketed by specific ranges of temperature and moisture.

As you make your way out of the barnacle zone, watch for sea lettuce and the inflated bladders of rockweed, as well as sea urchins, chitons, feather dusters (actually a type of worm), purple shore crabs, and flat porcelain crabs. Before we leave the tide pools, one word of caution. As I've suggested, many of these creatures are extremely sensitive to changes in sunlight or moisture. Therefore, it's important to not make drastic changes to their environment during your explorations. If you pick up a rock to look for a crab, for instance, be sure to put it back just as you found it. While you're poking around the rocks, don't forget to cast an eye up and outward once and a while. Besides spotting sea otters, you're likely to see western grebes, glaucous-winged gulls, ospreys, double-crested and pelagic cormorants, and perhaps even a bald eagle or two.

When you're ready to head back, carefully make your way eastward up the headland to a small footpath. Take a right here and you'll be on your way to a quick circle tour of Rosario Head, coming back out to the picnic area near the large totem in less than 0.3 mile. To the south you'll have fine views of North Beach on Whidbey Island, and to the southwest, the large, rocky promontory of Lighthouse Point.

NORTH BEACH

Distance: 2 miles
Location: Deception Pass State Park. From Interstate 5 north of Mount Vernon, take exit 230 and head west on Washington State Highway 20 for approximately 17.5 miles. Once you cross the bridge to Whidbey Island, turn right toward Deception Pass State Park Headquarters, and follow the signs to the West Point of West Beach parking area. Our walk heads east from this point, taking off from beneath a large totem that stands near the West Beach parking area.

There's a certain air of historical intrigue hanging on the cool salt air of Deception Pass—a wonderful mix of totem cultures and sailing ships and fishermen homesteaders. Indeed, your first steps along this trail will pass beside a beautiful bear totem. This is a replica of one used by a people known as the Haida, who lived north of here in the Queen Charlotte Islands, off the coast of British Columbia. As the interpretive sign at this totem says, the Haida sometimes came south

Great Horned Owl

into the Whidbey Island area to take slaves. This, however, is not the only reason the Haida left home. They were considered to be the most widely traveled of all the region's native residents, making regular forays in all directions to trade, fish, and hunt.

Outside of doctors and shamans, there were three classes of people in Haida culture: chiefs, noblemen, and commoners. Slaves, as you might expect, were at the beck and call of those in the upper tiers. As horrible a fate as being taken a slave would be, you probably

89

could have done worse than to be carted off by the Haida. Haida slaves were rarely beaten or tortured in the course of daily life as they were in many other cultures. What's more, Haida captives were usually allowed to marry and have their own families, and many were later ransomed and taken back home by their relatives.

Though the Haida ate a wide variety of seafood, they made a staple of the salmon they took from coastal streams and rivers with spears, dam-traps, and dip nets. For countless years the Haida, like the other cultures of the Northwest Coast, lived in relative harmony with the land, their populations balanced with the abundance of natural resources found here. In the end, however, they did not fare well under the advance of the Europeans. In the mid-1850s the Haida numbered about eight thousand; forty-five years later, barely six hundred were left.

Peregrine Falcon

Our walk begins by ascending a small rock promontory flush with tall Oregon grape, salal, and salmonberry, all of which, by the way, were food sources for the Haida and other coastal cultures. In 0.1 mile the trail drops into the park amphitheater, where you may have trouble finding it again. The easiest route is to head for the northeast corner of the amphitheater parking lot—in other words, the corner closest to the beach and to the Deception Pass bridge. Beyond this parking area the trail generally parallels the beach through a cool green forest of Douglas-fir and cedar, with occasional smatterings of shore pine, red alder, and madrone.

If ever you were to pick a spot to watch the dynamics of tides, this stretch of Deception Pass would be the place. Tides result from the gravitational relationship that exists between the earth, moon, and to a lesser degree, the sun. The moon has a fairly strong draw on the earth, actually pulling the oceans upward and then releasing them again each time it circles the earth. (Of course it also pulls on the land, but as the land is much denser, there is little response.) We can predict this pulling (high tide) and this releasing (low tide) because we know precisely how long the moon's journey takes. But you may wonder why, when the moon orbits the earth only once in a twenty-four-hour period, there are two high tides and two low tides each day. As it turns out, when the moon tugs at the earth, it has little effect on the oceans lying on the opposite side of the planet. In fact, centrifugal force makes them bulge away from the earth too (though to a lesser degree), thus causing another high tide. Low tides, then, can be thought of as simply marking the halfway point of two simultaneously occurring high tides.

As for the role of the sun, on the two days each month that it's aligned with the moon and the earth, the additional gravitational draw leads to a very high tide, known as a spring tide. On the two days each month that the sun is at right angles to the moon, we have very low tides, or neap tides.

Funneled through this narrow passageway, the tidal flows at Deception Pass are especially dramatic—roiling rivers of seawater charging alternately east or west at a fierce pace. On a strong ebb tide, 2.5 billion gallons of water boil through the narrowest part of the channel every hour. Obviously, the combination of fast water and narrow channel sets up some rather perilous conditions for navigators.

In fact Canoe Pass, which is the smaller of the two channels that lie underneath the bridge you see ahead, was so named by pioneers because nothing much larger than a canoe could safely negotiate it.

The many side trails off the main North Beach path can be confusing: Just keep heading east toward the Deception Pass Bridge, paralleling the beach whenever possible. In 1 mile the trail will enter a large beach-side picnic area. This is an idyllic spot, carved out of a magnificent forest of Douglas-fir, cedar, and Sitka spruce; the towering trunks planted in an airy, almost ethereal understory of sword fern. From this point follow the pathway down to the beach, and, if the tide is low enough, plan to return to West Point via the beach. In winter this is a fine place to look for bald eagles, which dine regularly on salmon as well as on a ducklike bird known as a western grebe. If you're here in March, check out the cliffs on your left for brilliant sprays of red-flower currant. Just about the time that coastal residents are suffering from terminal cases of winter drab, the red-flowered currant bursts on the scene and shouts "Spring!" It's one of the first of the blooms to appear, and a more beautiful beginning I can't imagine.

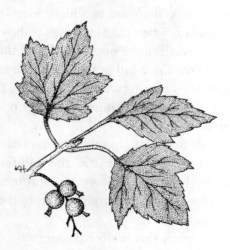

Red-flower Currant

POINT PARTRIDGE

Distance: 2 miles
Location: Fort Ebey State Park. From the Deception Pass
bridge at the northern edge of Whidbey Island, head south on
Washington State Highway 20 for about 16 miles, and turn right
(west), following the signs for Fort Ebey State Park. Once in the
park, you'll come to a T intersection. Turn left, and follow the
signs to the old gun battery emplacement. Our trail takes off near
a picnic area, on the north side of a high bluff overlooking the
Strait of Juan de Fuca.

The deep, fresh beauty of this slice of the Whidbey Island coastline
will reach up and grab you long before you take your first steps north
on the trail to Point Partridge. From the trailhead on a clear day you
can look across the blue waters of the Strait of Juan de Fuca to the
bold faces of the Olympic Mountains, rising from the breast of the
Olympic Peninsula like the gates of a strange and haunting spirit
world. Indeed, in coastal Indian mythology these mountains were
the source of many mysteries—from the fierce mountain monster
Tacobud, who swallowed those who came to the high country searching for game and wild berries, to the beautiful Valley of Peace, a place
high in the Olympics where once each year all nations could put
down their war clubs and gather in complete harmony. Rather at odds
with this latter vision of peace was the creation of Fort Ebey itself,
built during World War II and outfitted with two six-inch guns for use
against any enemy ships that might stray too close to the entrance of
Puget Sound. Although the guns are gone, you can still walk through
the dark concrete fortification tunnels, located at the south end of the
picnic area.

   This park takes its name from an early pioneer by the name of
Colonel Issac Ebey. Ebey served for a time as a customs collector for
the government, and in 1850 established a thriving commercial area
known as Ebey's Landing, which lies just to the south. As good as life
on Whidbey Island was to Colonel Ebey, his death was particularly
tragic. On a warm summer night in 1857, a Kake tribe of Haida
Indians climbed in their canoes and headed south out of the Queen
Charlotte Islands, bent on taking revenge for a battle fought with

U.S. troops near Port Gamble the previous autumn. During that skirmish twenty-seven Indians were killed, one of whom was a chief. Determined to even the score—one chief for another—the warriors made their way onto Colonel Ebey's farm on the night of August 11, shot him, and then fled back to Canada with his head in their hands. It was only through the extraordinary efforts of one of Colonel Ebey's friends, a steamship captain named Charles Dodd, that three years later the head was returned and buried with the body in Sunnyside Cemetery.

The beginning of our walk passes through a fine coastal mix of salal, Douglas-fir, ocean-spray, red-flowered currant, and an occasional rhododendron. If you're here from late April through June, you'll also see great clusters of yellow pealike flowers growing on a shrub with stiff green twigs. This is broom, and although not a native, it's one of the most common plants in all of western Washington. Broom is so named because during the Middle Ages it really was used as a broom (though never when flowers were on the plant, since to do so was to flirt with bad luck). The upper portions of the broom plant contain toxins, though during the 1500s and 1600s it was often used by people (including Henry VIII) as a diuretic and a laxative.

In 0.2 mile you'll see the smooth, terracotta-colored bark of a Pacific madrone tree on the right side of the path. This is one of the most beautifully colored of all the trees in the Pacific west. Just as the bark catches your eye even in a crowded forest, peeling away in strips during midsummer to reveal bright green layers of inner bark under-

Ocean Spray

neath, so too do old leaves add their share of color, bunches of them turning a burnt scarlet before dropping to the forest floor. As if that weren't striking enough, the madrone also sports lovely cream-colored, bell-shaped flowers from March to May, which are later replaced by yellow or orange fruits. A short distance past this Pacific madrone are nice clusters of ocean-spray, their foamy ivory flowers adding yet another shade of beauty to this high coastal ledge.

Notable by their absence are the plants you *don't* see along this path. While nearby Seattle receives about thirty-six inches of rain annually, this portion of Whidbey Island comes in with a some-what scanty eighteen. Coastal plants that require more moisture are either absent from here altogether, or else grow only in protected ravines.

Soon the trail begins a fairly gradual descent to ocean level, at 0.5 mile passing a quiet little hollow brimming with hemlocks, sword fern, and salal. Besides the occasional songs of the red-breasted nuthatch, western tanager, yellow-rumped warbler, western wood pewee, and pine sisken, the only other sound is the slow, rich rhythm of ocean waves, their volume softened a bit by the small hill that lies just to the west. The quiet reserve of this little woodland is broken rather suddenly in another 0.1 mile, when the trail emerges out onto a precipice teetering 200 feet above a rather narrow ribbon of rocky beach. Notice how misshapen the Douglas-fir and hemlock trees are that grow on this very exposed location, sporting branches primarily on the side nearest the trail. This kind of growth is sometimes called flagging, and it's a kind of pruning done to conifers by the winter winds that roar across this open ledge. Similar, but even more dra-matic flagging can be seen on trees that grow along the exposed highlands of the Cascade or the Olympic mountains.

From here the pathway continues to descend past some lovely wild rose bushes, finally reaching the Point Partridge picnic area at sea level in 0.9 mile. It's a short walk to the beach—a rather cobbly place littered with large, intriguing pieces of driftwood.

Fort Ebey State Park is part of the nation's first national historical reserve, established in 1978. Known as Ebey's Landing National Historic Reserve, this is an unusual mix of private lands (making up 90 percent of the reserve) and town, county, and state parks. The 17,000-acre complex is managed as a unit of the National

Wild Rose

Park Service. The reserve was created with support from local residents, who strongly agreed with the official intent of "preserving a rural community that provides an unbroken historic record from the nineteenth-century exploration and settlement in Puget Sound to the present time." While you're in the area, you may want to also visit historic Coupeville and the Admiralty Head Lighthouse, as well as do a bit more walking at Rhododendron Park, Ebey's Landing, or Fort Casey State Park.

DUNGENESS SPIT

Distance: 2 miles
Location: Dungeness National Wildlife Refuge. From about 4 miles west of Sequim on U.S. 101, turn north onto Kitchen-Dick Lane. (This will be about 1 mile west of mile marker 261.) Proceed for 3.35 miles to Voice of America Road, where you'll turn left. Follow this for 1.1 miles, passing through the refuge campground and finally into the large parking area for the Dungeness Spit trail.

Dungeness Spit, tracing a gentle arc for 5 miles into the salty waters of the Strait of Juan de Fuca, is the stuff that beach-walking dreams are made of. On one side of you will be the gentle slap of surf against the sand, while on the other, across a rugged backbone of driftwood, is an estuary fed by the Dungeness River—a favorite resting place for thousands of birds, and a nursery for no less than five kinds of salmon. If you're in the mood to just walk and walk some more, to put your feet on automatic and make a deep dive into the rhythms of the wind and the waves, then Dungeness Spit is the place for you.

Reaching the sand spit itself requires a 0.5-mile trek through a fine forest environment. Forming the woodlands are nice stands of Douglas-fir, cedar, alder, Pacific madrone, and grand fir, all underlain by patches of ocean-spray, Oregon grape, false lily-of-the-valley, Indian plum, and bedstraw. Also growing near the beginning of our walk, though not easily visible from the trail, is a large manzanita bush. A lover of dry lands, this beautiful tree provides evidence that much of the moisture that falls on the rest of the Washington Coast does not fall here; the nearby Olympic Mountains block many of the incoming storms, leaving Dungeness Spit with less than eighteen inches of rain a year.

At 0.4 mile you'll reach an observation deck framed by red-flowered currants and, on the back side, a nice pair of Douglas-firs. Here you'll find not only some good interpretive information, but also splendid views of the long, lanky curve of Dungeness Spit. This landform, like many others in the area, was named by the great explorer of the Northwest coast, Captain George Vancouver. He called it New Dungeness because it reminded him of another long spit of land, called simply Dungeness, which he'd passed many times in the British Channel. Nearly a century later, local pioneers referred to the arm of land that juts southward from the main spit by the rather unsettling name of Graveyard Spit. Supposedly, thirty Native Americans were buried here, all massacred by the Clallam Indians in 1875.

Having already passed through one of Dungeness's eco-systems—the coniferous forest—you'll have a good view of the refuge's other habitats when standing on this platform. These include estuaries, where the fresh water of the Dungeness River mixes with seawater; tidal flats, where, depending on the time of year you visit, you'll likely find scurrying groups of dunlins, sanderlings, and the ever-wary black-bellied plover; open ocean, which is the domain of whales, porpoises, and sea lions; and finally, the spit itself, which is an important nesting area for various shorebirds. All in all, more than

250 species of birds have been recorded at this refuge. In winter the place is especially enchanting—thick with the flutter and squawk of grebes, Canada geese, red-throated loons, and literally thousands of black brants, surf scoters, pintails, buffleheads, and goldeneyes.

Once on the beach, you can stroll to your heart's content. Though the spit can be busy on weekends, the farther out you go, the more potent the mix of sea and solitude becomes. The one sad note to all of this is that the protected areas of Dungeness just aren't big enough to serve the rush of life that comes and goes from these waters with each roll of the seasons. Right now there are several proposals for development along the private sectors of the harbor, some of which could seriously affect wintering wildlife populations. There will never be another place like Dungeness—for us, or for the wild creatures it sustains. Let's hope we have the wisdom to protect it adequately.

CAPE ALAVA

Distance:　7 miles

Location:　Olympic National Park. From U.S. Highway 101 at the village of Sappho, turn north onto Burnt Mountain Road. In about 10 miles you'll join Washington State Highway 112. Follow State Highway 112 through the town of Clallam Bay, and then turn south onto the Hoko-Ozette Road, which is located 0.5 mile past mile marker 13. Take the Hoko-Ozette Road for about 21.5 miles, where it will dead-end at a parking area near our trailhead. Follow the signs for the Indian Village Nature Trail and Cape Alava.

The coastal portions of Olympic National Park are the stuff that sea dreams are made of. Rugged headlands splay the cold ocean waves, while in the distance, dark sea stacks and volcanic islands topped with spruce can be seen rising out of the sea like the parapets of Avalon. This slice of coastal Washington has as many faces as there are variations in the weather. On any given day it can be sunny and smiling, somber and fogbound, or filled with the rage of winter winds that drive the waves hard against the coastal rocks. In all moods, however, this is a beautiful place—one of the last great untrammeled seashores in America. This particular trail was a favorite of former Supreme Court justice and conservationist William O. Douglas. He considered it "the most picturesque beach area of our whole coast line. . . . A place of haunting beauty, of deep solitude."

The lush weave of forest that greets you as soon as you set foot on this trail, washed in that wonderful perfume of cedar and Sitka spruce, attests that more than 100 inches of rain fall here each year. (Much of the trail is along a boardwalk that can be very slippery when wet; good tennis shoes are the best bet for safe passage.) If you haven't been in a moist area like this before, you're likely to be overwhelmed by the depth of green: the leathery green of salal and the soft green of licorice fern, sword fern, and Pacific yew; the fresh green of spring salmonberry and huckleberry leaves; and the dark, rich greens of hemlock and spruce. The real inheritors of this slice of earth are those trees and plants that can do well in shade. This is why, in a forest undisturbed by fire, wind, or disease, the very shade-tolerant cedars and hemlocks will sooner or later overtake the sun-loving broadleaf trees, leaving the latter to work life out on the edges of streams, roads, and other clearings.

As you make your way toward Cape Alava, notice the difference in water clarity in some of the small streams you pass. Some flow crystal clear, others run rusty. This coppery color is organic debris, and it's especially evident where catch pools have been created by logs falling across the watercourse. These pools also offer a habitat for several kinds of fish and insects that wouldn't be able to live, or at least thrive, in a stream that consisted of nothing but fast-flowing water.

At 0.1 mile you'll come to a split in the trail. Stay to the right here, following the signs for Cape Alava. If you're up for a hardy walk during low tide you could hit Cape Alava, make your way south for about 3 miles along the beach to Sand Point, and then return on the trail you see coming in from the left. The total distance for this walk would be a hefty 10 miles, but it's unquestionably 10 of the more beautiful miles you'll ever set foot on. Roughly 2 miles past this junction you'll come to a large clearing. This area is a remnant of Lars

Ahlstrom's homestead, and was the westernmost homestead in the continental United States. Ahlstrom came here in 1902 and stayed for fifty-six years before a foot infection finally forced him to leave. Look for patches of swamp laurel in this area, its flowers lending beautiful splashes of reddish-pink to the landscape. If you look closely at the swamp laurel flowers, you'll see that some of the anther stalks are curved backward, the tips held by the base of the petals. Insects landing on these "triggers" cause the anther to spring upward, letting loose a shower of pollen in the process.

At 3.4 miles, just after passing through a fine collection of skunk cabbage, you'll come out near the shore of beautiful Cape Alava. Your entryway to the sea is across a beautiful grassy parkland studded with Sitka spruce and scouler willow. This is a fine place to spot black-tailed deer, some of them so tame that you may think you took a wrong turn and ended up at the local petting zoo. Don't get too fresh with these animals, however; if it senses danger, a black-tailed deer will sometimes strike out with its front hooves.

Hopefully you've allowed plenty of time to explore this wonderful beach area. If it's low tide, take a close look at the potholes in the shore rocks for acorn barnacles, plate limpets, hermit crabs, sea urchins, roundworms, anemones, sea spiders, and rock whelks, as well as sea moss and sea tar. (The latter does indeed look like a patch of tar.) This coastline is also a wonderful place to spot some rather exotic birds. There's the rhinoceros auklet, which during breeding lets out a moan that sounds like a teenage cow whose voice has yet to break. Also here is the beautiful tufted puffin with its orange, parrot-like bill, the solitary pigeon guillemot, and the common murre, whose offspring begin their adolescence by making dramatic, forty-foot leaps into the sea from their ledge-top nests.

The "Indian Village" that you saw signs for when you were first starting this walk refers to a village that archaeologists excavated just to the north of here—an excavation that has proven to be one of the most significant ever done on the Northwest coast. From what archaeologists can piece together, around the year 1500 or 1600 a great mud slide engulfed a town of Makah Indians while they slept, sealing the people and their many possessions into a time capsule, in much the same way that volcanic ash has preserved communities in other regions of the world. The finds here have been spectacular.

They include intricate decorated baskets and cedar boxes, blankets made from a now-extinct "wool-producing" dog, ceremonial clubs, whale harpoons, and a sculpture of a whale's fin inlaid with hundreds of sea otter teeth in the shape of a thunderbird.

An even more amazing discovery at the Cape Alava dig, however, centered around pieces of metal that were completely different from those being made in Spain, Russia, or Great Britain—the only European countries that could possibly have been trading with the Makah at the time. (Sir Francis Drake is thought to have passed this area on a voyage he made in 1579.) Based on these pieces of metal, researchers now think that the Makah must have been trading with people not in Europe, but in Asia! The metal was perhaps carried across the Bering Strait by Eskimos, down through the Aleutian Islands and eventually into the intricate trade system of the Northwest, a system that generally ranged from northern California to Alaska.

Sitting here on this rugged, wind-torn coastline, it's easy to fantasize about the early explorers who drifted by in their wooden ships, the crew peering past the sea stacks and into the dark forest that rolled thick and green up the misty flanks of the Olympics. Explorers from Russia, Spain, and England were roaming this coastline on a fairly regular basis by the 1700s, many of them looking for a passage from the Pacific to the Atlantic. One of these early sailors, Captain James Cook, happened to trade some pieces of metal with the local Indians for otter skins that the crew needed for bedding. When Cook later sailed to China he was astounded to find that the Chinese were willing to offer the equivalent of a year's salary—$50 to $100—for a single otter pelt! Heavy trading, however, was still a few years off, stymied by wars raging in both Europe and the United States. When it did get going, however, it got going in a big way.

American ships typically came out of Boston and needed almost a full year to make the trip around Cape Horn, out to the Hawaiian Islands for provisioning, and then finally to the Northwest coast. Once loaded with pelts the crew sailed for China, where the furs were traded for spices, tea, and sometimes silver. A ship typically would then head back to Boston, making port there two-and-a-half to three years after its initial departure. Though at first profits were very high, this kind of commerce wasn't without serious cost.

Before long every sailor and his uncle were getting into the skin game; by 1820, the bulk of the Northwest sea otter population had been wiped out.

SECOND BEACH

Distance: 1.4 miles

Location: Olympic National Park. From the town of Forks, head north on U.S. Highway 101. At 0.1 mile past mile marker 193, turn left (west). In 7.8 miles you'll reach a fork in the road; stay left, and continue for 5.1 more miles. The trailhead for Second Beach will be on the left side of the road.

If you've had about all of U.S. Highway 101 you can stand, by all means make the 13-mile drive over to Second Beach, where, after only a 0.7-mile walk, you'll find yourself on an absolutely stunning seacoast. On the day I arrived here, a still afternoon with just a touch of gray in the sky, I thought perhaps I'd somehow passed through a sort of geography warp, landing not in America, but on a wild, rock-laden coast of Denmark. This was not the ocean, but the *sea*. Rather like some of the old-growth forests that still flank a few of the region's riverbottoms, Second Beach has a timeless, ponderous feeling to it. It must have been just this kind of coast that moved Shakespeare to write of living in a country "bound in with the triumphant sea, whose rocky shore beats back the envious siege of watery Neptune."

As you first begin this walk, look to the right of the path for a nice patch of false lily-of-the-valley. During May their shiny, heart-shaped leaves will have nice spikes of cream-colored flowers flying above them. On the other side of the trail you'll find a large conifer that appears to be standing on stilts. This kind of growth, which you'll see elsewhere along this trail, happens when a tree takes root on top of a log or stump. When the "nurse" log or stump finally rots away—a process that takes hundreds of years—the new tree is left looking as you see this one.

Continue past a nice forest of Sitka spruce, western hemlock, cedar, and red alder, all of which are underlain by a lovely mix of salal, salmonberry, skunk cabbage, sword fern, and deer fern. Shortly after you begin descending a series of wooden steps at 0.5 mile, you'll see a lush ravine on the right side of the trail. This is an especially good place to look for trillium, a plant with three large, deeply veined leaves and, from mid-April through May, a beautiful white or occasionally pinkish flower. Trillium is still sometimes referred to as birthroot, a name that stems from its use by Indians and pioneers to stop bleeding after childbirth. This plant has also had several magical properties attributed to it, including use as a love potion.

Before long you'll reach the bottom of the stairs, finding yourself in a world of wind and waves and sea stacks. To the right is a splendid "blowhole," where seawater shoots through a hole in the volcanic rock with every surge of the surf. Early mariners considered this section of coastline, from here northward for about 35 miles to Cape Flattery, to be one of the most dangerous on the entire Pacific coast. In the early days of fur trading, more than a few ships were ground into splinters as they tried to make their way into the mouth of the Quillayute River, a short distance to the north of where you now stand.

At that time, this rugged shore was still home to the Quillayute Indians. Historians believe that the Quillayute would

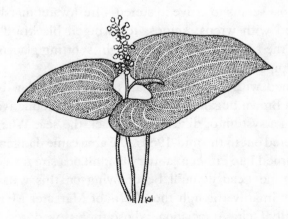

False Lily of the Valley

sometimes use these high, rugged offshore islands as fortresses, rolling rocks down on anyone either brave enough or stupid enough to pursue them.

BROWN FARM DIKE TRAIL

Distance: 5.8 miles
Location: Nisqually National Wildlife Refuge. From the city of Olympia, Washington, head north on Interstate 5 for approximately 7 miles. Turn off at Exit 114. At the end of the exit road turn left, and then right at a T intersection. Follow this road to Nisqually National Wildlife Refuge. Maps of the refuge and additional interpretive information are located near the parking lot.

Though 5.8 miles may seem like a long trek, along the Brown Farm Dike Trail it will pass beneath your feet with the greatest of ease. One can hardly go 100 yards along this trail without spotting something of interest: the deep scarlets of salmonberry blooms along the Nisqually River, or the flash of a northern flicker in a grove of cottonwoods; the splash of a river otter in McAllister Creek, or the grand swoop of a red-tailed hawk as it plucks a vole from the shaggy fields of Alson Brown's old farm. Indeed, on the back side of this loop nature almost seems to arrive in stereo—freshwater marshes on your left stitched with wrens, snipes, red-winged blackbirds, and bitterns, and the saltwater flats to your right sporting glaucous-winged gulls, sandpipers, brants, and scaups.

Armed with little more than horse-drawn plow-buckets, in 1904 Alson Brown began to turn this delta into productive farmland by building a system of dikes to hold back the sea. When the farm finally petered out in the mid-1960s, the area came dangerously close to being turned into either a sanitary landfill or a site for a cargo port. The grace and beauty you'll be enjoying on this walk has been preserved primarily through the efforts of Margaret McKenny and the Nisqually Delta Association, whose tireless work resulted in the establishment of the Nisqually National Wildlife Refuge in 1974.

Today this refuge provides either permanent or temporary homes for a whopping 300 species of fish, birds, reptiles, mammals, and amphibians. In a single winter, up to 20,000 birds will find food and shelter here. If you'd like to feast your eyes and ears on the migration parade that passes through Nisqually, plan to visit during mid-March through mid-May, or during mid-September through early December.

By the time you've walked 0.5 mile along the Brown Farm Dike Trail, the noisy bustle of Interstate 5 will for the most part have yielded to quiet patchworks of lowland marshes and fine weaves of cottonwood, broadleaf maple, and alder. Scattered along much of the trail are patches of Indian plum. This shrub is one of the first plants to get down to business in the spring, its brilliant green leaves and fragile clusters of small white flowers lending a special beauty to an otherwise drab forest. Like another early bloomer that grows a little farther down the trail, skunk cabbage, the flowers of Indian plum have a rather fetid odor. Though hardly an enticing smell to our noses, this skunky perfume is actually the perfect draw for the flies that will pollinate the plant.

This is also about the point where you'll join the lovely Nisqually River, which in various places is framed by fine patches of salmonberry. From here to the point where the path turns westward is

Common Snipe

Rufous-sided Towhee

a good stretch to watch (and listen!) for belted kingfishers, rufous-sided towhees, Wilson's and yellow-rumped warblers, cedar wax-wings, and song sparrows. If you enjoy birding, you may want to investigate the small 0.5-mile Ring Dike Loop, which takes off from the main trail at 1.2 miles into the walk.

An especially nice addition to the refuge, constructed for the Washington centennial in 1989, is a large wooden observation deck at 2.2 miles. Jutting out into the fringes of the mud flats, this is a wonderful place to survey the Nisqually Reach portion of Puget Sound. In fall you can witness a marvelous clatter of bird life coming and going here—herons, gulls, scaups, and ducks with seemingly no end.

The trail soon takes a southward turn up the muddy tidal reaches of McAllister Creek. The abundance of blackberries and wild roses here make this an ideal place to grab once again for your bird books. Continue to follow the small roadway south until it turns east, near an interpretive sign about the Medicine Creek Treaty of 1854, which granted fishing rights to native peoples of the region. You can still see Indian fishing nets in both McAllister Creek and the Nisqually River.

The Medicine Creek Treaty was engineered by the governor

of the territory, Issac Stevens, who met with the Indians of the Tacoma and Olympia regions of Washington at a halfway point known as Medicine Creek. Originally, the politicians of the region wanted to create one large temporary reservation to hold the people of all tribes until each could be shipped to a remote patch of farmland far away from settled territory. (At the time, Americans felt that all native peoples, no matter where they lived, should be pushed into farming.)

In the end, the native peoples wisely refused to let go of their traditional fishing areas, so three small reservations were created for them instead. One of the most outrageous facets of this entire treaty process was that Governor Stevens required all negotiations be conducted not in the tribes' own language, which he easily could have done, but in what was sometimes called "Chinook"—a kind of rough Pidgin English of a few hundred words developed by early traders. There was no way that even the basics of a treaty could have been defined adequately for the Indians using this language. The native people weren't the only ones who knew they were being manipulated; two years later, one of the governor's employees refused to go to

Wilson's Warbler

Cedar Waxwing

battle against the Indians because he felt it was this kind of official stupidity that had caused the fighting in the first place.

Ten years later, a heroic fellow named John Beeson began to voice strong objections to the deplorable treatment of the Indians in the Oregon Territory. When the Methodist church announced that, as far as they were concerned, the Indians of the region were still "wretched heathens, in the lowest depths of moral degradation," Beeson was quick to respond. "Let them," he pleaded, "at least have a religion that will not insult their common sense by presenting itself with whiskey and creeds in one hand and Bibles and bowie knives in the other." Beeson's stand was angrily attacked by his neighbors, and in the end he was forced to leave his farm in the middle of the night to escape being hung, or at least thoroughly beaten. He continued his fight for the native peoples of this region back in the East, and eventually even caught the ear of President Lincoln. "If we get through the war and I live," Lincoln supposedly told him, "this Indian system shall be reformed."

As you head back east along the last leg of our walk, notice the large crosslike structures that have been erected on either side of the path. These are raptor perches. You're most likely to see either a red-tailed hawk or a northern harrier sitting here, though visitors to the refuge on a cloudy winter day may also spot a short-eared owl—a beautiful bird that starts hunting for mice and small rodents long before it gets dark. Other birds sometimes seen on these perches include American kestrels, and rough-legged, sharp-shinned, and Cooper's hawks.

Rough-legged Hawk

LEADBETTER POINT

Distance: 1 mile
Location: Willapa National Wildlife Refuge. From the town of
Seaview, Washington, head north (at this point the road actually
goes east) on U.S. Highway 101. In 0.5 mile, turn left (north)
onto Sandridge Road. Follow this for 15.5 miles, to a T intersection at Stackpole Road. Turn left (west) onto Stackpole Road for
0.4 mile, past the Oysterville Store, and then make a right,
following the signs for Leadbetter Point. Park in the lot farthest
to the north, and pick up the trail that heads due north.

There's no doubt about it. Leadbetter Point, a unique mix of state
park and Willapa National Wildlife Refuge lands, is a bird-lover's
dream. Though winter is among the best times to visit Leadbetter,
much is happening here during other seasons as well. During peak
periods of migration in the spring and fall, for instance, there are
literally tens of thousands of birds—brants, sanderlings, turnstones,
and so forth—feeding and resting on the mud flats, marshes, and
beaches of the point. In late summer you can see sooty shearwaters
winging past the point on an incredible journey from the Aleutian
Islands to their nesting grounds off the coast of New Zealand. Since
shearwater parents leave their fattened chicks before they fledge,
young birds must make the long trip back to the Aleutians on their
own. At about the same time of year, young snowy plovers will be
attending their own survival school at the tip of Leadbetter Point.

You needn't give Leadbetter a miss just because you're not a
great fan of birds. You can not know an eagle from a sea goose and still
find the walking here to be wonderful—an easy stroll through a place
thick with a kind of wild serenity. (One caveat is in order. Hiking
here in the summer means sharing the place with lots of mosquitoes.
If you're here during May through September, wear lots of clothes,
eat lots of garlic, or bring a generous supply of bug repellent.)

A short distance from the parking area is an information sign
marking the beginning of a loop trail. We're not taking this loop walk
through the park, but will instead turn right here, toward the bay
side of the peninsula. The short path down the beach will pass
through an area thick with the leathery green mats of kinnikinnick.

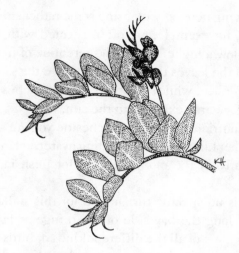

Beach Pea

While it's true that kinnikinnick leaves were dried and smoked by Indians (and later settlers) throughout North America, the name is actually an Algonquian word that means simply "smoking mixture." The leaves of this plant were typically mixed with several other kinds of plants, including red-osier dogwood, willow, and even tobacco. Folk healers have long prescribed kinnikinnick for treating infections of the bladder, an application thought to be made possible by the plant's high concentrations of an astringent known as arbutin.

Also along this pathway to the beach will be groves of shore pine (a variety of lodgepole pine), as well as some fine tufts of beach grass. Both of these plants are very good at stabilizing dune areas; even so, the forces of wind and water bring a great many changes to the face of Leadbetter Point from year to year. Once you reach the beach and head north, watch the sandy ridges and depressions to your left for several other plants that can easily be seen, including lupine, wild strawberry, beach pea, sea rocket, and gorse.

Also worth noting on this walk are two marsh plants that form lush green islands on the salt flats to your right. One of these is a kind of pickleweed, and the other is commonly referred to as arrowgrass. Despite the high level of nutrients found here, setting up shop in salty soil (the salinity here is roughly 5 percent) is not an option open to just any plant. Those that can manage it are called halophytes, and they make a living here only by using some rather specialized equipment. Leaves, for example, are often covered with hairs or a waxy powder that allow a higher intake and retention of fresh water. Some have glands on the leaves that actually remove the salt and deposit it on the plant's surface, while still others grow in shapes that reduce the amount of surface area exposed to the sun.

These nutrient-rich mud flats beside you are also prime habitat for many other kinds of life, including oysters, clams, and crabs. If you're here early in the morning, look for fresh raccoon tracks in the mud.

There is no specific turnaround for this walk. Simply make your way out along the bay side of the refuge as far as you'd like, trying to keep track of all the different kinds of birds you're likely to see along the way. Do keep in mind that the northern fringe of Leadbetter Point along the ocean beach side is closed to all traffic from April through August. This is to protect nesting snowy plovers, which are having increasing difficulty reproducing. Closing the area keeps people from inadvertently stepping on the snowy plovers' eggs (they blend in extremely well with the sand), or frightening the plovers off their nests, leaving the eggs vulnerable to predators.

Oregon

OSWALD WEST STATE PARK

Distance: 1.3 miles
Location: This trail takes off from the northernmost parking area in Oswald West State Park, which is located on the west side of U.S. Highway 101, 4.3 miles north of the town of Manzanita.

Oswald West State Park is a delight from stem to stern, for campers, for picnickers, and most certainly for walkers. Although on any summer day or pleasant off-season weekend it may take you a half-mile to fully escape the sound of cars speeding down Highway 101, the visual beauty of Oswald West starts with the very first step. The trail begins with a lazy traverse of a hillside thick with spruce, while down below you can hear the tumble of Short Sand Creek, at this point very nearly finished with its headlong dash to the sea. As you walk this stretch of pathway, keep your eyes open for the green bushy fronds of sword ferns, as well as the ivory, lemon, and lavender of fringecups, Oregon oxalis, and yellow violets. According to one legend, the world's first violets were created when Cupid made the mistake of telling his mother, Venus, that a group of young girls were more beautiful than she. Enraged, Venus bludgeoned the girls until they turned blue and shriveled into violets. These unlucky girls, then, were the first "shrinking violets."

This coniferous forest is also a good place to watch for pine siskins, a small finch that in most years can easily be seen in the pine,

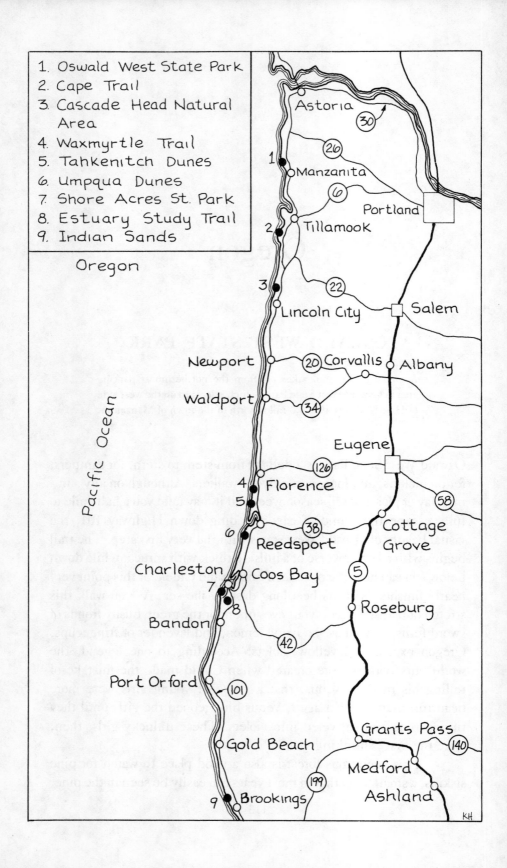

1. Oswald West State Park
2. Cape Trail
3. Cascade Head Natural
   Area
4. Waxmyrtle Trail
5. Tahkenitch Dunes
6. Umpqua Dunes
7. Shore Acres St. Park
8. Estuary Study Trail
9. Indian Sands

Oregon

Pacific Ocean

Astoria
30
26
1
Manzanita
6
Portland
2
Tillamook
3
22
Lincoln City
Salem
Newport
20
Corvallis
Albany
Waldport
34
Eugene
126
58
4
Florence
5
Cottage
Grove
6
38
Reedsport
Charleston
Coos Bay
5
7
Roseburg
8
Bandon
42
Port Orford
101
Grants Pass
140
Gold Beach
199
Medford
9
Brookings
Ashland

KH

Pine Siskin

spruce, and alder groves found along much of this coast. Besides being acrobatic in their feeding style—often hanging upside down to pluck seeds—pine siskins are also very sociable birds; if you see one, you'll probably see many. Because they're somewhat drab in color, one of the best ways to spot pine siskins is to look for the yellow patches visible on their wings during flight. You're also likely to see Steller's jays here, those raucous panhandlers that have made a profession out of working the nearby picnic area.

At 0.5 mile the trail forks; stay left. Soon after this junction you'll be afforded some fine coastal vistas, including a lovely pocket beach framed by a ragged green curtain of Sitka spruce. Just after a small observation point, the trail begins winding gently downward, reaching at 0.75 a fine beach-side picnic area—as idyllic a lunch stop as you could hope to find.

Steller's Jay

Rather than returning the same way you came, follow the pathway around to the southeast side of the picnic grounds, where you'll pick up a paved walkway leading up the south side of Short Sand Creek. The abundant moisture in this little ravine makes for a wonderful variety of plant life, including salmonberry, monkeyflower, bleeding heart (which you may recognize from your favorite garden shop), alder, skunk cabbage, salal, and devil's club. Salal, with its thick green leaves and pale pink, bell-shaped flowers, often forms vast, almost impenetrable patches of vegetation along the Oregon Coast. The berries of salal are quite tasty, not altogether unlike a blueberry, and were an extremely important food source for coastal Indians. Often the berries were crushed, formed into small cakes, dried, and later dipped in whale or seal oil. David Douglas, the noted botanist who "discovered" the salal plant in 1825, tried without success to turn it into a European commercial fruit crop. It did, however, eventually catch on as an ornamental shrub.

Devil's club, on the other hand, warrants a little more caution. The sharp spines growing out from the stems of devil's club made it the curse of early Northwest explorers, especially because in some people the scratches can cause troublesome allergic reactions. Devil's club was not entirely without redeeming qualities, however. Some Indians used it successfully to treat mild cases of diabetes, and the juice of the berries was reportedly a good remedy for lice.

When you reach the footbridge at 0.85 mile, turn around for a moment and savor the view downstream—Short Sand Creek dancing down lush green banks toward a jumble of driftwood, and behind that, the frothy, broken white lines of the ocean waves rolling forever into shore. At 0.9 mile is another trail junction, where you'll turn left. Follow this for just under 0.4 mile back to Highway 101.

If you live in a landlocked environ as I do, where the sea is far, far away, then you're likely to find the scenes in Oswald West State Park provide you with the perfect portable coastal daydream: something to cherish long after you've left this magic shore.

> For all at last returns to the sea—to Oceanus,
> the ocean river, like the ever-flowing stream of
> time, the beginning and the end.
>
> —RACHEL CARSON

CAPE TRAIL

Distance: 5 miles
Location: Cape Lookout State Park. From the town of Tillamook, head west on Oregon State Highway 6, and at the edge of town turn south onto Three Capes Scenic Drive. Cape Lookout State Park is about 12 miles south of Tillamook; Cape Trail is well marked.

Cape Lookout is one of the largest capes in the state of Oregon. Anchored to the lush green feet of the Coast Range, it forms a windswept, four-hundred-foot-high tail of basalt that runs for nearly 2 miles into the sea—a kind of final exclamation point before the continent yields to 64 million square miles of Pacific Ocean.

Actually, Cape Lookout isn't really Cape Lookout at all. Explorer John Meares gave that name to another cape 10 miles to the north, but chart makers in the middle of the nineteenth century are thought to have applied it inadvertently to this much more prominent landform. Before long the mistake was well entrenched in the minds of mariners, who doubtless would not have taken kindly to "fixing" something so important as a navigational chart merely for the sake of historical accuracy. Perhaps the ghost of John Meares was appeased, though, when years later it was decided to name his original Cape Lookout "Cape Meares."

This walk begins in a grove of young to middle-aged Sitka spruce. You could roam the entire North American continent and never find a more thoroughly useful and magnificent tree than the Sitka. In the right conditions, such as those on Washington's Olympic Peninsula or along the misty islands of British Columbia and southeast Alaska, the Sitka can grow at phenomenal rates, sometimes reaching a height of 200 feet in the course of a single century. It is a stately tree, with a straight trunk and a top of sweeping, tightly needled branches rising in gentle arcs toward the sky.

But what has long turned Americans toward the Sitka is not its beauty but its usefulness. It has a clear, consistent grain, and the highest strength-to-weight ratio of any wood in the world; pound for pound, it is every bit as tough as steel. This made it the wood of choice for, among many other things, the propellers, wing beams, and ribs of World War I airplanes. The vast majority of these parts were fashioned out of spruce cut from Oregon and Washington forests. On a more peaceful note, Sitka spruce has long been used for violin and piano sounding boards. In fact, it is the equivalent to the even-grained, elastic wood of the Norway spruce, for centuries the preferred material of some of Europe's greatest instrument makers.

The Sitka Spruce could well have done without some of this extraordinary popularity. There remains only a tiny fraction of the number of great trees that once blanketed this coast. That doesn't come as much of a surprise when you consider that even fifty years ago Sitka was being harvested in Oregon and Washington at a rate of nearly 250,000,000 board feet per year—more than ten times the optimum regrowth rate. Writing in 1950 about the high cuts of Sitka on national forest lands, botanist Donald Peattie voiced an opinion that is as pertinent today as it was forty years ago: "The spruce in the national forests constitutes a national reserve which could meet a national emergency. But it should not, in the judgment of the conservative, be called on to help out private industry just because the lumber and pulping companies are running short. They will have to solve their own problems and bring into line the rate of cut with the rate of natural reproduction."

In addition to Sitka spruce, by 0.5 mile the trail is firmly cradled by beautiful western hemlocks, while the ground is pep-

Salmonberry

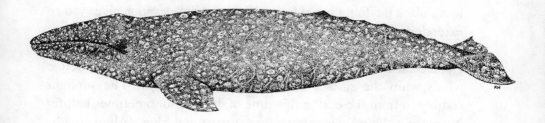

Gray Whale

pered with redwood sorrel, wild lily-of-the-valley, sword fern, and salal. As you walk through this lovely forest, keep your ears open for the melodic songs of chickadees, thrushes, and warblers. Early on a calm morning the songs can seem almost to drip like sweetener from the bushy green branches of the conifers. In all the diverse habitats of Cape Lookout State Park, which range from marsh and beach to headland and forest, there are more than 150 species of birds, including a number of beautiful sea ducks and passerines.

At just over a half-mile into the walk the trees on your left will fall away, opening up magnificent views to the south of Cape Kiwanda and Nestucca Spit. To the west is the blue wash of the open Pacific, stretching on and on into the haze of the far horizon. In the next mile you'll begin to spot growths of box blueberry and salmonberry, the latter a three- to ten-foot-high shrub with leaves composed of three double-toothed leaflets. The pink flowers this shrub produces, visible from March to July, are truly exquisite. Indian peoples of the region treasured both the fruit of the salmonberry, which they sometimes mixed with fish oil, and the young peeled shoots. The bark was also occasionally used to make a saltwater tea, reportedly effective in easing labor pains.

By 1.5 miles the trail levels out nicely, offering in the more open sections some wonderful views, to the south and to Netarts Bay and Cape Meares to the north. At just over 2.6 miles you'll reach the tip of the cape, a grassy, wind-blown point saturated with scenery—a wonderful place for everything from lunching to napping to whale watching.

Speaking of whale watching, Cape Lookout is about as perfect a place for doing so as you could ask for. Its elevation gives you an extended view, and shallow-water whales tend to go around it very close to the point. If you do decide to try your hand at spotting these grand creatures, you may want to be here early in the morning, before winds whip the surface of the sea into whitecaps. The sunlight coming in from the east at this time of day is also sometimes helpful in spotting the whales as they first surface and blow. (Alternatively, overcast skies will eliminate the problem of glare.) Gray whales have an uneven, splotchy color about them, with ridges along the back just forward of the tail. A whale with a tall dorsal fin and a striking black and white color pattern is a killer whale; these whales are often seen in groups. And finally, those that have large, square heads and wrinkled skin, and that blow water at a forty-five-degree angle, are sperm whales.

CASCADE HEAD NATURAL AREA

Distance: 2.5 miles
Location: Nature Conservancy. From U.S. Highway 101, approximately 7 miles north of Lincoln City, turn west onto Cascade Head Road (Forest Road 1861). This turnoff is made from the top of a 700-foot divide. Follow Forest Road 1861 for 3.3 miles to the sign for the Nature Conservancy North Trail.

If Robert Frost had been ambling around western Oregon instead of the woods of New England, he might well have ended up writing love poems to alders instead of birches. The mature red alders leaning gently over much of the trail to Cascade Head lend to the land a sense of grace and suppleness unmatched by almost any other kind of northwestern woodland. More than just exquisite form, red alders also boast a wonderful mix of colors on their bark. Young trees

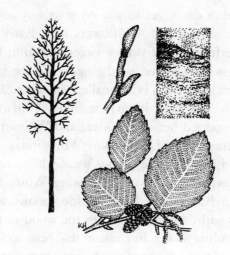

Red Alder

start out with smooth white bark, not unlike that of a birch or aspen. But as the tree matures the trunk becomes thoroughly laced with mottled brown furrows and ridges, as well as the dark green mosses that flourish in the 100 inches of rain that fall here each year. (Where is the red in all this vast color scheme? It's out of sight, along the inner bark.) While alders are quick to start growing on areas cleared by wind or fire, they will eventually be overtaken—typically in fifty to eighty years—by Sitka spruce and western hemlock.

Candy Flower

If the trees don't get to you on your way to Cascade Head, then surely the shrubs and wildflowers will. Early on in the walk there's a wonderful array of yellow violet, trillium, false lily-of-the-valley, candy flower, coltsfoot, wild ginger, and the beautiful blooms of Oregon oxalis. This latter is also called wood sorrel, and during the Middle Ages it was well known to most Christians because it bloomed in the period between Easter and Whitsuntide. (The seventh Sunday after Easter is known as Whitsunday, or "White Sunday," so named because the clergy wear white, the color of Pentecost. Whitsuntide is the week following White Sunday.) In the period between Easter and Whitsuntide monks would end their psalm readings with "Alleluia!"—thus the wood sorrel soon become known as the alleluia flower. Because at that time so few people could read, the blooming and dying of plants was a common way of marking special periods of the Christian calendar.

At 1 mile you'll find beautiful thickets of salmonberry, which from about March through early June contain brilliant red or dark pink, five-petaled flowers. The first of the edible berries typically ripen by the first of July, and in some years it's not uncommon to see fading flowers and ripening berries on the same plant. These berries actually come in two colors, red and a translucent orange. Although the numerous species of birds that dine regularly on these fruits don't seem to care in the least which color they eat, most people find the orange berries to be better tasting.

At just over 1.1 miles is a nice mix of young alder and spruce, and then, all of a sudden, the trail delivers you to the magnificent,

Oregon Oxalis

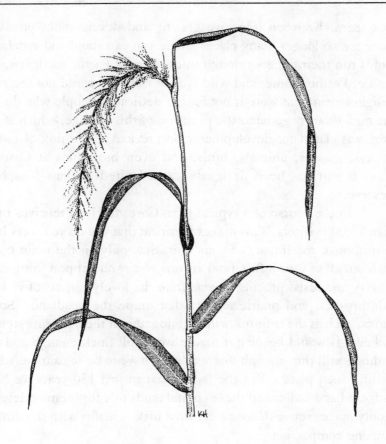

Wild Rye

windswept promontory of Cascade Head. From here the world tumbles into a brilliant mix of sea and sky and prairie headland. To the south you can see the beautiful Salmon River, making its last lazy meanders after a fast dance down the steep green flanks of Saddlebag Mountain. Beyond the Salmon River to the south, just east of Lincoln City, is Devil's Lake. According to Indian legend this lake was once the home of a giant sea monster that on occasion gobbled up unwary visitors.

Continue to our turnaround point at the highest point of land, which lies just past marker post number five. Many of the plants you'll pass along this last stretch of trail are natives of the Oregon coastal prairies—something that is far more unusual than it might at first seem. Between intensive grazing and development pressure, there are no longer many places where you can stand and watch the winds run their fingers through thick shags of Pacific reedgrass, red fescue, Pacific brome, and wild rye. In fact, you could not see such delights even here were it not for the dedicated people who during the mid-1960s negotiated the purchase of this acreage, which at the time was slated for development. So precious is the mix of forest, flowers, grasses, animals, birds, and even butterflies at Cascade Head that it has been designated as a United Nations Biosphere Reserve.

In the course of a typical year, Cascade Head receives more than 10,000 visitors. This makes it critical that you do your very best to minimize the impact of your visit. Stay only on the main trails, pack out all of your refuse (and anyone else's you happen to stumble across), and resist picking flowers from the lovely carpets of violets, paintbrushes, and prairie rockets that drape the headland. (Some plants, such as the trillium, will die altogether if the flowering stem is picked.) It would be nice if nature were still thick enough and our numbers still thin enough that we didn't have to be so cautious when visiting such places. But the fact is that in just 150 years we have badgered and bulldozed these coastal lands to a frightening degree. It only makes sense that we treat what little remains with the utmost care and compassion.

WAXMYRTLE TRAIL

Distance: 2.2 miles

Location: Oregon Dunes National Recreation Area, Siuslaw National Forest. From Florence, Oregon, head south on U.S. Highway 101. In about 8 miles, turn right (west) at mile marker 198, following the signs for Siltcoos Dunes and Beach. One mile from this junction you'll see the Stagecoach Trailhead on the left (south) side of the road. Park here. To reach Waxmyrtle Trail, follow a footpath that runs along the south side of the road you came in on, until you reach the entrance road into Waxmyrtle Campground. Cross the bridge over the Siltcoos River, and immediately take a right.

Waxmyrtle Trail, a slow, beautiful meander along the elevated southern banks of the Siltcoos River, is actually one of three pathways in this area that are often referred to as the "Stagecoach Trails." The name speaks of a time before the 1920s, when travelers would roll up and down the hard-pack beaches during low tide on their way to and from the towns of Florence, Coos Bay, and Reedsport. (And a Cadillac of a ride it was, compared to the rocky, rutted roads that most Oregon Territory stagecoach passengers had to endure.) This walk begins very near the point where these early beach buggies made their crossing of the Siltcoos River.

As noted above, to reach the Waxmyrtle Trail you must work your way up the footpath that parallels the entrance road, and then cross a bridge to the south side of the Siltcoos River. This is not a trail that seems in any kind of hurry to reach the ocean. The path winds to and fro, gently rising and falling along the twists and turns of the Siltcoos River, taking you either through or very near some fine forest, estuary, deflation plain, and foredune environments. This is the perfect walk not only to clear some of the Highway 101 traffic cobwebs out of your head, but also to acquaint yourself with several of the more common plants and birds of the Oregon coast. (There are nearly 250 species of birds alone to be seen here, including more than 100 kinds of songbirds!)

As you settle into the forested portion of Waxmyrtle Trail, you'll find yourself surrounded by a lovely weave of broom, salal, Sitka spruce, false lily-of-the-valley, bracken fern, red-flowered currant, evergreen huckleberry, lodgepole pine, ocean-spray, black twinberry, and, of course, western wax myrtle. Wax myrtle, a delightful little evergreen tree that produces wax-coated berries early in the fall, is sometimes referred to as bayberry. If this name sounds like

Great Blue Heron

126

something right out of a candle shop, it should. Early American settlers routinely boiled the berries from several eastern varieties of this tree and then used the wax as an additive for scented candles.

At just over 0.3 mile you'll come to an open, grass-covered bench overlooking the Siltcoos River. To the west lies the Pacific, its broken lines of waves gliding in for smooth landings on a long, flat line of golden sand. Directly across from where you're standing, on the north side of the Siltcoos, is a wonderful estuary habitat. If you've never had the pleasure of seeing a great blue heron feeding before, this is a good place to look. Though we tend to think of these hauntingly beautiful birds as residents of wetland environments like this one, that's not where they spend all of their time. They build large stick nests high in the canopies of trees, commonly using cottonwoods, alders, and even redwoods and Douglas-firs. In the spring adult birds can be seen making trip after trip from their treetop nests to their fishing grounds and back again, bringing food to their ever-hungry chicks. The effort involved in such food shuttling is nothing to sneeze at, especially when you consider that great blue herons sometimes nest 20 or even 30 miles from their feeding grounds!

By 0.65 mile the trail has descended to river level again, beginning a trek through a medley of sandy hummocks and foredunes. As you walk this stretch, keep your eyes open for lovely mats of purple pea, as well as beach grass, yellow lupine, and coast strawberry. Likely to be flying overhead east of the foredunes are ospreys, northern harriers, and, during spring migration, a whistling swan or two en route to their breeding grounds in Alaska or the Canadian Arctic.

If you spend much time on this, or virtually any other of Oregon's magnificent beaches, sooner or later you may find what's commonly referred to as a "drift bottle." These are glass bottles weighted at the bottom (pop, wine, and beer bottles are often used) that have been cast into the sea by researchers so that they might better understand the movements of ocean currents. Each of these bottles will have a special return card in it, which you should fill out and mail back as instructed. Besides helping the researcher who launched the bottle, you'll probably receive a background sheet that will tell you when and where the bottle was first set adrift. Serious beachcombers have collections of drift bottles, some of which had come from as far away as Russia and Japan.

TAHKENITCH DUNES TRAIL

Distance: 4 miles
Location: Oregon Dunes National Recreation Area, Siuslaw National Forest. From the town of Florence, Oregon, head south on U.S. Highway 101 for about 13 miles, and then turn right into the Tahkenitch Campground. (The turnoff for this campground is 0.6 mile south of mile marker 203.) Once in the campground, follow the loop road to a parking area near camp site number 30. Our trail takes off from here.

To walk from Tahkenitch Campground out to the mouth of Tahkenitch Creek is to capture the essence of the Oregon Dunes National Recreation Area. Here you'll see dark green coniferous forests and the curling yellow crests of shifting dunes; the pale flush of trillium and the shout of ocean waves. While not a particularly difficult hike as far as the terrain is concerned, there's a substantial amount of sand walking involved here—an activity that will certainly tax you more than any stroll down a typical forest pathway.

The first portion of this trail is usually thick with a steady drone of traffic from Highway 101. After a junction at 0.25 mile, though, where you'll head to the right, the traffic quickly fades and the rush of wind and the lilt of bird song begin to take over. In no time at all you'll find yourself wrapped in a thick green cloak of hemlock, Sitka spruce, grand fir, and Douglas-fir, with an understory of salal, evergreen huckleberry, and rhododendron. This latter plant, incidentally, produces clusters of pink flowers in June that are arguably as beautiful as those of any shrub in America. For all their beauty, though, not only are the leaves and blooms of rhododendrons poisonous to consume, but honey made from their flowers is toxic as well.

At about 0.75 mile you'll reach the edge of a hill that offers splendid views to the west. Immediately in front of you is a series of oblique and parabola dunes. These are framed in back by a thin strip of lodgepoles, then a line of much smaller foredunes, and finally, the mighty Pacific itself. Sand is initially carried to this shore in the arms of ocean waves—the result of coastal rivers dumping sand into the sea, as well as of waves constantly grinding down the sandstone that comprises many of the coastal headlands.

Longshore currents move these grains of sand generally southward, while high tides and waves then bring them onto shore. Once they dry, prevailing winds take over. Any wind over about eleven or twelve miles per hour is enough to make the sand grains begin to dance. Each grain typically moves only a few inches at a time, skittering along until it comes to rest on a soft surface, like that of a dune, or hopping ever onward over things that are hard. Dune sculpting is influenced a great deal by seasonal winds, which blow out of the northwest in summer and the southwest in winter. The stronger winter winds give dunes their basic shape, while the summer winds tend to form sharp cross-ridges. Driven by these winds, dunes actually migrate toward the northeast at a rate of anywhere from five to fifteen feet per year.

The reason that the dunes are so expansive in this particular region is that this is one of the few places along the coast where prevailing winds can transport the sand grains inland—in some places, for two-and-a-half miles—without having them intercepted by high cliffs and ridges. As a result, this has become the largest dune-covered coastal plain on the entire West Coast, and certainly one of the most dramatic in the country.

Shortly after you gain this wonderful ocean vista you'll find a series of posts just to the south, forming a line that heads straight for the beach. These are the trail markers. They will take you across the dunes, past the deflation plain (a place where winds have scoured the sands out down to the water table), and finally to the east bank of Tahkenitch Creek. From here you can stroll up and down the beach as you wish, lulled into the finest of stupors by the hiss of ocean waves.

UMPQUA DUNES

Distance: 4.5 miles

Location: Oregon Dunes National Recreation Area, Siuslaw National Forest. From Reedsport, Oregon, head south on U.S. Highway 101 for approximately 8 miles. At 0.25 mile past mile marker 222, turn right (west), following the signs for North Eel Campground. Our trailhead takes off from the back side of the north campground loop, approximately 0.4 mile from the junction of the campground entrance road with U.S. Highway 101.

The Walrus and the Carpenter
were walking close at hand:
They wept like anything to see
Such quantities of sand:
"If this were only cleared away,"
They said, "it would be grand!"

"If seven maids with seven mops
Swept it for half a year,
Do you suppose," the Walrus said,
"That they could get it clear?"
"I doubt it," said the Carpenter,
And shed a bitter tear.

—LEWIS CARROLL

If the Walrus and the Carpenter were that easily upset by "quantities of sand," they can count themselves lucky that they never set eyes on the Umpqua Dunes. These are the highest, broadest dune fields in all of Oregon Dunes National Recreation Area—four square miles of golden troughs and rippled ridges that, at least when you're in the very middle of them, can absolutely overwhelm you. Rising up to a height of 400 feet, these dunes are the childhood vision of an Arabian sand desert come to life. A line of mangy, squawking camels making their way along a nearby crest would seem anything but out of place.

Our walk begins through a short stretch of coniferous forest, the understory thick with wax myrtle, salal, evergreen huckleberry, broom, and rhododendron. When in bloom, the rhododendron growing in the ravine on your right is especially beautiful, with tufts of pink petals floating on leathery green leaves. Also in this ravine can be seen the smooth, copper-colored trunks of the Pacific madrone. This is a hardwood member of the heath family whose Spanish name, *madrono*, means "strawberry tree." It was given this name in 1769 by a member of the Portola expedition, who recognized the tree as being similar to one found in his native Spain.

At 0.1 mile is a pathway coming in from the right; stay left. (This is about fifty yards past an intersection with a stairway heading uphill on your left.) The area around this latter junction is also a good place to get a close-up look at a couple of Pacific madrones, and at the crooked red limbs and evergreen leaves of hairy manzanita. At 0.2 mile you'll find yourself on the edge of the great dunescape—an ocean of sand piled into a graceful collection of rippled hummocks, ridges, and soft yellow valleys.

Because the volume of drifting sand makes it impossible to put marker posts here, those interested in walking the entire distance to the ocean should first climb to the top of the highest dune for a better look at the lay of the land. Gazing to the west, you'll see a tree island, not far from the ocean itself. Your plan should be to head to the northern edge of this tree island, at which point you'll pick up a line of trail posts running to the north. Follow these for a short distance, and then cross over the deflation plain to the beach itself.

Salal

This deflation plain—an area where the sand has been scoured away by the wind down to the water table—is an entirely different world from that lying on either side of it. Here the land is thick with rushes, sedges, willows, and silverweed. It makes a fine place to break for a while and watch the abundance of birds and small mammals that can usually be found here.

A word of caution is in order for this walk. It's very easy to become disoriented when crossing this vast expanse of dunes, turning what was supposed to be a short walk into an unsettling afternoon of aimless wandering. The trickiest part of the walk is not making it out to the ocean, but making it back again. As you're heading out, you should pay close attention to what the scene looks like behind you. There are, for example, a couple of liquid storage tanks visible to the east on the other side of Highway 101 that you could aim for on your return trip. If all this sounds like more of an adventure than you're up for, know that you can still have a delightful time just ambling around the edge of this dunescape, never getting far from the lovely fringes of the transition forest.

SHORE ACRES STATE PARK

Distance: 2.2 miles

Location: Our trailhead is located approximately 3.6 miles west of Charleston, Oregon, on the Cape Arago Highway. To find the beginning of the walk, continue just past the entrance to Sunset Bay State Park Campground, to a small parking area on the right side of the road. (This pull-off will be adjacent to a sign that says "Oregon State Park Botanical Garden ½ Mile.") Our walk takes off from this parking area, along the Oregon Coast Trail.

If your time allows for only one short walk along the Oregon coast, it would be hard to imagine a better one than this. After an easy stroll along a particularly wild, jagged edge of the continent, this short section of the Oregon Coast Trail will bring you to the heavily manicured, yet nonetheless magnificent site of the old Simpson estate. Even though the great Simpson homes are no longer here, it doesn't take much imagination to see why during the first quarter of the twentieth century this was considered to be the finest estate in all of Oregon.

At the beginning of this walk you'll pass fine clusters of salmonberry, which in April frame the path with a striking splash of scarlet-colored blossoms. Early coastal peoples not only relied heavily on the berries of this plant for food, but also on the young shoots. As was true throughout the country with other kinds of edible plants and trees, the tribes of the Northwest sometimes had individual family ownership of certain salmonberry patches; barring their destruction by fire or disease, these patches became sustainable food sources to be passed down from generation to generation. Another plant growing here that was an important food source for early peoples was salal, a shrub that sports thick evergreen leaves and pink, bell-shaped flowers. In most areas, the sheer abundance of salal made private ownership less of an issue than it was for salmonberry.

Fifty yards down the path you'll come to a junction; bear to the right, following the Oregon Coast Trail. At just under 0.2 mile is an overlook of a splendid little pocket beach framed on both sides by rugged headlands. Notice how the waves flow over these beautiful terraces, first submerging them, and then gently pouring off their lips in thin, frothy veils.

Steller's Sea Lion

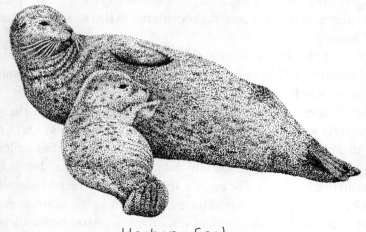

Harbor Seal

Gray whales can sometimes be spotted offshore during their fall migration to calving and breeding grounds in Baja California, or during their spring swims to feeding grounds in the cold waters of the Arctic. A mile south of this point, along a line of reefs that lie halfway between Shore Acres and Cape Arago, you stand a good chance of seeing harbor seals, elephant seals, and Steller's sea lions. The Steller's sea lion is an enormous mammal that takes its name from George Wilhelm Steller, who was the naturalist on Vitus Bering's great expedition to Alaska in 1740 to 1742. (You may recognize Steller's name from the Steller's jay—that large, raucous bird that sports a crest on its head and is often seen flitting through the coniferous forests of the Northwest.)

Because the Steller's sea lion lacks a thick coat of underfur, it has never been on fur trappers' most-wanted lists. Its habit of occasionally preying on squid, halibut, crabs, and other valuable fish, however, have hardly won it any friends among commercial fishermen. Sea lions breed in small colonies after what are often fierce battles between the males to establish dominance. These males may look like Sumo wrestlers, but this is no staged event. In fact, it would be hard to find a single harem bull that doesn't wear more than a few scars around his neck from wounds inflicted by opponents' teeth. Pups are born singly, usually in June or early July. Life can be rather uncertain for these youngsters during the first few weeks of their lives. Sometimes they're washed off the harem rocks by large waves and cannot get back up again; sometimes they are even crushed under the weight of careless bulls, some of which weigh in at a whopping 2,000 pounds. Steller's sea lions do most of their feeding at night, along a band of ocean that extends roughly 10 to 15 miles out from the shore.

The trail continues to meander by the cliff side beneath growths of Sitka spruce and lodgepole pine, offering countless perches from which you can enjoy this wild, rugged coastline. At 0.5 mile, and again at 0.9 mile (near the more groomed portion of Shore Acres State Park), pay special attention to the tilted slabs of siltstone, sandstone, and shale that rise thirty to forty feet out of the breakwater. The wind and storm patterns present along this stretch of coast during fall, winter, and early spring turn these slabs into launching ramps for incoming waves, sending them exploding into the air in magnificent showers of glittery spray. Such surges are the forte of this wet, unbridled symphony—nature's equivalent to the crash of cymbals and the bellow of brass.

At 1 mile you'll be on the groomed picnic grounds of Shore Acres State Park. A visitor podium stands near the cliff edge, and offers a wealth of interesting interpretive panels on the history of this splendid estate. Louis Simpson, son of timber and shipping magnate Asa Mead Simpson, first came upon this place early in the twentieth century while out cruising for commercial timber. He fell in love with it immediately, and managed to buy it from the owner—who happened to be somewhat down on his luck at the time—for the paltry sum of $4,000. Over the years two separate mansions were built here (the first one burned). They sported magnificent entry halls, bedrooms, gymnasiums, and a seventy-five-foot-long Roman bath complete with fresh water and seawater—either of which came hot or cold.

Portions of the Simpson Estate were often open to the public, most especially the magnificent botanical gardens. As family fortunes began to wane, the property was eventually sold to the state, which razed the second mansion in 1948 because it could no longer afford its upkeep. Seven acres of the gardens, however, have been maintained in splendid fashion. No less than 60 different rose varieties can be seen here, 400 kinds of trees and shrubs, and 1,200 annuals. Approximately 1,000 bulbs are planted each spring. If you happen to miss the blooming season, don't worry. During the last three weeks of December the grounds are lighted and the garden house fully decorated for the holidays—a display of some 40,000 lights.

ESTUARY STUDY TRAIL

Distance: 2.75 miles

Location: South Slough National Estuarine Reserve. From the town of Charleston, Oregon, head west on the Cape Arago Highway for 0.1 mile, and turn left onto Seven Devils Road. Continue south on this road for about 4.3 miles, following the signs for South Slough National Estuarine Reserve. Our walk begins on the Plant Identification Trail, located behind the reserve's visitor center.

South Slough National Estuarine Reserve was the first national estuary in the United States, and it is without question one of the most engaging natural areas you'll find anywhere in Oregon. It's a place that always seems to be erupting with life, no matter what time of year you happen to visit. Among these 5,000 acres are fine, thick weaves of plants growing in the upland forests, and a delightful variety of birds inhabiting the salt marshes and tidal mud flats down below. South Slough is one of the relatively few large, marine-dominated estuaries in this country that has remained essentially unbroken by development. To date more than 200 million acres of the world's estuaries have been lost, most of them to the kind of "reclamation" that has consumed so much of the Coos Bay estuary system just to the north. (For a time the town of Coos Bay was actually known as Marshfield, as it was built on filled-in marsh.)

An estuary is, in simplest terms, a place where a freshwater river joins the saltwater of the ocean. Largely because of a phenomenon known as the detritus cycle, in which large amounts of energy are made available through the decomposition of plants, estuaries are unmatched when it comes to sheer quantity of food produced. South

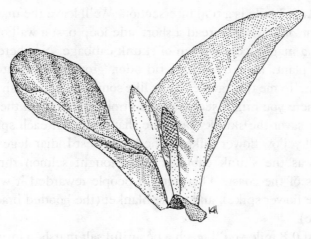

Skunk Cabbage

Slough is, in fact, more than five times as productive as a cultivated cornfield or wheat field, and seven times more productive than a forest. This rich base of detritus material, along with an abundance of phytoplankton, creates a platform upon which many larger, more familiar creatures can exist. We now know that estuaries are crucial nurseries for literally millions of fish; about twenty-two species of commercially harvested fish and shellfish are found at South Slough alone. This area is also wintering ground, breeding area, or stopover point for hundreds of thousands of waterfowl. Indeed, one of the more painful environmental lessons of this century has been that to destroy what at first might seem like a worthless patch of mud and marsh, is to yank the threads from one of the most important webs of life on earth.

Our walk begins along the Plant Identification Trail, located just behind the South Slough Visitor Center. This visitor center, by the way, is an excellent place to learn more about the intricate workings of estuaries. You can also pick up a small interpretive brochure highlighting some of the habitats you'll find along this walk. On the back side of the Plant Identification Trail is a small amphitheater; turn off here on a side trail, following the signs toward Sloughside Pilings. The path will begin a steady descent through growths of Port Orford cedar, red alder, evergreen huckleberry, salal, and raspberry, that mix finally giving way to a cool, quiet slice of coniferous forest.

At 0.7 mile is a trail intersection. We'll leave the main path at this point, following instead a short side loop past a wall of salmonberry to a magnificent garden of skunk cabbage. Nowhere will you see this plant, named for its fetid odor, growing in greater size or profusion. To me this ravine seems like some sort of odd fairyland—a place where you might see newts and trolls standing on their tiptoes to better savor the skunky perfume that pours out each spring from these tall yellow flower spikes. One Northwest Indian legend claims that it was the skunk cabbage that brought salmon runs to the residents of the coast. The grateful people rewarded it with a war club (the flower spike), and a fine blanket (the hooded bract around the spike).

At 0.8 mile you'll reach a beautiful salt marsh, a lovely mix of sedges, arrowgrass, bulrush, and spike grass. At the edge of the marsh is a wooden platform from which you can get a wonderful view of some common feathered residents and visitors to South Slough. Be very quiet as you approach, and you may spot whimbrels, greater scaups, harlequin ducks, green-winged teals, wood ducks, great blue herons, common mergansers, cattle egrets, Brandt's cormorants, kestrels, yellowlegs, and, if you're lucky, even an osprey or a bald eagle. Besides being a very important habitat for birds, salt marshes are also very effective as water purification systems. A salt marsh like this one can trap the sewage produced by thousands of homes, ultimately removing the nitrogen as well as much of the phosphorous from such waste.

Continue north through "the Tunnel"—an arched wall of hemlock, yew, cedar, salal, and evergreen huckleberry. At 1.25 miles you'll intersect the main trail again near a restroom. Turn right here, and follow the signs for Sloughside Dike. Very soon you'll find yourself on a narrow dike that stretches into the water for about 0.1 mile before dead-ending at a set of pilings. These pilings are the last remains of an old railroad trestle. The railway line was built here in order to carry raw logs to this point and then dump them into the slough; they were then tied together and towed in great rafts to mills located in nearby Marshfield and other points along the bay. Logging activity actually drove most of the settlement here at South Slough. Not only did the lands cleared by timbering lend themselves to

Osprey

settlers coming in and establishing farms, but the logging employees were a ready market for beef, milk, butter, eggs, and vegetables.

South Slough was established under the National Estuarine Reserve Research System. Under this program scientists are to make intensive studies of several estuarine systems around the country, and their findings then made available to federal, state, and local policy makers. (One big problem with deciding how to manage these vital ecosystems is that we still know very little about them.) Though this system has not been without its share of problems, it remains one of the finest programs to come out of the federal hopper in many years.

INDIAN SANDS

Distance: 0.6 mile
Location: Samuel Boardman State Park. This walk takes off
from a parking/picnic area along U.S. Highway 101 about 6 miles
north of Brookings. You'll find the turnout on the west side of the
highway, 0.5 mile north of mile marker 353.

The trail to Indian Sands drops like a shot off of the busy Highway
101 corridor, leading you in just 0.2 mile to a weird, wonderful world
of sand. Here are sandstone headlands and delicate dunes, sharply
eroded cliffs and soft hummocks topped by purple beach pea and
shaggy mats of shore pine. If you're in the market for aimless wandering you can simply meander up and down a wonderful maze of
convoluted escarpments and coulees. Alternatively, those in a more
linear mood can pick up the Oregon Coast Trail at the point where
you first come out into the sandscape—the route marked by a series
of wooden posts with yellow bands.

True to its name, Indian Sands is a place that was visited by
various coastal Indian tribes in both historic and prehistoric times.
The archaeological sites here include a midden (a refuse pile) measuring more than three feet deep. A great many arrow and spear points
have been found, as well as various knives and scrapers—some of
them from people who were traveling through this area close to 3,000
years ago. (It's rather odd to consider that while these people were
sitting here flaking rock into points, the Hebrew elders were just
beginning to write the books of the Old Testament!)

Interestingly, although the finds here have been rich, none so
far have included the kinds of things you might think would be found
in a coastal fishing site, such as fish bones, shells from harvested
bivalves, and so on. One theory suggests that when the people who
made these artifacts were here, not only were there no fish—there
was no ocean! When the last ice age finally ended about 11,000 years
ago, there's strong evidence to suggest that this coastline was 300 or
even 400 feet lower than it is now. The ocean waters rose very slowly
as continental ice melted over thousands of years. Such a theory

140

assumes, of course, that the land itself remained fairly stable, not going through any major settling or uplifting during the period.

The people who lived along the Oregon coast 3,000 years ago were well cared for by the bounty of the land and the sea. There were a great many plants to be had, including an abundance of strawberries, blackberries, salmonberries, and huckleberries, not to mention ferns, skunk cabbage, and various seeds, greens, and nuts. Chinook salmon were taken along the coastal rivers in the summer, followed by coho salmon and steelhead trout. Perch, smelt, herring, and flounder were available in any season. While inland game animals were almost certainly abundant, they do not seem to have made up nearly as much of the coastal Indian's diet as did fish.

Sitting here high above the ocean, it's fun to speculate about what the real story of this place was. As you're wandering about the area, don't be surprised if you end up discovering a small piece of an arrow point or scraper laying in the soft, sandy hummocks and eroded ravines. If you do, examine it to your heart's content, but then put it back where you first found it. Researchers hope to launch a significant archaeological investigation in this part of the state park sometime soon; if they're to ever figure out the twists of this cultural tale, then they're surely going to need every piece of the puzzle left in place.

THE MOUNTAINS

To lovers of mountains, the Northwest high country is like waking up on your seventh birthday to a banquet table lined with birthday cakes. The only real question is, where do you begin? These rocky folds are without question among the great mountains of the world. There are the towering, snowy reaches of Ranier and the dry yellow hills of the Seven Devils; the tortured wrinkles of the Coast Range and the long, high swells of the Lost River Range. You can have granite and you can have basalt, alpine meadows or ponderosa parklands, wet or dry, green or gray, in the absolute middle of nowhere or a mere stone's throw from the back side of the city.

No matter which Northwest range you happen to be talking about, the country is for the most part so vast and tightly folded that it seems you can always manage to cut off a little slice just for yourself. Indeed it has been the incredible ruggedness of this land, a good share of it far too impenetrable for exploitation, that has allowed much of the Northwest high country to remain in such pristine condition. Idaho, for example, most certainly would not be blessed with the 2.3 million-acre Frank Church–River of No Return Wilderness if the region were not too twisted and remote to be used for other purposes.

For those who enjoy the more puzzling aspects of natural science, sorting out the geological events that created the Northwest high country can be a lifetime affair. Here were vast island arcs scraping against the edges of an ancient continent, and volcanoes tossing ash and lava bombs across a landscape already blackened by eruptions. The greatest known flood in the history of the world occurred here, and glaciers ground the mountains into what are arguably the most rugged alpine headwalls and cirque basins on the continent. In all it is a dizzy spin of uplift and erosion, the crunch of tectonic plates and the grind of glacial ice—even, according to some geologists, a giant meteorite that crashed into the southeast corner of Oregon, giving birth to the vast sweep of the Columbia Plateau. Of

145

course, while piecing together such puzzles are fun for some, you hardly have to understand such tangled webs to come out of these peaks with a smile on your face. Indeed, you might just agree with Walt Whitman, who once cautioned that "you must not know too much, or be too scientific about birds and trees and flowers; a certain free margin, and even vagueness . . . helps your enjoyment of these things."

A simpler pattern you may enjoy tracking across these trails, however, is the relation of so much of what you encounter on the face of a mountain to elevation. The higher you go, the cooler it gets. And, since cool air masses can't hold as much moisture as warm ones, when mountain ranges force them upward they begin to condense into clouds, often loosing their cargo on the high slopes in the form of rain or snow. This is precisely how the Cascades manage to snatch precious water from the inland Northwest. It's also how Mount Ranier—standing so incredibly tall against such moist coastal air—produces some of the snowiest conditions in the world. As you're driving to these trails, notice how dramatically things change the higher you get. Increasing moisture and decreasing temperatures cause not only the types of trees to be different, but also the kinds of shrubs, groundcovers, and wildflowers spreading from their feet. And that, in turn, means the types of birds, mammals, insects, and amphibians will change too.

But first and foremost, just enjoy these highlands. Much has changed, after all, since Lewis and Clark first punched their way across the rugged folds of the Bitterroots, since Alexander Ross of the Hudson's Bay Company trudged up the Sawtooth Valley to the headwaters of the Salmon River. The same mountains that for early explorers were laced with the constant threat of death, in modern times seem thick with the promise of aliveness.

> In such places standing alone on the mountaintop it is easy to realize that whatever special nests we make—leaves and moss like the marmots and birds, or tents or piled stone—we all dwell in a house of one room—the world with the firmament for its floor—and are sailing the celestial spaces without leaving any track.

> —JOHN MUIR

146

Washington

BAGLEY LAKES

Distance: 2.2 miles
Location: Mount Baker–Snoqualmie National Forest. From the town of Bellingham, Washington, drive east for approximately 60 miles on Washington State Highway 542 (the Mount Baker Highway). Our walk takes off from a parking area located on the right side of the road, directly across from the main Mount Baker Ski Area building.

Admittedly, it was downright sporting of Captain George Vancouver to name magnificent Mount Baker peak after the third lieutenant in his expedition who was the first to spot it through a spyglass in April of 1792. But the native peoples who lived in this area tended to be much more pragmatic in assigning names to things. Nooksack Indians, for instance, knew this mountain as Koma-Kulshan, meaning a white, shining, steep mountain. Indeed, Mount Baker towers 10,778 feet above the sea, supports a dozen glaciers and more than 40 square miles of shimmering ice fields, and is in places steep enough to put the fear of falling into nearly anyone. Clallan Indians, who most times saw the mountain from a greater distance, just called it P-Kowitz, or "white mountain."

As for the pretty pair of alpine lakes you'll be visiting on this walk, I certainly would have fallen into the old habit of giving them one of those classic but sorely overworked mountain names: Heather

147

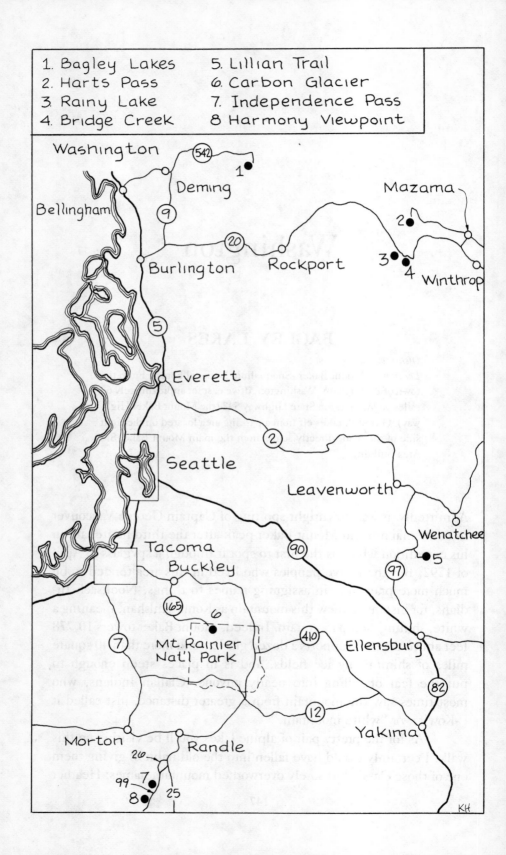

1. Bagley Lakes   5. Lillian Trail
2. Harts Pass   6. Carbon Glacier
3. Rainy Lake   7. Independence Pass
4. Bridge Creek   8 Harmony Viewpoint

Washington

Bellingham

Deming

Mazama

Burlington

Rockport

Winthrop

Everett

Seattle

Leavenworth

Wenatchee

Tacoma
Buckley

Mt. Rainier
Nat'l Park

Ellensburg

Yakima

Morton

Randle

KH

Lakes, Diamond Lakes, Upper and Lower Looking Glass Lakes, or something along those lines. Such titles seem to do a better job of leaping out at you when you're sitting in your kitchen on a winter night pouring over maps, dreaming of the North Cascades high country. But alas, these two pockets of mountain water are known as the Bagley Lakes, named in honor of a heck of a good engineer and all-around nice guy on the Bellingham Bay and British Columbia Railroad.

Since we're on the subject of names, you may wonder about "Nootsack"—the name of the beautiful river you followed for much of the way to this trailhead. This was a name commonly used by early explorers for an Indian people who lived to the west, along the distant sunrise shadows of Mount Baker. *Noot* is roughly the word this nation used to mean "people," while *saak* meant fern, or specifically, the bracken fern. Depending on how you choose to put it together you end up with either "people of the bracken fern," or more commonly, "fern-eating people."

Before you assume that these people were either living in a place with a very dull pantry, or else had pretty easy-to-please palettes, perhaps we should take a closer look at just what the bracken fern has to offer. Though there is some controversial evidence to suggest that bracken fern can actually be toxic, the young fiddlehead stems it produces are quite delicious, offering a taste not altogether unlike asparagus. The Nootsaaks were fond enough of bracken that they'd often burn areas in the forest to encourage its growth. This

Bracken Fern

practice, by the way, also helped bring deer—also fond of young bracken stems—into an area where they could be more easily hunted.

It would be a mistake to think that native peoples were the only ones to make use of this most common of the American ferns. When times were tough during the Middle Ages, people pulverized the underground portion of the stems into flour for bread. American settlers and Indian peoples alike also used bracken as a treatment for worms.

Now that we've gotten our name tags on straight, let's head down the trail. A rather steep, precipitous path winds quickly down and across the north end of Lower Bagley Lake, where you can get down to some serious walking. Woven underneath the wind-tusseled branches of the spruce-fir forest are thick mats of huckleberry, bilberry, false hellebore, valerian, bistort, showy sedge—and, since this is the Heather Meadows area, plenty of white mountain heather. These mountain heathers aren't really true heathers, like those found in Europe, but their dense, matlike growth and small needlelike leaves are quite similar. When you come across a mat of heather on this walk, get down on your knees and take a close look at the exquisite urn-shaped flowers that hang off the plants, looking like carefully crafted bells from some Middle-Earth fairyland.

As you make your way to the small ridge dividing the two lakes at 0.7 mile, keep your ears open for the "Eek!" of the pika, or rock rabbit, which lives in the cold gray jumbles of talus that flank so many of these lush alpine meadows. At 1.1 miles you'll reach the fringe of Upper Bagley Lake, on the very edge of the 125,000-acre Mount Baker Wilderness. Although at this point you're only a couple of good stone throws from what in winter is a hustle and bustle ski area, this tiny alpine pocket, laced with braids of cold water and high-country wildflowers, can truly seem a million miles away.

It was the famous British botanist David Douglas that in 1827 first named these stunning mountains the Cascades, taking the title from the waterfalls he'd seen far to the south along the Columbia River. Other names were tried, such as the Snowy Mountains and the President's Range, but in the end it was the Cascades that stuck. More than a century-and-a-half later that name strikes images in the hearts of American mountain-lovers, not so much of waterfalls (although there are plenty of those), but of icy lakes and glacier-scoured cirques and basins—some of the best of what remains of the unfettered Northwest.

HARTS PASS

Distance: 2 miles

Location: Okanogan National Forest. From the town of Winthrop, head northwest on Washington State Highway 20 for approximately 10 miles, turning right onto a road that leads to the village of Mazama. (This turnoff is a short distance before mile marker 177.) In Mazama, turn left on County Road 1163, which becomes Forest Road 5400. At a point 19 miles from this last turn, turn left onto Forest Road 500, toward Meadows Campground. Continue past the campground to the end of the road, which is approximately 1.7 miles from Forest Road 5400. (This is not, incidentally, a route for trailers or extra-wide vehicles.) The braid of trails heading south can be somewhat confusing; the best way to hit the right path is to head up behind and to the right of a large information sign that marks the beginning of the trail.

Although this walk is just a tiny slice of the sprawling wonderland traversed by the 3,000-mile-long Pacific Crest Trail, it is most definitely the stuff that wildland fantasies are made of. All around you on this path the world seems to be exploding into mountains: a crisp, rugged collage of rock and timber and sky. Despite the long twists and turns of the road getting here, this is a very gentle walk, easily done by even young hikers. It's a place to let your mind drift across the very top of the world, to clean out the cobwebs with a cool rush of mountain wind.

The body of these mountains is a rich mix of metamorphic rock—quartz, marble, gneiss, and schist that were squeezed and heated by magmas lying deep within the inner reaches of the earth. In eons past the land that forms the spine of the Coast and Cascade ranges—a ridge that stretches from northern California into southern Alaska—ground its way higher and higher into the sky, in this particular area reaching a point 8,000 feet taller than where it first began. Yet in the end it was not such grand swells of earth that gave the North Cascades their rugged, distinctive beauty. For that we can thank the general cooling periods that gave rise to the glaciers. Glaciers are the master sculptors of many of the northern hemisphere's greatest mountain systems. At one point all of western Washington almost to Seattle was covered in a vast sheet of ice, which in places grew to be thousands of feet thick. The steep, knifelike ridges, the headwalls and amphitheaters, the grand U-shaped valleys like that of the Methow River far below you, all were carved by these great tongues of ice grinding their way downward through the heart of the Cascade high country.

The beginning of our walk meanders along a classic mix of coniferous forest, to the east broken by wide reaches of alpine meadows filled with wildflowers. In early October the tattered quilts of western tamarack lining much of this mountain slope turn a soft gold. Soon they'll fall from the trees, to be replaced anew the following spring. In a short distance the path crosses a marvelous talus slope, which in summer runs thick with the "Eeek! eeek!" of the pika, or rock rabbit. Its cries of protest at being disturbed may seem overdone, but keep in mind that it does have a lot of work to do. Before this short, sweet summer comes to a close it must cut bushels and bushels of grass and leaves, lay them out carefully on the rocks to cure, and then store them away in an underground pantry to feast on this winter.

The views become better and better as you make your way

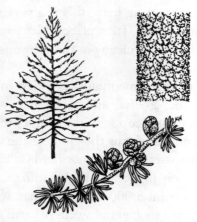

Tamarack

upward, the route tossed with tamarack, red heather, willow, phlox, yarrow, pussytoes, and white moss heather, the latter plant hung with exquisite bell-shaped white flowers. The mix of meadow and forest that surround Harts Pass is a wonderful place to look for flowers of all kinds. In fact, there are reportedly about six dozen flowering plants in this immediate area—more than you'll find in almost any other roof-top slice of the North Cascades.

The view at our turnaround point—a small saddle reached at 1 mile—can only be described as glorious. To the west are saw-toothed ridges, steep, scoured ravines and polished headwalls, all blending together to form the rugged eastern fringe of North Cascades National Park. The lower reaches of the slopes here are wrapped in spruce and fir, but as you move upslope these yield the stage to the tenacious tamarack. In fall it looks as though the mountains have donned an old, tattered green scarf fringed with a thick border of gold.

As you make your way back down the trail you may notice a fire tower to the north, atop Slate Peak. This is one of many such towers throughout the Cascades. For decades lookouts have been used as a means of early fire detection across much of this country; at the peak of their popularity there were ninety-three of them in the North Cascades alone. One of them, named Desolation, was where Jack Kerouac came to spend a wild, lonesome summer of writing.

Back in the 1930s, when the chief of fire control for the state of Washington heard that the Russians were doing mass parachute jumps, the notion dawned on him that such a thing just might be a perfect way to go about fighting forest fires. He wrote off to Moscow for information, had it translated, and before long was conducting experiments that involved dropping sandbags—and then men—into the meadows and forests surrounding Winthrop. (It was this little experiment, incidentally, that gave birth to the American military paratroopers.) Thinking that $191 a month for jumping out of a plane sounded a whole lot better than $135 for being a "ground pounder," a young firefighter by the name of Francis Lufkin became part of the first smokejumping team. He admits that the whole idea was pretty hard for the old rangers to accept. "We had quite a job selling smokejumping," he says, "because they used to think we were nuts."

RAINY LAKE

Distance: 2.2 miles
Location: Okanogan National Forest. Take Washington State
Highway 20 (the North Cascades Highway) east out of Rockport
or west out of Twisp to Rainy Pass. Turn south onto Forest Road
500 and follow it for 0.1 mile to the Rainy Lake trailhead and
picnic area. Rainy Lake is handicapped accessible.

There's no getting around the fact that unless you walk the trail to
Rainy Lake early or late in the day or during the off-season, you're
going to have some company. But because this lovely trail is paved
and level, it's perfect for those who aren't able to navigate dirt paths.
Besides, the lake itself is splendid—a small jewel set in the vast
green and gray folds of the high Cascades.

Before the path enters the cool shade of the spruce-fir forest,
where the trees' trunks and branches are wrapped in thick cloaks of
lace lichen, it passes nice smatterings of horsetail and false hellebore.
You'll recognize this latter plant by its veined leaves and its tall stem,
which at this altitude reaches a height of about three to four feet. The
range of uses for false hellebore is amazing. Alkaloids in the plant
have been used for centuries to lower blood pressure and heartbeat.
If you're a gardener, you may recognize the name "hellebore" as a
type of insecticide; in fact the insecticide is made of this plant, dried
and ground into a fine powder.

Also growing in this area are nice clusters of lupine, rue
anemone, and pearly everlasting. The last of these you've probably
seen time and again in dried flower arrangements. Framing this
vegetation, on the far side of the North Cascades Highway, is the
rugged flank of 7,790-foot Whistler Mountain. Rather than being
named for a person, some historians suggest that Whistler Mountain
instead takes its title from the hoary marmots that live there. The
habit these fat, furry vegetarians have of emitting a shrill whistle
whenever danger approaches has earned them the nickname of
whistle-pig. Hoary marmots often make their homes in jumbles of
rocks high in the mountains, where the weather allows them to be
active only a few months out of the year.

At 1 mile, the thick curtain of forest will begin to lift and the first shimmers of Rainy Lake will begin to appear in the distance. Before you actually reach the lakeshore, however, take note at 1.1 miles of the beautiful ribbon of ferns on either side of the trail; at one point coursing down the hillside ravine like a great green river. Ferns of all types were widely used by Indian peoples throughout the Northwest—the fronds as liners and coverings, and the roots and young fiddleheads as food. In medieval times there were many European cultures that believed ferns bore a single golden flower that bloomed only on Midsummer's Eve. Anyone lucky enough to find the flower (and many people looked) was assured riches beyond his wildest dreams.

Rainy Lake is a classic Cascade Mountain alpine lake, right down to the rugged glacial headwall that was carved out by Lyall Glacier. While serious glacial sculpting and scouring took place during the ice age of 12,000 to 20,000 years ago, many of the glaciers here in the Cascade high country did manage to gain some additional muscle during another, mini-ice age that occurred just 3,000 years ago. A glacier is formed during extended periods when more snow falls during the winter than melts during the warm seasons. No matter how massive they get, however, glaciers don't barrel down the mountain like an icebound freight train. Their work—nothing less

False Hellebore

than shaping virtually every dramatic cirque, horn, or U-shaped valley you see before you today—is a slow, patient business, usually involving movement of no more than several feet per day.

BRIDGE CREEK

Distance:　2.8 miles
Location:　Wenatchee National Forest. Head west from the town of Winthrop on Washington State Highway 20. The parking area for our walk is located on the right (north) side of the highway, just west of mile marker 159. The trail takes off directly across from this parking lot, on the south side of the highway.

If you love the mountains, it's almost impossible to drive the North Cascades Highway without feeling an itch on the bottoms of your feet to get out and do a little walking. The perfect cure lies along the Pacific Crest Trail, at Bridge Creek. You will have to contend with some highway noise for the first half-mile or so, but after that the trail makes quick progress into a world marked by the cool, almost ethereal silence of a mature spruce-fir forest, punctuated here and there by the gush and gurgle of streams tripping their way down the mountain toward Lake Chelan.

　　This is a wonderful walk on which to familiarize yourself with

Black-capped Chickadee

156

some of the more common plants of the high Cascades. Within the first 0.25 mile of trail you'll pass silver fir, Engelmann spruce, grand fir, willow, huckleberry, and trailing rubus, along with a fine show of wildflower blooms during the warm months of summer. The reason for the great diversity of vegetation here is you're standing very close to the crest of the Cascade Range—that high, cold line of peaks that wrings such great quantities of snow and rain from the bellies of the clouds. After passing this divide clouds descend into warmer air, where they can hold on to more of whatever precipitation they have left. The lands that lie to the east of the Cascades, especially those at lower elevations, are left to make the best of life in the rain shadow.

One of the most enchanting, unexpected aspects of this trail on the day that I walked it had to do not with trees or mountain vistas, of which there were plenty, but of the thousands of spider web strands that were flying like silken banners in the first fresh light of the day. Though sometimes you may think otherwise, spiders do not build webs to catch on your nose and eyes as you walk down the trail early in the morning; they build webs to snare insects to feed on. The strands used for constructing these webs are formed from a protein-based liquid that the spider draws out of its underside. When the time comes that the spider no longer needs one of the lines it has cast, it simply eats it, thus "recycling" valuable material.

At 1 mile into the walk you'll intersect connector trails to Copper Creek and Stiletto Peak. At this point you're just a mile away from North Cascades National Park, and less than 30 miles from beautiful Lake Chelan, which is where all of the bright, frothing streams you see around you are heading. If you've ever doubted the raw power of the glacial ice to actually shape the high country, then Lake Chelan should convince you once and for all. The bowl of this lake, scooped out 20,000 years ago as if it were so much sherbet, is 50 miles long and a phenomenal 1,528 feet deep, which makes it the seventh-deepest lake in the world.

Lake Chelan basin is remote country. The population along its upper reaches is served not by road but by ferries, which make regular runs to Stehekin Landing delivering groceries, clothing, hardware, and so forth.

Very soon dramatic views begin to open up to the southeast of the rugged Cascade crest, capped along this section by the cold,

157

ragged summits of Lincoln Butte, Twisp Mountain, and Hock Mountain. Not 4 miles to the east of where you now stand, at a windswept saddle called Copper Pass, Alexander Ross became the first European to cross the roof of the Cascades in 1814. Ross had his share of excitement as a trapper working under George Simpson of the Hudson's Bay Company, crisscrossing the vast reaches of the Columbia watershed in search of beaver. After foolishly invoking the ire of the Snake Indians while trading in what is now southern Idaho, though, Ross's men were summarily robbed of all their goods. Ross himself was demoted, and not long afterward gave up the trap line to become a schoolteacher.

At 1.4 miles you'll reach a fine open slope, the airy views courtesy of an avalanche that steamrolled through here several years ago. The sudden addition of sunlight has provided a wonderful growing opportunity for plants that wouldn't be able to make it in the shade of the great conifers. Look for alder, raspberry, red elderberry, lady fern, and Sitka mountain ash. This is our turnaround point, though you can certainly continue on for more of the same, hitting the national park boundary in 0.6 mile.

LILLIAN TRAIL

Distance: 2.2 miles
Location: Wenatchee National Forest. From U.S. Highway 2 west of the town of Wenatchee, turn south onto U.S. Highway 97. In approximately 22 miles, near the top of Swauk Pass, turn left (south) onto Forest Road 9716. Follow this for 3.8 miles, and turn left onto Forest Road 9712. In 5.7 miles you'll reach our trailhead (trail number 1204), on the left side of the road. (Note: A short distance to the east of this trailhead is a small road that actually parallels our trail. If you can't find a parking place on Forest Road 9712, you may want to pull onto the shoulder of this small road and walk back to our trailhead.)

I should tell you from the start that the Lillian Trail just isn't fast-food walking—the kind where you make a quick turn off the highway, grab a few yards of trail, and get back on the road again before the rubber on your tires has had a chance to cool. The 10 miles of twisting, sometimes confusing dirt roads that must be navigated to get to this path create an experience more suitable for those who consider themselves eclectic, gourmet walkers: the kind of people who like to cruise the back streets of strange towns for home cooking instead of always heading for the Golden Arches.

Those who do have the time and patience to take this trail, however, will be rewarded with a marvelous perch from which to gaze into hundreds of square miles of that dry, delicious landscape that lies east of the Cascade Mountains—a complex symphony of rock and timber, sage and sky.

Like the scenery, the forest you'll be walking through on your way to the turnaround point is a strange, hard-to-define mix. Engelmann spruce, subalpine fir, and lodgepole pine are all common, but in places these are seasoned with sprinkles of whitebark pine and ponderosa. Underneath all that are sparse, yet still engaging gardens of yarrow, grouse whortleberry, pearly everlasting, and pyrola.

As you make your way along the first portion of this walk you'll see many conifers draped with the dark, stringy hairs of black tree lichen. While this plant could hardly be classified as appetizing, it is indeed edible. In fact, there was a time when the sweet taste of black tree lichen was enjoyed by a great many Indian families living in this region, especially during winter when other plants were scarce. After

Subalpine Fir

the tree lichen was cleaned it was baked in a fire pit, a process that changed it into a smooth black mass. This could be eaten as it was, or else dried in the sun and ground into a sweet powder that would later be used as an additive to other foods.

Two of the trees along this trail that serve as "hat racks" for black tree lichen are the subalpine fir and Engelmann spruce. Notice how in particularly thick stands the lower portions of these trees are bare of vegetation, lined instead with only the spikes of dead, gray limbs. This phenomenon is actually a kind of self-pruning. It makes little sense to put effort into growing needles in this dark understory, when almost all the sunlight—and thus the energy—is to be had topside. In some forests these rows of dead limbs will rise for more than 100 feet, leaving just a tuft of food-producing vegetation waving high overhead.

At 0.4 mile you'll join the road that's been off to your right. A short distance later, take off to the right and begin a moderate climb for 0.3 mile. There are nice lodgepoles in here, a few of the young ones sporting dark patches of a sticky substance on the tips of their lower branches. This is actually a mold that sometimes takes hold when one of the supple lower branches of a conifer is pinned down to the ground for a prolonged period of time by heavy snow. Of course, as the tree grows, it will have fewer branches down low that can be caught in this compromising position. (One reason mountain conifers tend to have supple branches rising to a point, like a cone, is so they can shed snow.)

At 1.1 miles you'll come out of the forest into a small opening. On your left will be a faint trail leading in just twenty or thirty yards to a beautiful outcropping. Follow this to our turnaround point, on the edge of a high, windswept rim of sandstone that offers dazzling views of the country lying to the north, east, and west.

CARBON GLACIER

Distance: 6.8 miles

Location: From the town of Buckley, Washington, head south
on State Road 165. In 10.5 miles you'll come to a fork; take the
left branch, following signs toward the Carbon River entrance to
Mount Ranier National Park and Ipsut Creek Campground. Our
trail takes off from a parking area on the east side of Ipsut Creek
Campground, which lies 13.2 miles from this last road junction.

> *The swift red flesh, a winter king—*
> *Who squired the glacier woman down the sky?*
> *She ran the neighing canyons all the spring;*
> *She sprouted arms; she rose with maize—to die.*
>
> —HART CRANE

Given that Mount Ranier contains the largest mountain glacier system in the continental United States, it would be hard to find a more
appropriate place to rub elbows with these great sculptors of the high
country. At about 4 square miles in size Carbon Glacier is the second
largest in the park, as well as the most accessible. Top honors for size
go to Emmons Glacier, at 5 square miles the largest glacier in the
country outside of Alaska. Altogether, there are more than 30 square
miles of ice covering various portions of this mighty mountain, radiat-
ing out from its high flanks like the spokes of a great wheel.

Glaciers do not necessarily form in conditions of extreme cold,
but rather when, over many years, more snow falls in the winter than
can melt in the summer. As these layers of snow become deeper and
deeper, their own weight eventually begins to compact them into
hard glacial ice, which begins to move slowly downslope because of a
certain amount of flexibility in its bottom layers. (Research in Glacier
National Park has found that glaciers generally start to move when
the thickness of their ice grows past 100 feet.) There was a time when
the Ranier ice sheets were literally thousands of feet thick; as they
bulldozed their way downslope they cut the beautiful, deep
U-shaped valleys and the staggering vertical cliffs you see today,
including the magnificent Willis Wall, which lies at the head of
Carbon Glacier. So while forces deep inside the earth may have

created this mountain in the first place, it was the glaciers that lent real beauty to its final form, slicing and polishing it like a sculptor pulling lines across a lump of clay.

Our trail begins in a lovely forest of Douglas-fir, the bottom-lands cut by an abundance of watercourses, each one more choked with blooms, leaves, and fern fronds than the next. Deer fern, wood fern, and sword fern are all common, as are foamflower, bunchberry, queen's cup, star-flowered Solomon's seal, twisted-stalk, and huckle-berry. At about 0.2 mile, just past a small footbridge, is a trail junction; bear to the left toward Carbon Glacier, making a 0.1-mile climb up a small hill. Once on top the path will carry you along a bench overlooking a wonderful stream bottom—a sublime, almost ethereal mix of sun and shade that is forever fingering the plush carpets of fern, devil's club, and, in summer, the silky green leaves and pink flower spikes of corydalis. (The formidable thorny stalks and leaves of devil's club, incidentally, are very common along such stream bottoms. This caused early explorers, who routinely traveled in such corridors, no end of pain and misery. Though beautiful in a rather exotic way, it's probably safe to say that devil's club is one of the kinder names given to this plant; even its species name—*horridus*—hardly speaks well for it.)

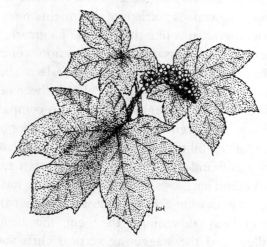

Devil's Club

Maidenhair Fern

At 0.75 mile the trail comes out into an opening at the edge of the Carbon River, the long, green flanks of 5,000-foot-high Chenuis Mountain rising to the northeast. Watch trailside for vanilla leaf, hemlock, alder, and coltsfoot. At about 0.5 mile farther along, you'll come across a fine avalanche path on the right side of the trail. Avalanche paths are wonderful places to stumble across when hiking in the mountains, primarily because the absence of trees allows the growth of a unique collection of plants that wouldn't otherwise be there. This is a fine spot to see salmonberry and alder, and beneath their branches, lovely splashes of foamflower, Siberian miner's lettuce, columbine, and maidenhair fern. The leaves of the latter plant, incidentally, were used by both Northwest Indians and European herbalists to treat congestion, coughs, and other irritations of the throat and chest.

Your reward for making the slow, steady climb to the 2.5-mile mark will be a wonderful view of Mount Ranier. By now the feeling has grown more and more mountainous, though trilliums, ferns, violets, vanilla leafs, and maples remind you this is a long way from the dry alpine country that lies to the east. The open sky is pierced by peaks and ridgelines, and thin veils of water pour off the steep sides of Chenuis Mountain. The air is one minute brisk with the breath of Carbon River and Glacier, and the next warm, almost sultry—thick with the smell of moisture-loving plants.

One of the plants you'll see along the right side of the trail here is vine maple, a modest tree that, during the summer, can often be overlooked among the more stately species of maples and conifers common throughout this area. But come fall this is one of the loveliest of all the northwestern trees, its leaves lighting paths of red and gold through the deep reaches of the forest. Beautiful or not, French fur trappers sometimes referred to the vine maple as the "devil of the forest"—a name bestowed on it for the sole reason that its low-growing trunks often tripped them as they made their way along portage trails. Indian tribes of this region used the branches of vine maple to make scoop nets for catching salmon. If you're here in the spring or early summer, look for pretty clusters of red to purple flowers drooping from the ends of the short twigs.

At 3.2 miles you'll cross Cataract Creek, busy living up to its name by leaping and tumbling from the reaches of Mist Park in a ribbon of utter froth. Our turnaround point comes 0.2 mile later, at a cable bridge crossing the Carbon River. From here you can look upstream right into the face of Carbon Glacier, which is not white as you might suppose, but a muddy, ashen gray from tons of sediment and till. If you want to get an even closer look, just cross the bridge and take a right, climbing rather sharply to a point beside its leading edge.

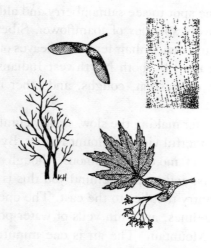

Vine Maple

INDEPENDENCE PASS

Distance: 0.5 mile
Location: Mount Saint Helens National Volcanic Monument, in
the Gifford Pinchot National Forest. From the town of Randle on
U.S. Highway 12, head south on Forest Road 25 for 20 miles to
Forest Road 99, and turn right (west). Follow this for 12.2 miles
to Independence Pass Interpretive Trail, located on the right side
of the road.

The eruption of Mount Saint Helens on that fine Sunday morning in
May 1980 was hardly a complete surprise. Two months earlier there
had begun a series of shallow earthquakes on the north side of the
mountain, followed by eruptions of steam that ripped a crater through
the volcano's ice cap. More and more earthquakes began to rumble—
thousands of them, in fact—and a crater began to form at the summit, rapidly growing to 1,000 feet in diameter. A large bulge started
to swell on the volcano's north flank. On some days it grew more than
eight feet, a certain indication that viscous magma was rising high
into the cone. Officials became increasingly concerned. First they
closed the mountain itself to visitors, and then an ever-widening
circle of land around it.

But when at 8:32 A.M. on May 18 an earthquake began to
rumble on the mountain, no one—scientist, visitor, or landowner—
could have helped but be dumbstruck at the magnitude of the events
that unfolded. Almost immediately the entire north side of the volcano began to give way, steamrolling down the mountain at 150 miles
per hour, filling in less than ten minutes a 20-square-mile slice of the
North Fork Toutle River Valley to an average depth of 150 feet—the
largest landslide in recorded history. Later, flows of gas, ash, and
pumice, some of them measuring 1,100 degrees Fahrenheit, poured
out of the volcano, killing virtually every kind of life on the northern
fringe of the mountain. Even 15 miles away the blast thundered
along at speeds of 200 miles per hour, snapping three-foot-thick
Douglas-firs as though they were toothpicks. In terms of forest alone,
the various blow-down areas contained enough timber to build
300,000 two-bedroom houses.

By the time the main Mount Saint Helens eruptions were over, enough ash had fallen to bury a football field 150 miles deep. Some of it had been spewed so high that it actually circled the earth in just fifteen days. Two hundred homes were damaged or destroyed, as were 27 bridges and 185 miles of road. More than thirty ships were stranded in the Columbia, volcanic debris having choked the river into a channel one-third as deep and wide as it had been before the blast. Fifty-seven people were dead or missing. After 123 years of silence, Mount Saint Helens had spoken with a roar heard around the world.

Since the time of the original blast, an easily visible lava dome has been built within the crater, which currently measures more than 1,000 feet high and 3,000 feet wide. Such features are quite typical, and are formed in two ways: First, when magma rises into the core of the dome, making it swell; and second, when the hard crust of the dome breaks, allowing the molten rock to pour out and form rounded piles of lava. At the current rate of growth, it's conceivable that this lava dome could grow enough to fill in the excavated crater in only about two hundred years.

This short walk climbs for 0.2 mile to the top of a ridge that will afford you splendid views of both Mount Saint Helens and Spirit Lake, much of it choked with downed timber. Though the regrowth of plants is not as far along here as in other parts of the monument, you will see fireweed, dwarf bramble, huckleberry, and some valiant little

Fireweed

166

Pacific silver firs lending welcome splashes of green between the gray lines of fallen timber. These plants represent the beginning of a roughly two-hundred-year-long process to reestablish the kind of old-growth forests that existed in the undisturbed areas of the monument before the eruption. (Though no human-aided reforestation is being done within the monument, on nearby national forest lands more than ten million trees have been planted on about 14,000 acres. The survival rate has been very good, generally approaching 70 percent.)

Upon gaining the ridge, continue along it for another fifty yards to an interpretive sign framed by benches. The sign here is especially helpful to first-time visitors, as it outlines the location of several natural features visible from this vantage point, as well as where some of the structures lost in the blast used to stand. No matter how many feet of videotape you saw flash across your television screen a decade ago, no matter how many pictures you stared at in magazines and newspapers, there is simply no way to really comprehend the awesome, fantastic force of the Mount Saint Helens eruption until you stand here and see the results for yourself. In this one vast scene, consisting of miles and miles of toppled trees and ash-laden valleys lightly peppered with tufts of green, is the whole story of Mount Saint Helens—a 40,000-year cycling of violent destruction, countered by the slow, patient push of new life.

HARMONY VIEWPOINT

Distance: 2.8 miles
Location: Mount Saint Helens National Volcanic Monument, in the Gifford Pinchot National Forest. From the town of Randle on U.S. Highway 12, head south on Forest Road 25 for 20 miles to Forest Road 99, and turn right (west). Follow this for 13.6 miles to Harmony Viewpoint, located on the right side of the road.

The staggering effects of the Mount Saint Helens blast are readily apparent to anyone driving Forest Road 99 through the monument. But to walk off the lip of Harmony Viewpoint and onto the vast Spirit

Lake basin is to feel completely immersed in this incredible natural wonder. Likewise, standing on the northeast shore of Spirit Lake looking toward the collapsed face of Mount Saint Helens can be almost overwhelming. From this vantage point, even on a bright June day the volcano seems tired and haggard, her once-shimmering white flanks thick with a gray drizzle of ash. Whether in fact she is too tired to blow her stack yet again, sending her recently constructed, thousand-foot-high lava dome spewing into the Washington sky, remains to be seen.

Yet as stark as the images along some of this walk can be, as you make your way down the trail from the overlook parking area it's hard not to be amazed at the amount of life springing from the steep slope beneath the highway. To some extent this face was spared the full impact of the blast because of the protection offered it by the high ridge on your left. Also in its favor is that it faces generally northward, an orientation that allows it to retain more precious rain and snowfall than its warmer south-facing counterpart on the other side of the valley.

Besides the patches of fireweed, huckleberry, and dwarf bramble that can be seen reclaiming other nearby areas, you'll also find alder, western mountain ash, trailing blackberry, and elderberry. In spring and early summer the flowers along this trail are an absolute delight, made even more so by being the lone splashes of color in a landscape that, at least from a distance, can be generally defined in shades of brown and gray. Look for the large single white flowers of

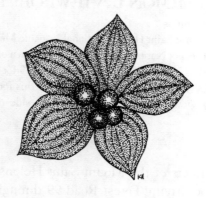

Bunchberry

168

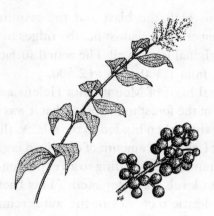

False Solomon's Seal

trillium and queen's cup, as well as the ivory-colored clusters of blooms that mark vanilla leaf, devil's club, false Solomon's seal, and western mountain ash. At a crook in the trail at 0.6 mile, near a place where a small spray of water trickles down an outcrop of rock, the flower show gets even better. Here you'll find the soft rose-colored petals of bleeding heart, the pleated petals of Oregon fairy bells, and a little further down the trail, a fine weave of bunchberry. This latter plant is a member of the dogwood family, those prized trees that bloom so beautifully throughout much of the eastern and southern United States. In August this little plant turns even more showy, sporting clusters of bright red berries. Though humans don't seem to enjoy its fruits, white-tailed deer consider them a delicacy.

By 1.1 miles the path you've been following will have largely faded into a gray, barren mound of ash, leaving you to follow a series of posts to the shore of a small inlet stream. This little watercourse, its edges lined with lavender tufts of lupine and the scarlet of red monkeyflower, seems completely unimpressed by the scope of destruction that spread all around it. It gurgles strong and clear into Spirit Lake, freely offering up its waters to various grasses and willows that are slowly working to reclaim the land.

On May 17, 1980, Spirit Lake was still a clear, cold mountain lake—generally high on oxygen and low on nutrients. But the blast the next day changed all that. For starters, part of the volcano's north side actually fell into the lake, raising the water level by almost 200 feet. In addition, both the blast and the resulting debris caused waves to form that crashed against nearby ridges to heights up to 600 feet above the original lake level! The actual surface area of the lake almost doubled, from 1,300 acres to 2,500.

The lateral blast of Mount Saint Helens actually heated the organic material of the forest to the point that it was broken down into organic carbon, which then binded to the ash. As this carbon-rich ash sifted into Spirit Lake, the amount of dissolved organic carbon in the lake increased dramatically, leading to an explosion of bacterial activity. Soon, oxygen levels were depleted. (This bacterial activity was speeded up by drastic increases in the water temperature; the day after the blast, Spirit Lake had a temperature of 91 degrees; a full 40 degrees higher than it would normally have been at that time of year.) Gradually these new nutrients were depleted and temperatures dropped. Oxygen was stirred back into the water by wind and by the mixing that occurs in lakes due to seasonal temperature changes.

Because Spirit Lake was so close to the inner blast zone, the fish and amphibian life in its waters was destroyed. However, at the time of the blast various kinds of frogs and toads were hibernating in the bottoms of other, more protected lakes and streams. Their progeny quickly found their way into Spirit Lake, and have been successfully reproducing there for many years. Similarly, certain insects came into the blast zone very quickly. A great many ant colonies survived beneath the ground, while beetles and ballooning spiders (spiders that travel on the winds using silken "parachutes") arrived here in great numbers. It wasn't long before Roosevelt elk and black-tailed deer were also seen in the area, having migrated in from surrounding lands to feed on the surviving vegetation.

Though it can seem like a slow process to those of us who measure time by hours and weeks and months, there has in fact been a tremendous resurgence of life here at Mount Saint Helens. In fact, one of the biggest surprises to scientists was how many species survived what at first seemed like total devastation. In turn, the survival of these species in the months and years that followed was aided a great deal by the large amounts of organic material that remained wrapped in the shattered landscape.

Oregon

SOUTH IMNAHA RIVER

Distance: 4.4 miles
Location: Wallowa-Whitman National Forest. Near the town of
Joseph, Oregon, head south on Forest Road 39 for about 28
miles, and turn right (west) onto Forest Road 3960. Our trailhead
is 9 miles down this road, taking off from the northwest corner of
Indian Crossing Campground.

If you've been among those who have thought of eastern Oregon as a
seamless braid of dry, chalky desert, then you'll find the Wallowa
Mountains to be a dazzling dose of attitude adjustment. Nearly 60
percent of the peaks in the state that are higher than 9,000 feet are
not in the Cascades, as you might expect, but here in the heart of the
Wallowa's 300,000-acre Eagle Cap Wilderness. From the summit of
9,595-foot Eagle Cap peak, glaciated valleys rimmed with alpine
lakes tumble down in all directions, drained by such enticing watercourses as the Lostine and the Minham rivers, Sheep Creek, Eagle
Creek, and, the centerpiece of this walk, the South Fork of the
Imnaha River.

   Before we hit the trail, let's take a closer look at a couple of the
engaging names that mark much of this landscape. The name Imnaha, a version of which shows up as early as 1814 in the published

171

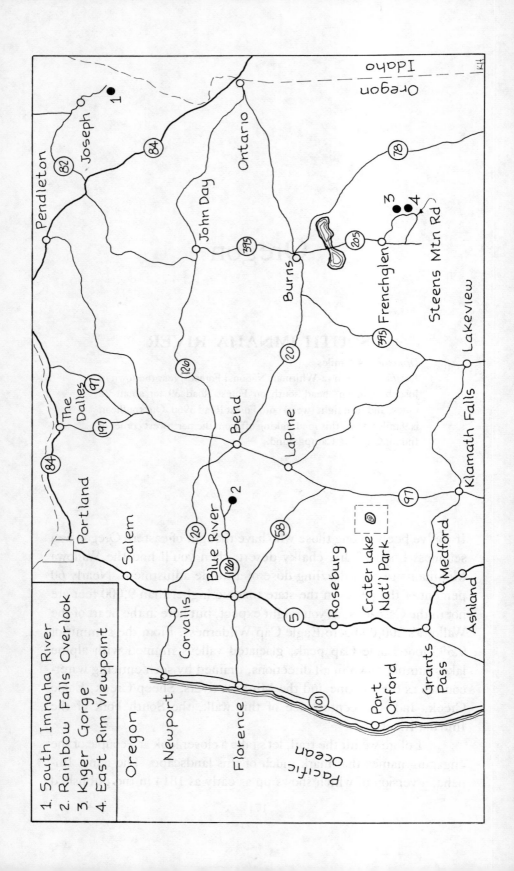

1. South Imnaha River
2. Rainbow Falls Overlook
3. Kiger Gorge
4. East Rim Viewpoint

journals of Lewis and Clark, comes from a subchief known as Imna. Native Americans in the area referred to lands held under a certain chief by using that chief's name, adding "ha" onto the end of it. Thus, Imnaha means the lands ruled by Imna.

As for the name Wallowa, which has been given to a town, county, lake, river, and mountain range, several historians seem satisfied that it derives from a Nez Percé Indian word for a set of stakes used in a fish trap. These stakes were set up in roughly the shape of a triangle pointing upstream, with smaller wooden slats woven between them. Fish would swim into the narrow opening, but then could not swim out again.

Since we've touched on the Nez Percé, you may be interested in knowing that these mountains were the homeland of the great Chief Joseph, who in 1877 led his people on a staggering 1,700-mile journey through the rugged folds of the northern Rockies in order to escape pursuit by federal troops. Six years earlier, Joseph's father had implored him from his deathbed never to sell the Nez Percé lands. "This country holds your father's body," he counseled, referring in part to the beautiful Wallowa River Valley to the northeast of here. "Never sell the bones of your mother and father." Young Joseph was a man of extraordinary peace and patience, but the writing was on the wall. The whites would have this land, and the Nez Percé would go to reservations whether they wanted to or not. But for a brief visit to

Cassin's Finch

his father's grave in 1900, when Joseph left the Wallowa Valley that July morning with 700 followers and 2,000 horses, it was the last time he ever saw his beautiful, beloved homeland.

Each step of this walk seems better than the last, and how it begins is no small slice of wonder. The forest here is a stately blend of ponderosa pine, Douglas-fir, and Engelmann spruce, their feet cloaked in fine mats of huckleberry, violet, pipsissewa, lupine, anemone, strawberry, and, in early spring, glacier lilies. By the time you reach the boundary of the Eagle Cap Wilderness at 1.1 miles, the scene has taken on the aspects of a dream. Old, cinnamon-colored ponderosas stand in parklands stitched with grass and wildflowers, huddled like grand old men at the feet of the Imnaha Divide. In spring a small runoff stream comes charging through the park, glacier lilies spilling yellow up and down its eroded banks. To your left the Imnaha fast-steps ever eastward, heading over an increasingly steep fall of land toward Hell's Canyon, the deepest gorge on the North American Continent, from there to begin a slow, deep meander to the Pacific Ocean.

Continue walking for another 0.7 mile. Here the trail will cross a small inlet fringed with false hellebore, willow, and currant, then deliver you to the north bank of the Imnaha. This is a perfect place to look for the tracks of animals that live here, including elk, deer, beaver, and porcupine. From this point the path winds through a pocket of bracken fern spiked with tamarack, and at 2.1 miles reaches the junction with the trail to Blue Hole and Twin Lakes. Follow the Blue Hole Trail for 0.1 mile to a small campground. On the south side, tucked into a bold outcrop of rock, is the chasm we're looking for. Here the Imnaha roils and rolls deep and dark, the whispers of eddies belying the real power held between these walls.

Much of the grand scenery in this valley is due to the effects of glaciation 12,000 to 20,000 years ago. Now we're not talking about a mere popsicle dribbling down the valley; at one point, the campground where you parked your car was covered with over 2,000 feet of ice. While the finer points of how the Blue Hole chasm itself was formed are not completely clear, the river is choked into this narrow slot largely because the rock here is hard, erosion-resistant Clover Creek greenstone. The falls themselves may have been partly the result of uplift (you are standing on a major fault line), or pockets of

American Elk

175

rock may simply have been peeled away by the actions of both river and glacier.

Far upstream lie the high, wind-scoured granite peaks of an alpine world that resembles the Rocky Mountains, while downstream are dry, pine-clad basalts and volcanics. And overhead the sky seems to be forever burning up with blue, spiked on occasion with the wings of raptors riding on waves of mountain wind.

RAINBOW FALLS OVERLOOK

Distance: 2.4 miles
Location: Willamette National Forest. From the town of Eugene, Oregon, head east on State Highway 126, continuing past the town of Blue River. Turn right (south) 0.7 mile east of mile marker 53 onto Foley Ridge Road, also known as Forest Road 2643. Follow this for 6.4 miles, and bear right onto Forest Road 460. This road ends at our trailhead in 0.3 mile.

Most people are too busy paying their respects to the more traditional approaches of the Three Sisters Wilderness to give this delightful little forest pathway the slightest attention. But if easy, uncrowded walking and breathtaking vistas are what you're after, this is the place to find both. Although the first 0.4 mile of trail is through an old forest cut, the land has come back with bells on, cloaked in a fine wash of willow, Oregon grape, star flower, fir, hemlock, cedar, bracken fern, and thimbleberry. Because there are really two forest communities here—one middle-aged and one fairly young—this is the perfect walk for getting a feel for the changes that occur as a forest matures.

If you haven't already become acquainted, two plants that you may want to watch for during the first 0.4 mile of the walk are snowbrush and thimbleberry. Snowbrush has shiny evergreen leaves with three main veins fanning outward from the stem. The underside is soft and hairy while the top is often gummy, hence another one of the plant's common names—sticky laurel. When things begin to heat up around here in July and August, you may discover that the leaves of the snowbrush have curled along their center veins. This isn't a sign of ill health, but rather a little trick the plant has developed to avoid the drying effects of the sun. The elk and deer that inhabit the Cascades consider snowbrush to be a choice winter browse; if you're here after a rough winter, you may see that the stems of these plants have been chewed down considerably.

Thimbleberry is another plant of note here, and it forms a hip-high wall of large, maplelike leaves at just under 0.4 mile. Though the plant's species name, *parviflorus*, means "small-flowered," its beautiful white blooms are often a good 1.5 inches across. In mid- to late summer thimbleberry sports lumpy, bright red berries. Each "lump" has developed independently from separate ovaries, coming together as they grow into what appears to be a single berry.

Shortly after this thick veil of thimbleberry you'll enter a mature forest of firs and hemlocks. If you're here in June and look off to your left you'll see the showy pink to purple blooms of red rhododendron, each cluster perched atop a rosette of long, shiny evergreen leaves. Some people have called this the most beautiful shrub in the western United States, and looking at it in bloom, it would be hard to argue. (You won't hear any objections from the state of Washington; in 1949 they made it their state flower.) Rounding out the bloom parade along this stretch of the trail are trillium, bedstraw, pathfinder, star-flowered Solomon's seal, three-leaved anemone, and, at about 0.6 mile, some lovely clumps of vine maple.

Soon a striking canyon begins to open up on your right, the rim lined with a loose weave of firs and spiked with several Pacific

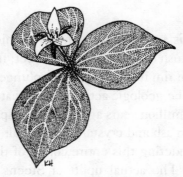

Western Trillium

madrone; the smooth, polished trunks of this latter tree rising like dancers caught in the middle of a delicate movement. The sculptor responsible for the canyon below is Separation Creek, which, although you can't see it, can be heard hissing away on its mad dash to join the McKenzie River. The trail ends at our viewpoint, an absolutely magnificent perch along the northwest boundary of the Three Sisters Wilderness. Once you get to the overlook, carefully make your way to the southern-most rock outcrop, where you'll have a glorious view of Rainbow Falls to the west, as well as North Sister, Husband, and South Sister peaks. (This mountain range is a real family affair; Brother, Wife, and Middle Sister peaks can be found nearby.)

Please note that this final stretch of path out to the southern rock outcropping is narrow and steep. It is *not* a place for young children.

KIGER GORGE

Distance: 1.2 miles
Location: Steens Mountain Recreation Lands. From the town of Frenchglen, south of Burns approximately 61 miles on Oregon State Highway 205, head east on the Steens Mountain Road. In about 23 miles you'll come to a small road taking off to the left (north) to the Kiger Gorge Viewpoint. Follow this for 0.5 mile to the viewpoint, and begin your walk eastward along the rim of the gorge.

Steens Mountain is a tilted sandwich of volcanic rock ripping out of the Oregon sagebrush to a height of 9,773 feet; from the sharp, windy crest of the eastern rim it is a long, dizzy plunge to the Alvord Valley lying far below. The geologic activity that created Steens Mountain began roughly 15 million years ago, in a great spew of volcanism that covered the area in ash and crystal-laden basalt to a depth of several thousand feet, rendering this entire corner of the state a flat, rather featureless plain. The actual uplift of Steens Mountain occurred eight million years later, during a grinding collision between two large continental "plates" that were floating on the molten interior of the earth. Steens Mountain rose, while the valleys on either side of it actually subsided. Finally, it was only about 20,000 years ago that glaciers came on the scene. And really, it was the work of glaciers, not uplift, that turned this mountain from something great into something truly magnificent.

Steens was the only place in all of southeastern Oregon that held glaciers during the last ice age. And yet Kiger Gorge, on the northeast corner of the mountain, is easily one of the best views of glacial handiwork to be found anywhere in the country. The sheer enormity of this gently curving U-shaped valley is overwhelming—a sculpture that would seem more at home in the icy folds of Norway than hanging here above the Great Basin desert. Also impressive glacial gorges are Blitzen, Little Indian, Big Indian, Wildhorse, and Little Wildhorse canyons. Those of you who enjoy photography will likely end up running out of film long before you can capture all the moods that roll across these gorges on a single summer day.

Steens Mountain used to be known simply as Snow Mountain, a name it certainly deserves, as it's a rare year when you can make it all the way around the loop road before early July. But the name of the mountain was to change not long after Major Enoch Steens arrived on the scene in 1860. He was a man with a mission: to develop a wagon road from nearby Lake Harney to Eugene City, in the rich Willamette Valley to the west. But one day while he was deep

Yarrow

179

in the throes of plotting his route, word came of an Indian attack against an army surveying party. Steens dropped his road-building project like a hot potato and headed east, where he established a fortified camp on Silver Creek, west of present-day Burns. Later that summer Steens had a row with a band of hostile Snake Indians, and ended up driving them up and over this mighty mountain. Happy miners and settlers referred to it as Steens Mountain from that time on.

In addition to being a wonderful place for drinking in the scenery, Steens Mountain is also a botanist's dream. A phenomenal 600 species of plants have been found growing over many life zones, including four that grow nowhere else (Davidson's pentstemon, Cusick's draba, Steens mountain thistle, and Steens paintbrush). As you make your way eastward along the rim of Kiger Gorge, keep your eyes peeled for buttercups, yarrow, phlox, silky phacelia, milkvetch, needle-leaved sandwort, mat buckwheat, stonecrop, and pussytoes.

At a point about 0.2 mile from the parking area, you'll be able to look down on a beautiful little lake set in a high basin at the head of Kiger Gorge. In the right light, and with a little wind blowing across it, it looks very much like a shimmering cache of precious gems, just a little too remote to ever reach. Also visible in the very bottom of the gorge is a thin, silvery braid of water known as Kiger Creek. This stream dances its way to the northwest for more than twenty miles, not resting until it reaches Diamond Valley, just south of the parched volcanic domes of Diamond Craters.

Continue to follow the faint trail around the rim. In another 0.2 mile you'll have to jog around a large cut in the headwall of the canyon. Our turnaround is at a very small alpine water pocket that lies just to the north of this jog. (Because of the very fragile nature of this environment, it's extremely important that you stay on the faint path already in place.)

Whether this great mountain is "supposed" to be here or not, there can be no mistaking that it represents the high country in all its glory—the brace of cold wind, the whistle of the marmot, the small pockets of snow still shining under an August sun. The poet Byron was right when he said that "high mountains are a feeling." When you stand atop a place like Steens, you wish that feeling would never end.

EAST RIM VIEWPOINT

Distance: 2 miles
Location: Steens Mountain Recreation Lands. From the town of Frenchglen, which lies approximately 61 miles south of Burns on Oregon State Highway 205, head east on the Steens Mountain Road. In about 26 miles you'll see a road taking off to the left (east), with a sign pointing to the East Rim Viewpoint. Follow this to the end—about 0.4 mile—and begin walking north on a faint path that winds along the top of the rim.

This short, rim-top ramble will bring you about as close as you'll ever get to realizing that old mountain notion of being able to "look all the way into tomorrow." (A shorter, but still expansive view—perhaps a look back at roughly this morning—can be had merely by turning around and facing west.) The east face of the tilted, thirty-mile-long Steens Mountain uplift nosedives so sharply into the desert 5,000 feet below that if you have even the slightest case of acrophobia you may want to consider chaining yourself to your car before you venture anywhere even close to the rim.

One of the first things you'll spot lying at the foot of this mountain is the thin skin of sand, sagebrush, greasewood, hop sage, and shadscale that cloaks the Alvord Desert. This is a hot, fabulously desolate place—the driest environment in the state of Oregon. But the small family groups of nomadic Indians who roamed here thousands of years ago fared better than you might imagine. While these people did eat jackrabbits, seeds, roots, rodents, lizards, and other offerings of the desert, they were also close to a variety of richer environments. Bighorn sheep, elk, and deer could be hunted in the uplands, while salmon were plentiful in the Malheur River to the north. The wetlands of Malheur provided them with ducks, geese, and coots. The fact is this region, as dry as parts of it may appear, has more water and a greater variety of elevation-determined ecosystems than any other in the Great Basin Desert.

Even so, as a group of pioneers headed for the lush valleys of western Oregon in 1845 found out, the skills needed to prosper in any kind of desert environment cannot simply be figured out as the need arises. While resting at Fort Boise after crossing the hot, dry reaches of southern Idaho's Snake River Plains, a number of weary

Bighorn Sheep

emigrants found themselves set upon by a man named Steve Meek. (This was the brother of Joe Meek, the famous trapper). Meek boasted he knew a fine shortcut across the Oregon Desert that would shave 200 miles off the regular path of the Oregon Trail, and further, that he would happily guide them over it for the trifling sum of $5 per wagon.

Saving 200 miles meant eliminating about two weeks of travel, and to people who'd been on the trail for four months already that was a tempting proposition. A large group agreed to try. Unfortunately, Meek somehow lost his way near the Malheur River, and for six long weeks the party ambled around in loosely woven circles through the sand and the sage. By the time they finally reached the Columbia River, twenty people had died; another twenty were so sick they died shortly thereafter.

If all this were not enough to ensure a kind of immortality for the ill-fated trip, a strange story that later surfaced about the discovery of gold nuggets would. One of the wagon train members, a man named Dan Herron, supposedly picked up a couple of pieces of shiny metal while looking for cattle he'd lost near the head of the Malheur River. He took the stones back to show the others, who promptly judged them as worthless. (According to one version of this story, Dan later used them as fishing weights.) Four years later, at Sutter's Fort in California, a group of men who knew what they were talking about told poor Dan that this was in fact gold after all. Several of them—Dan among them—took off immediately to search for the spot where he'd found the gold, but it was never found again.

The "blue bucket stories" were variations on this theme. In one version, a thirteen-year-old girl spots the nuggets while washing at a stream. Fascinated by the colors, she gathers up the biggest of the stones and takes them back to the wagon train, accidentally leaving her blue bucket by the stream. Then, so the yarn goes, one day years later when she gives them to her own children to play with, her brother sees them and pronounces them real gold. Eventually this story, or similar versions of it, became so widespread that the wagon train was dubbed "the blue bucket train." Although the stories had no basis in fact, more than a few people ended up combing this area, looking for that little blue bucket—a signpost on the way to Easy Street.

As you make your way above the steep, fluted ravines and

rocky ledges of the eastern face, keep your eyes out for bighorn sheep down below. These animals were at one time plentiful in the area, but hunting and other human-related pressures caused them to vanish from the mountain by 1915. Eleven bighorn were taken from Hart Mountain National Wildlife Refuge in the early 1960s and placed here along the east slope, where they did very well. Sixteen years later there were 150 animals plying a vast portion of these rugged cliffs and ravines, and today there are 250 to 300.

Watching a bighorn spin dizzy pirouettes here on the sheer edge of oblivion is an experience you'll never forget. Except during their breeding season, bighorn sheep spend most of their day in a cycle of eating and resting, the young sometimes scrambling after each other in a rock-bound game of chase. No matter how relaxed a band of bighorn might appear, however, bighorns are always in a state of alertness. Their exceptionally acute eyesight allows them to detect the slightest movement, and they will dash for cover if they feel at all threatened.

Typically just one ewe comes into estrus at a time, usually during November or December. If she catches the attention of more than one ram, the two males will square off in one of those skull-crunching duels that almost hurt to watch. What we rarely see on television nature shows, though, is that rams don't just use their horns against each other: If they get a chance to kick their opponent in the flanks, they'll do it. Six months after breeding, a single lamb is born to the females, delivered in the most out-of-the-way, inaccessible places imaginable.

Bighorn do not seem to do well in stressful situations. Under conditions of overcrowding, for example, what would normally be a minor illness may quickly lead to death. For this reason, managing these magnificent animals has in many parts of the West been a tremendous challenge to wildlife agencies.

In just under a mile you'll reach our turnaround point, a steeply cut ravine heading off to the southeast. (On the other side of the road is Little Blitzen Gorge—yet another example of the staggering power of glaciers.) At this point you may just want to take a seat and stare out into the incredible vastness that tumbles eastward from this alpine island; a view that extends past the boundaries of Oregon, and well into the vast high deserts of northern Nevada and southern Idaho.

Idaho

MINERAL POINT

Distance: 0.9 mile

Location: Kanisku National Forest (within the Idaho Panhandle
National Forests). From the town of Sandpoint, Idaho, head
south on U.S. Highway 95 for approximately 6 miles. At 0.2 mile
past mile marker 469, turn left (east) onto Sagle Road. Follow
this for approximately 7.3 miles, at which point you'll reach a
small road taking off to the right, with a sign that says "Mineral
Point—6 miles." Take this right fork and proceed for 1.5 miles,
turning left at Garfield Bay on a village street going uphill. At 0.3
mile from this last junction, take a right. Our trailhead is 3.6
miles down this road; whenever you come to a fork, follow the
Forest Service signs for hiking trail number 82.

This lovely interpretive trail was constructed in 1989 to honor Brent
"Jake" Jacobson, a forty-one-year-old Forest Service law enforcement officer who was gunned down while pursuing two fugitives in
northern Idaho during the winter of 1989. Jake was the first Forest
Service law enforcement officer ever killed in the line of duty. It
would be hard to imagine a finer tribute to him than this 0.9-mile
nature path, hung on a lush, forested hillside high above the shining
waters of Lake Pend Oreille. An interpretive brochure has been
produced by the Sandpoint Ranger District that corresponds to numbered posts along the trail; be sure to pick one up before you begin
your walk.

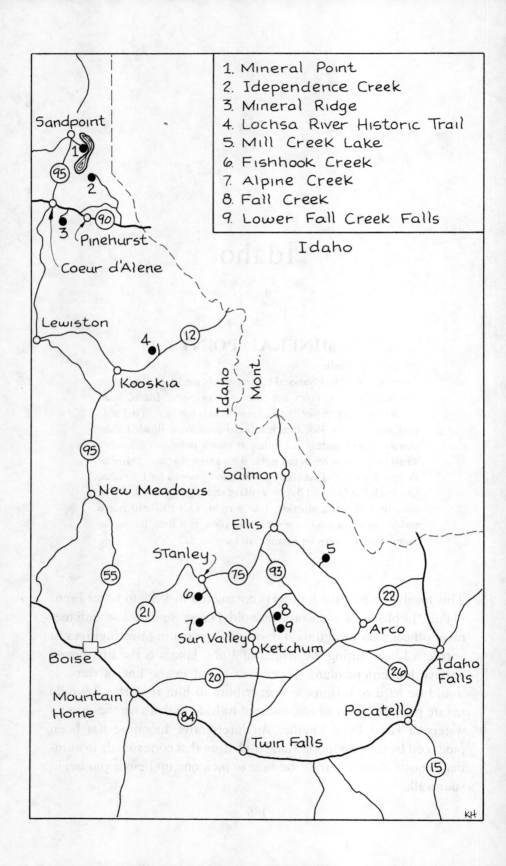

1. Mineral Point
2. Idependence Creek
3. Mineral Ridge
4. Lochsa River Historic Trail
5. Mill Creek Lake
6. Fishhook Creek
7. Alpine Creek
8. Fall Creek
9. Lower Fall Creek Falls

Idaho

Sandpoint

Pinehurst

Coeur d'Alene

Lewiston

Kooskia

Idaho

Mont.

Salmon

New Meadows

Ellis

Stanley

Sun Valley

Ketchum

Arco

Boise

Mountain Home

Pocatello

Twin Falls

Idaho Falls

KH

Columbine

One of the striking features of the Idaho Panhandle forests is how lush they can be. This path begins in a beautiful tapestry of Douglas-fir, maple, and ponderosa pine, then carries you in 0.4 mile to a bottomland thick with moisture-loving western red cedar and Pacific yew. Along the way the path is lined with mats of twisted-stalk, Oregon grape, columbine, fireweed, violet, lupine, false Solomon's seal, fringecup, trillium, strawberry, and calypso orchid.

You'll have gone less than 0.1 mile before coming to the first good view of Lake Pend Oreille—a perch that in the spring is backed by cream-colored serviceberry blossoms, as well as the warm yellow heads of arrowleaf balsamroot. Lake Pend Oreille is in places more than 1,000 feet deep, apparently excavated by great tongues of glacial ice that flowed south out of Canada more than 100,000 years ago. (Major ice flows were again pouring out of Canada as recently as 12,000 years ago, though many geologists think that this far south they would not have been formidable enough to excavate a basin 1,000 feet deep.)

While the actual excavation of the Lake Pend Oreille basin is certainly nothing to sneeze at, it pales in comparison to another icy phenomenon that occurred on this site—one of the most spectacular geological events in the world. The great lobes of ice that flowed down from Canada eventually formed a mammoth ice dam along the

187

Fringe Cups

eastern edge of Lake Pend Oreille, cutting off the flow of water from the Clark Fork River. Foot by foot the Clark Fork drainage began to fill, forming a lake (known as Glacial Lake Missoula) that reached a depth of over 4,000 feet! And then an astounding thing happened. The block of ice that formed the dam began to float and then break into pieces, causing the sudden release of 500 cubic miles of water, which is thought to have thundered across the land at a speed of 45 miles per hour. (Some researchers have speculated that at maximum flow, the release was ten times the volume of water present in all the world's rivers combined!) This raging wall of water scoured out deep ravines throughout eastern Washington, filled the Columbia River Gorge with 1,000 feet of churning water, and caused enormous floods as far west as Oregon's Willamette Valley. This process of ice damming, filling, and then flooding happened not once, but dozens of times, though the force and power of that first great release was never equaled again.

From this vista point the trail continues to descend through the forest, soon reaching another splendid lookout: the memorial site for Brent Jacobson. After this the path descends more quickly, reaching the cedar bottoms at just over 0.3 mile. At this point you'll come to a fork in the trail. Turn left, and proceed past a shaded garden of trillium, bedstraw, and pipsissewa. Indian peoples of the Northwest used solutions made from pipsissewa for a variety of ailments, including as a tea to relieve fever and as a wash for sore eyes. Many of the settlers who adopted the plant relied on it most heavily as a treatment for kidney disorders, a use which science has verified to some extent in recent years. Pipsissewa is found not only in moist coniferous forests across North America but in Asia and Europe, as well.

From here the trail will make a small loop through beautiful groves of ponderosa, Douglas-fir, western red cedar, and yew. This is a quiet, sheltered world, rich in the natural magic that still weaves itself across so much of the green, rounded face of the Idaho Panhandle.

Pipsissewa

INDEPENDENCE CREEK
NATIONAL RECREATION TRAIL

Distance: 3.6 miles

Location: Coeur d'Alene National Forest (within the Idaho Panhandle National Forests). From Interstate 90 west of Pinehurst,
take exit 43 and head north on Forest Highway 9, a road that
follows along the south bank of the Coeur d'Alene River. In about
23.5 miles you'll see Forest Highway 9 heading off to the east;
continue north along the Coeur d'Alene River on Forest Road
208. Continue on road 208 for approximately 30 miles, at which
point you'll make a right turn onto Forest Road 3099. (Note:
Don't panic if, at about 4 miles before this junction, Forest Road
208 suddenly changes its number, becoming Forest Road 6310.)
Follow Forest Road 3099 for 0.3 mile, and then turn left onto
Forest Road 825—a narrow two-track road that heads down a
slight hill. Our trailhead is about 0.9 mile from this last junction.
(Those with large vehicles could park at the intersection of routes
3099 and 6310; this would add 2.4 miles to the walk, round-trip.)

Those who intend to take this warm, sun-drenched stroll up Independence Creek may want to arm themselves with a Coeur d'Alene
national forest map. There are many ways of getting into this area,
from the wild shores of Lake Pend Oreille to the banks of the Clark
Fork; from the flanks of Honey Mountain to the North Fork of the
Coeur d'Alene River. No matter how you come, though, getting to
this trailhead will involve some serious driving time; why not spend
your off-trail time day doing some creative cruising in the back
country?

The route you'll be walking follows an old wagon road that
was built sometime around 1910, in an effort to connect Lake Pend
Oreille and nearby mining camps with Independence and Tepee
Creek valleys. Over the next twenty years this route was traveled by
homesteaders, loggers, and Forest Service rangers and fire fighters.
Most of the improvements that were made along Independence
Creek during this period, from cabins and corrals to a splash dam
used to raise the water level for floating logs, have long since disappeared. Today there is only a wonderful weave of clear water, rounded
mountains cloaked in conifers, and meadows spiked with thick mats

of grass and wildflowers. If there's any walk in this book where you'll ignore the suggested turnaround point and just keep on going, this will likely be it.

Our walk begins with a 0.5-mile climb through a pleasant forest of Douglas-fir, white pine, and an occasional cluster of aspen. This is also the place to see huckleberry, Oregon grape, violet, and pipsissewa, as well as large swaths of false box (also known as box myrtlewood or myrtle box leaf). False box is a shrub that's often found in profusion in Douglas-fir, aspen, and lodgepole forests. It typically grows one to three feet high, and sports opposite, toothed evergreen leaves and tiny clusters of raspberry-colored flowers. Both white-tailed and mule deer seem to be big fans of false box, especially in the winter, when other foods can be hard to find.

Another evergreen shrub that you'll see along the more moist sections of this walk is snowbrush—a shiny green plant with three distinct veins running up from the base of each toothed leaf. Like

White-tailed Deer

191

false box, snowbrush is heavily grazed by local deer during the winter; if you look closely, more than likely you'll see broken stems where the animals have been browsing. An interesting quality of this, and many other species of *ceanothus*, is its flowers contain a glucoside called saponin, which has properties very similar to soap. Indeed, early Indian peoples, and later settlers, used snowbrush blooms extensively as a cleansing agent.

As you begin to descend the small divide you gained at 0.5 mile, the character of the landscape undergoes a splendid transition. Sweeping views begin to open up of the soft, wild mountains to the west, out of which Independence Creek comes pouring like a river of jewels. After crossing a fine little stream at 0.8 mile framed with willow and false hellebore, the path rounds a very open, south-facing slope from which you can gain striking views of Independence Creek both upstream and downstream. The added warmth afforded this hillside due to its southern exposure causes it to bloom earlier than other sections of the trail, with scattered gardens of Oregon grape, lungwort, blue-eyed Mary, phlox, blue violets, and larkspur.

At just over one mile, the trail will drop down off this sunny slope into a young conifer forest sprinkled with trillium, goldthread, and coarse tufts of bear grass. Every five to seven years bear grass puts forth a towering three-foot-tall stalk, atop which rests a raceme of beautiful white flowers. The leaves of this plant are extremely tough, and are virtually ignored as a food source by almost all big game species but the hearty Rocky Mountain goat. Indians throughout the Northwest dried and bleached the tough, shiny basal leaves of beargrass and then wove them into baskets.

In another 0.2 mile the path joins the grassy north bank of Independence Creek. From here the stream will be an almost constant companion, offering you literally dozens of cool, quiet places to rest or picnic. At 1.6 miles you'll cross Mirror Creek and pass by Emmerson Ridge Trail taking off to the right, and in another 0.2 mile, reach our turnaround on the wild green shores of Emmerson Creek. If you'd like to grab an even bigger scoop of solitude than that afforded by the Independence Creek Trail, make your way up through the cool shade of Emmerson Creek for 100 yards or so, where there will be no one to bother you but an occasional dipper, white-tailed deer, mountain chickadee, ruby-crowned kinglet, and, if your

Lynx

luck is very good, the regal, reclusive lynx. The lynx is perhaps as little known as any mammal in America. It's frequently confused with the bobcat, but bobcats are not found in thick woods like this one, but in open patchworks of shrubs and forest edges. Lynx have a range of 6 to 8 square miles, and subsist on a diet of squirrels, mice, birds, and, whenever possible, snowshoe hares. In fact, in some regions snowshoe hares are such an important part of this animal's diet that the death rate of young lynx kittens exactly mirrors drops in the hare population.

MINERAL RIDGE
NATIONAL RECREATION TRAIL

Distance: 3.1 miles
Location: From Interstate 90 east of Coeur d'Alene, Idaho, head south on Idaho State Road 97 for 2.3 miles. At this point you'll see the Mineral Ridge picnic area and trailhead off to your left. (If you cross the bridge over Beauty Creek, you've gone too far.)

While on any given weekend the Mineral Ridge Trail can be rather thick with people, those who can rouse themselves to make the trek early in the morning will end up sharing the walk with few others. This is also, by the way, the time of day when you'll hear a particularly splendid chorus of bird song, the performance courtesy of local nuthatches, chickadees, wrens, jays, and thrushes. Although the Mineral Ridge Trail does make a steady climb of 735 feet over about 1.5 miles, there's no shortage of engaging diversions and rest stops along the way—pungent coniferous forests, clusters of wildflowers and blooming shrubs, and beautiful views of shimmering Lake Coeur d'Alene. This was the first recreation site in Idaho to be developed by the Bureau of Land Management. Started in the winter of 1963, it's a showcase of what this agency can do for recreation when they put their pocketbooks to the task. (The BLM has produced a trail guide for this walk that corresponds with numbered posts along the path; be sure to pick one up at the trailhead information sign.)

The trail rises through a nice mix of ponderosa pine and Douglas-fir, spiked here and there with a few hemlocks, white pines, and tamaracks. If you can make it here during blooming season, you'll also be treated to the showy blossoms of pea vine, strawberry, Oregon grape, long-flowered lungwort, white clover, fairy slipper, and waterleaf. This latter plant, which is also known as ballhead waterleaf, produces its ball-shaped cluster of violet flowers early in the spring, before the soil on Mineral Ridge has had a chance to dry out. The young leaves of waterleaf are very succulent, and were a popular cooked green with settlers and Indian peoples alike.

At about 0.8 mile you'll reach marker post 11 at Radio Viewpoint, beside which is a bench perched on the edge of a hill sprinkled with arrowleaf balsamroot. As the BLM trail guide explains, this and many other areas along Mineral Ridge were mined extensively during the first few decades of the twentieth century, particularly when metal prices were high during World War I. As you walk this path you'll occasionally see shallow depressions on either side of the trail. These are the remains of Mineral Ridge mining activity.

When we think of mining, it's often with a romantic image of a lone prospector kneeling beside a stream cradling a gold pan in his weathered hands. The panhandle of Idaho certainly had its share of loners as late as the early 1880s, some of whom were farmers from the Palouse country to the west who worked their claims around the planting and harvesting of their crops. But the "easy pickings" quickly disappeared. What's more, it was silver, not gold, that formed the lion's share of wealth in the Coeur d'Alene mining district—a mineral that had to be mined through expensive tunneling operations, and then refined. All this meant that by the late 1800s, mining in this region was not a personal adventure but strictly big business; a game where powerful eastern corporations called the tunes that miners were supposed to dance to. If something happened in the industry to tarnish profits, it was the miners who were expected to take it on the chin. When silver prices started to fall at the same time that railroad freight charges were rising in the 1890s, for example, mine owners responded by making sharp cutbacks in miners' wages. When workers banded together and struck as a protest, they were fired and replaced by nonunion members, most of whom worked under the protection of armed guards.

The tension between management and labor grew worse and worse in the Coeur d'Alene district until, in the summer of 1892, angry debate was replaced by gunfire and dynamite. Just as it seemed that the miners might win the battle by having rounded up the nonunion workers and ousting them from the district, Governor Norman Willey decided to end the war altogether by declaring martial law. State and federal troops descended on the district en masse, imprisoning more than 300 people in bull pens—not just miners, but virtually anyone corporate spies had identified as "sympathetic" to the miners' plight. Most ended up staying in these hot, stinking prisons for more than seven weeks, waiting for a hearing. Eventually, twenty-five union leaders were sent to Boise to stand trial; many later did time in prison. (Federal troops were sent in once again seven years later after union members dynamited the Bunker Hill and Sullivan mine complex; that incident led to nearly 700 men being sent to the bull pens.)

The Coeur d'Alene became the biggest mining district in the entire state of Idaho, and one of the most lucrative of the entire western United States. More than a third of all silver produced in this country comes from this mining district; to date, over a billion ounces have been plucked from the nooks and crannies of these rolling mountains.

Continue climbing for another 0.5 mile to the 2,875-foot summit of Mineral Ridge, and turn left. A short distance after gaining this ridge you'll reach Caribou Cabin, a structure built in 1918 that offers fine views of Wolf Lodge Bay to the north. If you happen to be here in early spring, scan the steep hillsides just below the Caribou Cabin for the beautiful nodding yellow bloom of the glacier lily. Although the bulbs of this plant can be eaten raw or cooked, they are often so difficult to unearth that few Indian tribes ever made them a mainstay on their spring menus.

From here the trail makes a pleasant traverse of this high, forested ridge, the quilt of conifers broken here and there by serviceberry, wild rose, ocean-spray, and ninebark. At marker post 22, just before the trail begins a sharp descent back to the parking area, you'll find a bench offering a spectacular view of Lake Coeur d'Alene. While you might assume that this lake is the product of glaciation, like some of those to the north, that's true only indirectly. When what we consider to be the first great ice age poured out of Canada about 100,000 years ago, the mammoth sheets of ice actually stopped before they got this far. In their wake, however, was a moraine of till and outwash debris that ultimately dammed the St. Joe River. Eventually the St. Joe Valley filled with water, creating the magnificent body of water you see before you today.

LOCHSA RIVER HISTORIC TRAIL

Distance: 2.5 miles
Location: Clearwater National Forest. From U.S. Highway 12, turn north on the Fish Creek Road, located at about mile marker 120. Shortly after making this turn you'll see the trail crossing a wooden bridge on your left; continue down the road until you've found a suitable parking place.

September 16, 1805
I have been wet and as cold in every part as I ever was in my life, indeed I was at one time fearful my feet would freeze in the thin moccasins which I wore.

> WILLIAM CLARK, writing from
> the Lolo Trail, about 25
> miles from this trailhead.

September 17, 1805
The snow melted so that the water stood in the trail over our moccasins in some places. Very slippery, and bad traveling for our horses. We ascend very high and rocky mountains; some bald places on the top of the mountains, high rocks standing up and high precipices.

> JOSEPH WHITEHOUSE, member of
> the Lewis and Clark expedition.

September 18, 1805
This morning we finished the last of our colt. We supped on a scant portion of portable soup, a little bear's oil, and about 20 pounds of candles form our stock of provisions, our only resources being our guns and horses. This is but a poor dependence where there is nothing upon earth but ourselves, a few pheasants, small grey squirrels, and a blue bird of the vulture kind about the size of a turtle dove or jay bird. Used snow for cooking.

> MERIWETHER LEWIS, about 15
> miles to the northwest. (The
> "blue bird," incidentally, was
> a Steller's jay.)

197

The following day, September 19, the Lewis and Clark party reached Sherman Peak, which is a high promontory lying just 6 miles to the north of where you now stand. To their utter delight they gazed out on not just another tumble of mountains, but on a great tract of prairie that their Indian guide Toby assured them held the long-awaited Columbia River. Party member Patrick Glass tells of the feeling running through the men on that autumn morning: "When this discovery was made there was as much joy and rejoicing among the corps as happens among passengers at sea who have experienced a dangerous protracted voyage, when they first discover land on the long looked for coast."

At first glance, it may not be completely apparent why the Lolo Trail gained such an infamous reputation among explorers and trappers. Actually, as former regional forester Ralph Space points out in his fine book *The Clearwater Story*, there were several reasons. Perhaps foremost is that timber grows thick in these mountains, and that riding on a trail not regularly maintained is like poking your way through a pile of pick-up sticks. Also, a number of major saddles cut this route, requiring that travelers make a series of steep climbs and descents, some of them over 1,000 feet high. General O. O. Howard—a pious Army man who was often referred to as the "praying general"—summed up well why travel on the Lolo Trail was a painstaking affair: "Conceive this climbing ridge after ridge, in the wildest wilderness, with the only possible pathway filled with timber, small and large, crossed and criss-crossed; and now, while the horses and mules are feeding on unnutritious wire grass, you will not wonder at only sixteen miles a day."

The walk along the Lochsa River Historic Trail traverses a cool forest for about a mile, finally coming out on a series of flower-bedecked slopes that offer wonderful views of the Lochsa River to the southwest, as well as the high, rugged ridges of the Selway Bitterroot Wilderness to the south. The first 0.6 mile of the walk requires a steady climb, though the grade is certainly not enough to worry about. Helping to ease the ascent is a delightful array of the region's more common plants, including Douglas-fir, white pine, and mountain hemlock. This is also a good stretch to see ocean-spray, queen's cup, twisted-stalk, twinflower, serviceberry, thimbleberry, pathfinder, strawberry, bedstraw, bunchberry, and both sword and

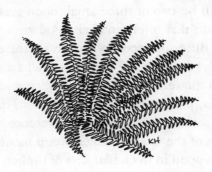

Sword Fern

maidenhair ferns. Pathfinder, incidentally, is a one- to two-foot-high plant with large, arrow-shaped leaves. One of the best ways to identify pathfinder is by its leaves, which are green on top and silver beneath. It was this coloration that led to the plant's common name of pathfinder: It's very easy to follow the path of someone who steps through a patch of these plants, since the silver side of the turned leaves shows up from yards away. Another common name for pathfinder is silver-green.

This entire area, incidentally, was completely burned during a fire in 1934. A heroic effort by a crew of about 200 Civilian Conservation Corps men kept the Lochsa Ranger Station—just east of where you turned off the highway for this walk—from burning to ashes. Indeed, by the morning of August 18 nearly everything *but* the station was reduced to smoldering ashes. At one point a large spark landed on the fire hose, causing it to burst; it was only the frenzied efforts of men carrying bucket after bucket of water and operating hand pumps until they dropped from exhaustion that saved the Lochsa Station.

The Lochsa River Historic Trail is a "reborn" pathway, just completed in 1990. It runs along the length of the Lochsa River from Split Creek Trailhead (mile marker 111) to Sherman Creek (mile marker 123). Built in the mid-1920s, the trail was used for nearly forty years by the Forest Service to supply both fire lookouts and the Lochsa Ranger Station, which lies just to the east. The route is also part of the Idaho Centennial North-South Trail, which runs the entire length of the state.

There will be two or three small open areas along the early section of the path that offer tantalizing views of the Lochsa River and the Selway Bitterroot country to the south, but the real glory comes at about 1.1 miles. Here the forest melts away into meadows strewn with wildflowers—scarlet gilia, yarrow, Saint-John's-wort, stonecrop, clarkia, paintbrush, and pentstemon, to name but a few. Now add to this a magnificent view that stretches both up and down the silvery twists of the Lochsa River, steep mountains running up on either side wrapped in thick blankets of timber, and a bright blue ribbon of summer sky stretching overhead. This is wild Idaho. And you can see why many consider it to be one of the best places on earth. If you continue around the next lobe of mountain you'll come to Otter Slide Creek—a beautiful mountain stream, and an excellent place to have lunch on a warm summer day.

MILL CREEK LAKE

Distance: 5 miles
Location: Challis National Forest. From U.S. Highway 93 at the tiny town of Ellis, turn southeast along the north side of the Pahsimeroi River, following a road that leads through the village of May. Follow this for approximately 53 miles to Sawmill Canyon Road, which takes off on your left. Continue for 10.2 miles, and turn right onto Forest Road 171. Proceed 1 mile down this road to the trailhead.

Although the 1,200-foot climb to Mill Creek Lake over 2.5 miles of trail is not exactly a walk in the park, the grade is in most places fairly pleasant—certainly manageable by anyone who takes time to enjoy the beauty found along the way. This central slice of the Lemhi Range is a land of stream corridors thick with vegetation, as well as of vast mountains of talus that sprout little but ragged patches of lichen. There are cool groves of spruce and aspen and parched huddles of lodgepole pine and Douglas-fir, not to mention trailside gardens peppered with larkspur, rue anemone, squaw currant, and sage.

Sticky Geranium

The first stretch of this trail is through a loose weave of aspen riddled with the blooms of columbine and sticky geranium. Besides holding some of the most beautiful pink flowers you'll find anywhere in the forest—here blooming in June and July—the leaves of sticky geranium are widely eaten by deer, elk, moose, and bear. Just after crossing Mill Creek, notice at 0.1 mile the large dead snag standing beside the trail. While most of us don't give such dead timber a thought, its value to the wildlife of the forest is tremendous. Hairy woodpeckers will often be found raising their young in large nesting cavities ten to twenty feet off the ground, which they excavate from wood that has been softened over time by fungi. Once the wood-pecker family has moved out, it may well be taken over by a moun-tain chickadee or even a saw-whet owl—a beautiful, fairly approachable bird that at night flies through the conifer forest hunt-ing rodents. Up and down much of the length of such snags you can often see the holes of where woodpeckers have been feeding on carpenter ants. The broken branches of snags are frequently used as perches; this snag alone may have three dozen species of birds resting, feeding, or hunting insects from its stubby branches at various times of the day.

After leaving the creek and climbing gently through a very quiet corridor of Douglas-fir, aspen, squaw currant, and fireweed, you'll pick up the cool tumble of Mill Creek once again at 0.5 mile. When you reach this point, notice the increase in the variety of plants that make their homes along this stream corridor. This is due not just to the additional moisture, but also because of the extra light avail-

Yellow-bellied Marmot

able to them here. Look for a classic mix of Idaho montane plants, including willow, sedges, rue anemone, cow parsnip, and saxifrage. Soon you'll leave Mill Creek's pleasant company once again, and make a dry, fairly healthy climb along a bench that parallels the stream channel. Along the way the path makes a slow, rather delicious transition between forest and mountain, passing on occasion jumbles of talus where aspen and dwarf juniper are struggling for toeholds, as well as increasingly rugged outcroppings of rock framing the west side of the ravine.

If you stop for a breath as you near the 2-mile mark, turn around and take a drink of the fine view opening up to the southwest of the long, lonely Pahsimeroi Valley and the Lost River Range. The name Pahsimeroi, incidentally, is thought to be of Shoshone origin, meaning roughly "single grove of trees near the water." Indeed, this dry, yawning reach of the Pahsimeroi Valley did at one time have but one grove of conifers standing in it, not far from the Pahsimeroi river. The first American explorer to stumble into the Shoshone homelands across the continental divide not far to the northeast, was a now rather famous fellow named Meriwether Lewis. The Shoshone not only didn't seem to resent the trespasser, they greeted him with bear hugs, later traded horses with him, and offered no small amount of valuable advice about what lay ahead for the expedition along the rugged rivers and mountains of Idaho.

Little could those Shoshone have known the tide of humanity that would soon follow. Fifty years later there were hundreds of wagons and livestock by the thousands crossing Indian lands nearly every summer day, decimating the range, pushing the Shoshone to the walls of their traditional territories, beyond which they could go no farther without inflaming other tribes. During the Civil War federal troops were few and far between; military leaders and their civilian volunteer contingents often took drastic, ruthless measures to quell the Indians. At one point, traveling from California to Utah to protect emigrants moving west on the wagon trails, Colonel Patrick Edward Connor developed a particularly appalling way of dealing with the angry Bannocks and Shoshone. At the mere suggestion of robbery, kidnapping, or an attack on white settlers, Connor sent one of his men to round up every Indian he could find in the area where the incident occurred. He then sent word to their main tribe, demanding that the guilty be handed over. If they were not, he executed the hostages. Hundreds and hundreds of Indians were shot down this way, many of whom had had no part in any aggression against the whites.

By 2.1 miles the trail has entered a flat area lined with pockets of springwater, surrounded by vast fields of talus—a great place to

Bushy-tailed Woodrat

see pikas scurrying around the rocks. Mill Creek Lake, lying at 8,350 feet, is reached soon afterward. It lies in a small pocket framed by a vast jumble of rock, the scene spiked here and there with Douglas-fir, whitebark pine, and shaggy tufts of currant and bunchgrass.

FISHHOOK CREEK

Distance: 5.5 miles
Location: Sawtooth National Recreation Area. About 5 miles south of the town of Stanley, turn west, following the signs for Redfish Lake. Approximately 2 miles down this road you'll come to a split; follow the left fork, and then make a quick right turn into the backpackers' parking area. We'll begin our walk on trail number 101, which first crosses the paved road that runs along the northern edge of the parking lot.

If you never quite make it out of the easy chair to another single place mentioned in this book, at least make it to the Sawtooth Valley. The lands that rise along the first 30 miles of the Salmon River—the White Cloud Peaks to the east and the Sawtooth Mountains to

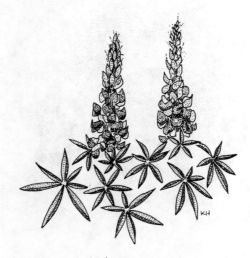

Lupine

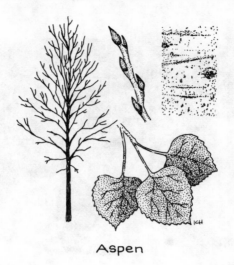

Aspen

the west—are quite simply as splendid as the American West gets. To walk the shores of the region's shimmering lakes, or daydream in the shadow of these rugged, weather-scoured peaks is to open yourself up again; to find yourself in a place where both head and heart seem to sizzle from bolts of sheer, unfettered splendor.

If you arrive at the parking area on a typical summer day, you may begin to wonder just how many other people are going to be gulping down shots of the Sawtooths at the same time you are. Don't worry. This first stretch of pathway actually serves those people going to Marshall Lake or up the North Shore of Redfish Lake, which is also a beautiful walk. By the time a mile passes under your feet things will have quieted down considerably.

The lovely, fast-stepping waters of Fishhook Creek will be on your left by about 0.15 mile, framed by lodgepole, fireweed, lupine, paintbrush, and tufts of aspen and sage. This creek is a major feeder for Redfish Lake, which gets its name from the numbers of Kokanee, or "landlocked" salmon that live there. When it comes time to spawn, these fish turn a beautiful crimson color and begin migrating up the Redfish Lake feeder streams toward "home"—to spawn in the very same places where they themselves started life. The female lays her eggs in excavated depressions called "redds"; immediately thereafter the male fertilizes them. Both adults then die. This is a miniature version of the magnificent tale played out by the Chinook

Black Bear

in the Salmon River just to the east. Those fish swim more than 900 miles to their birthplaces, guided upstream by an uncanny ability to "taste" minute amounts of their home waters in the heavy flows of rivers like the Columbia and Snake.

About 0.3 mile into the walk you'll see a small footbridge on your left crossing Fishhook Creek. Immediately on the other side, off in a pocket of trees to the left, are the remains of an old grizzly-bear trap built by a nineteenth-century trapper. The door was held open by a wooden prop, to which was attached a piece of cording that went over the length of the trap and through a hole in the back side, where it was tied to a piece of bait. The bear crawled into the trap to fetch the bait, yanked on the rope, and thereby pulled the prop from the door. At first glance you may think the trap was much too small to hold a bear, but that was the real beauty of it. If the bear had been able to stand erect he could have used his powerful forelegs to tear the trap to shreds, but in the crawl position his legs were pinned beneath him, where they did him little good. On the north side of the trap you can see a small hole where the trapper stuck in the barrel of his gun to finish off his hapless victim.

At 0.5 mile is the junction with the Redfish Lake Trail, which takes off to the left. You continue straight, entering a fairly homogeneous lodgepole forest, the open areas to the right peppered with tufts of bunchgrass and scattered blooms of lupine and arrowleaf balsamroot. At 1 mile is a trail taking off to Marshall Lakes—a very exposed pathway that on a hot summer day can bake the energy right out of you. Once again we continue straight, into a remarkably quiet, peaceful stretch of pathway. For the next 1.75 miles this is a daydreamer's delight—a gentle meander through a vast quilt of lodgepole huddled in the green grass of summer, with occasional glimpses of Fishhook Creek gliding gently through the long hush of the forest.

Perhaps it's the long walk through a landscape that, while peaceful, is devoid of anything particularly bold or remarkable, that makes the view in 2.75 miles at the wilderness boundary such a bolt out of the blue. There in front of you is a thick riparian meadow laced with beaver runs and cloaked in flowers. And beyond that are the magnificent Sawtooth Mountains, their feet and shoulders wrapped in thick, but tattered blankets of spruce and fir.

Red Squirrel

Though I've been fortunate enough to have walked in almost every mountain range in the continental United States, never have I found one that can reach in and massage the knots out of my soul better than the Sawtooths. English literary critic Charles Lamb once wrote a letter to William Wordsworth, responding to an invitation by the great Romantic poet to go on an outing together. "Separate from the pleasure of your company," he said, "I don't much care if I never see a mountain in my life." Poor Lamb! He'd never been told—never even imagined—that there was a place with mountains like these.

ALPINE CREEK

Distance: 4.2 miles
Location: Sawtooth National Recreation Area. Heading north on Idaho State Highway 75 past Galena Summit, turn left (west) 0.5 mile past mile marker 168, following the signs to Alturas Lake. Follow this road for 6.5 miles, where it will end at the Alpine Creek trailhead.

The name Alturas, which graces the beautiful lake that you passed on the way to this trailhead, at one time was used for this entire region. Alturas is a Spanish word which means "mountainous

Lodgepole Pine

208

Western Tanager

heights," though on occasion writers have interpreted it to mean "heavenly heights." Perhaps this latter translation is more appropriate, since this slice of Idaho is about as close to heaven as a person can get. If you came here from Ketchum and took the time to peer down from Galena Summit to the rugged line of peaks that spill northward along the Salmon River, you'd likely agree with the 1937 WPA guide to Idaho, which called that view "one of the most remarkable in the West." (In the 1920s people would sometimes tie logs onto the rear bumpers of their Model T's to slow their descent down Galena Pass. For years piles of these logs were visible at the bottoms of both sides of the pass.)

True to form, this walk is a precious trip into a stunning collage of rugged mountainscapes, most of them cradled either by cool green forests of lodgepole, spruce, and aspen, or meadows choked with paintbrush, cinquefoil, and sage. Though there are some short steep sections to the trail, it's a path that can be negotiated by nearly anyone. Besides, there are plenty of mountain chickadees, Clark's nutcrackers, and even an occasional western tanager to keep you company while you catch your breath.

We'll be starting our walk in a classic lodgepole forest, underlain by bright green tufts of grouse whortleberry. The lodgepole is among the most hearty and tenacious of all the pines, and the only one found in both Alaska and Mexico. True to its name, the lodgepole did in fact form the framework for early Indian lodges, and early Europeans in the region wasted no time putting them to use as

Golden-mantled Ground Squirrel

well. The excellent strength-to-weight ratio of these trees made them perfect for everything from fences to corrals to mining timbers.

At just over 0.3 mile you'll cross into the Sawtooth Wilderness, where the trail settles into a few serious climbs through a forest of lodgepole, spruce, and an occasional patch of willow. Things will begin to open up at 0.75 mile, patches of sunlit ground washed in the soft green hue of thimbleberry leaves. Suddenly the path comes out onto the edge of a wonderful talus slope, where willow, aspen, and dense clusters of twinberry are all managing to carve out good lives among the jumble of rocks. This is a perfect place to listen for the "Eeek!" of the pika, a small rabbitlike rodent who will undoubtedly be scurrying about cutting grasses and drying them on slabs of rock, building a good store of tasty hay for the long winter ahead.

This area near the talus slope is also a good place to look for fireweed—a tall, spindly plant which in mid to late summer sports beautiful lilac-colored blossoms. Fireweed produces seeds with light, silky hairs that are perfect for catching free rides on the autumn winds. In the best of cases those seeds end their journeys on burned or otherwise disturbed areas, which they then go about reclaiming with amazing speed. In fact, fireweed was often the first life to be seen growing amidst the bombed-out rubble of World War II England.

From here the path will skirt glorious mountain views, on occasion passing through thin ribbons of forest. At 1.9 miles you'll reach a long swell of open land on your left that runs thick with carpets of cinquefoil, paintbrush, and various grasses all the way down to Alpine Creek. Slightly upstream from this is a wild-looking braid of beaver ponds skirted by dark huddles of spruce. It was the beaver, incidentally, that first brought Hudson's Bay Company trapper Alexander Ross into this country in 1824, the last stop on a splendid journey along the Wood, Boise, Weiser, and Payette rivers. But while Ross's trip may have been exciting for the country he traversed, it was not the most successful in terms of economics. To add insult to injury, a band of Iroquois trappers working for Ross so infuriated the Snake Indians with their high-handed "terms" (supposedly handed down by Ross himself) that the Snakes promptly robbed them on the spot. What could have been a sterling career for Ross with the Hudson's Bay Company was suddenly on the rocks. Nevertheless, the journals that this hearty explorer kept on his treks throughout central Idaho are among the best and most detailed to ever come out of the fur trade era.

Our turnaround point is at 2.1 miles, where the trail joins Alpine Creek. If you're not ready to stop this delightful mountain foray, however, by all means continue up the valley, where toward the end of another 2-mile stretch you can climb into the lovely Alpine Lakes basin.

Western Blue Flag Iris

211

FALL CREEK

Distance: 3.75 miles
Location: Challis National Forest. From the Sun Valley Mall, head northeast on Trail Creek Road for approximately 22 miles to Forest Road 135 (Copper Canyon Road), and turn right. (Note: Trail Creek Road crosses Trail Creek Summit, which is not recommended for vehicles pulling trailers.) Continue on Forest Road 135 for 2.1 miles, then bear right onto Forest Road 136. Follow this for 3.6 miles to a small campground on the right side of the road. Park here, and begin your walk eastward on a two-track road marked with the number 503.

A lot of people drive the first 0.6 mile of this route, parking at the point where a wooden footbridge crosses the stream. But the feeling that came from walking through this yawning sagebrush steppe, Fall Creek singing beside me, and the soaring Pioneer Mountains ripping into the burnt blue of a scrubbed summer day, left me no choice but to abandon my car near the campground and get down to the delights of hoofing it. In fact if you really want to do right by this region, camp for a couple of days at Fall Creek Campground or down the road at Wildhorse Campground and walk all over the place. You can go south along Wildhorse Creek toward the magnificent ramparts of Hyndman Peak, or, for the more ambitious, continue this walk by following the Right Fork of Falls Creek to the beautiful, glacier-scoured Sur-

Rabbitbrush

Broom Snakeweed

prise Valley. This is a brilliant land of sage, spruce-fir forest, and fast-stepping streams—Idaho at its astounding best.

The two-track road rambles gently along the south side of Fall Creek through sagebrush, rabbitbrush, and broom snakeweed. Though such vegetative mixes tend to fly by the car window in a dry, dull blur of green, close examination reveals a special kind of beauty. For instance this is often where you'll find the lovely scarlet blooms of paintbrush, a plant that purposely sets up shop next to sagebrush in order to steal nutrients from its root system. You may also see the yellow, star-shaped blooms of stonecrop, as well as the white umbrella-blooms and fernlike leaves of yarrow. Yarrow has a long history of healing. Indeed its genus name, *Achillea*, refers to a similar plant that Achilles used to stop the bleeding of his soldiers' wounds at the battle of Troy. (Another nickname for yarrow is "soldier's wound-wart.") Scientists researching the chemical composition of yarrow have identified an alkaloid named achillein, which does in fact reduce the clotting time of blood. Early Indian tribes of this region used yarrow for other medicinal purposes as well, including as a tea for breaking fevers and colds.

At 0.6 mile you'll cross to the north side of Fall Creek on the footbridge mentioned earlier. (Going straight will take you to Lower Fall Creek Falls; see page 215 for a description of this walk.) As you enter the mouth of the canyon you'll find beautiful old Douglas-fir and whitebark pine trees, as well as a few clusters of aspen nicely tucked into the lower reaches of the valley. At 1.1 miles you'll reach a fork, where you'll stay left. This point begins a moderate to steep climb. When you get winded, just turn around for a few minutes and drink in the splendid view of Hyndman Peak, Duncan Ridge, and Phi Kappa Mountain in the Pioneer range off to the southwest. The town of Sun Valley is on the other side of that high divide, less than 20 miles as the hawk flies from where you're now standing.

While you're resting on the upslope you might also want to scan the trees for Clark's nutcrackers, a rather large gray and white bird that flits and flies through this slice of forest with great abandon. These curious, raucous birds love pine seeds, and in fact have a special pouch under their tongue to allow them to carry off several at one time. Not that they're purists when it comes to food. Nutcrackers are perfectly capable of nabbing insects on the wing, ferreting out various kinds of bugs from beneath the bark of conifers, and—perhaps their greatest talent—flying into picnic sites and helping themselves to whatever tidbits the humans have abandoned. Clark's nutcrackers are found throughout the piney mountains of the West, from southern British Columbia all the way to Baja, California.

At 1.7 miles, after completing the steepest section of the climb, you'll find yourself at a fork; stay right. Just over 0.1 mile farther you'll reach our turnaround point, as the path rounds the outside edge of a small hill onto a fine promontory high above Fall

Clark's Nutcracker

Creek. From here there are grand views to the west of the Pioneer Mountain highline, and to the east, the rugged, glaciated cirques and horns that flank the edge of the Copper Basin cowboy country. Directly below you Fall Creek has carved out several blue-green pools—a chain of brief, beautiful pauses before it tumbles onward to its rendezvous first with Wildhorse Creek, and then with Big Lost River to the north.

LOWER FALL CREEK FALLS

Distance: 2.8 miles

Location: Challis National Forest. From the Sun Valley Mall, head northeast on Trail Creek Road for approximately 22 miles to Forest Road 135 (Copper Basin Road), and turn right. (Note: Trail Creek Road crosses Trail Creek Summit, which is not recommended for vehicles pulling trailers.) Continue on Forest Road 135 for 2.1 miles, then bear right onto Forest Road 136. Follow this for 3.6 miles to a small campground on the right. Park here, and begin your walk eastward on a two-track road marked with the number 503.

Because the first 0.6 mile of this easy walk overlaps with the Fall Creek trek (see page 212), you may want to combine the two into one outing. Although both paths go in the same general direction, the floodplain of Fall Creek is an entirely different world than that found on the high, pine-covered ridgeline traversed by Fall Creek Trail.

Instead of crossing the footbridge over to the north side of Fall Creek at 0.6 mile, continue straight on the small road that runs along the south side of the stream. After 0.2 mile of forest the road ends and becomes a trail, descending onto a beautiful bottomland peppered with young aspen and lodgepole pine. Here and there you'll see gigantic boulders sitting among the young trees. These are known as glacial erratics, and they were carried here from the mountains on the cold, massive shoulders of glaciers that ground down through the high reaches of Fall Creek 15,000 years ago. (Some of the rocks in this area have also been brought here by high water; we'll take a closer look at those flood-related events in a moment.)

There are two features in this region that serve as unmistakable fingerprints of glacial action. The first are known as moraines, which are long ridges of gravelly debris—often covered with dryland plants such as sage—that generally mark the outline of the glacial outflow. The second and much more obvious clues are the dramatic, deeply serrated peaks that mark so much of the central Idaho high country. It's hard to imagine that solid rock could be sculpted like so much clay, but that's exactly what these massive sheets of ice—some easily 2,000 feet thick—were capable of doing. Indeed, while great uplifts along various fault lines may have been responsible for the high country ending up where it did, a great deal of the rugged, breathtaking grandeur that marks so much of these lands is due to the glaciers.

After 0.2 mile of lightly forested bottomland the path breaks out onto a flat sagebrush plain, a good place to look for paintbrush, larkspur, yarrow, stonecrop, blue flax, and lupine. This open area, which is often bathed in brilliant sunlight, lasts for about 0.4 mile, after which the path enters a fine woodland that cradles the edge of Lower Fall Creek Falls.

This is really quite a striking waterfall—terraces dappled with clear, icy pools, the water pouring off the escarpments in big, broad strokes. Mosses flourish here. On the upper reaches of the cascade conifers can be seen leaning out over the stream, giving a tattered green cast to the scene that in some ways seems more reminiscent of western Oregon than of central Idaho. Even in low water this waterfall is impressive; in high water it can seem like the very source of the mountain thunder.

In August of 1984 a tremendous rain fell in the Fall Creek and Wildhorse drainages: ten inches in less than half a day. This one stream swelled to an unbelievable discharge rate, sending a 25-foot-high wall of water crashing down the valley; at its peak, it was kicking out more than the average flow of the Missouri River! Rocks and trees and massive scoops of soil were torn from the banks and sent crashing down from the mountains in a scene of almost unparalleled fury. The trail that used to ascend beyond these falls to your right was wiped out altogether. When the waters cleared again it was a much different place indeed. Several upstream meadows were washed away completely, while steep, bare escarpments stood where only gentle hills

Red-shafted Flicker

had been before. With the flick of a storm, the land had in a single day gone through erosional changes that would normally have taken centuries to complete.

Impressive as it was, the flood of 1984 almost pales in comparison to one that struck just twenty years earlier. This time the floodwaters raged all the way to U.S. 93, wiping out all the bridges along the way. Trailers, pickups, buildings, and heavy equipment at the Cordero Mine were either washed away or buried in gravel. (The mine did rebuild. Alas, their new "flood-proof" bridge floated away in the flood of 1984.) Surprise Valley Lake, which lies in a beautiful mountain valley just to the south of here, was absolutely choked with debris, its outflow completely changed.

Sir Walter Scott may have been talking about Caledonia when he wrote in *Lay of the Last Minstrel* about that "stern and wild" place, that "land of the mountain and flood." Something tells me, though, that Fall Creek and the mighty Pioneers would have served him just as well.

> O Fall Creek! stern and wild,
> Meet nurse for a poetic child!
> Land of brown heath and shaggy wood;
> Land of the mountain and the flood!

Yes, I rather like that.

THE DESERT

A thousand fantasies
Begin to throng into my memory,
Of calling shapes, and beck'ning shadows dire,
And airy tongues that syllable men's names
On sands and shores and desert wildernesses.

—JOHN MILTON

The American deserts have been among the last of our ecosystems to be embraced. For years we have dropped bombs on them and used them to test our atomic weapons; overgrazed their native grasses and buried in their folds our nuclear waste, sure that no one would ever care. The deserts have long been, and to many people remain, unfortunate landscapes—places made ugly simply by virtue of their lack of human amenities. And of all the American deserts, perhaps the Great Basin, whose fringes extend into southeastern Oregon and southern Idaho, has been appreciated least of all.

Of course, if you've spent much time in these places, if your senses have been sufficiently honed to pick the precious from among the overwhelming, you know that these arid lands are amazing places. Here are rugged, cobbled canyons where young golden eagles take their first daring leaps into the sky, and thin earthen canvases that in spring explode with the reds of skyrocket and paintbrush, the lemons of primrose, balsamroot, and sunray, the ivories of sego lily, fleabane, and pincushion. And here too is silence and space beyond imagining—two shrinking American commodities that in the end perhaps will be what saves the desert after all.

Engaging enough in their own right, what adds so much delight to the deserts of southeastern Oregon and southern Idaho is

221

that they are framed by such contrasting landscapes. The shimmering black basalt desert of Craters of the Moon is even more profound when backed to the north by a line of snow-capped peaks—the distant mountains approaching, as William Merwin once described it, like sails from a wingless kingdom. From the hot sands of Oregon's Alvord Desert rises the mammoth 9,733-foot Steen's Mountain, while a short distance to the northwest is a braid of marsh, lake, and rimrock comprising one of the richest bird sanctuaries in America.

As you walk through the high deserts of the northwest, look for some of the themes that seem to run through the life of the desert. Notice the small size of the leaves here, as well as how many of them, instead of being smooth like the plants of the forest, are covered with fine hairs—designs meant to conserve water. See how a landscape that seems almost devoid of animals during the day becomes filled with activity under the cool blanket of darkness. Notice the number of burrows you see in the ground—homes that are cool in the summer and warm in the cold basin winters.

Many ecologists claim that most of the country of southeastern Oregon and southern Idaho is not really a desert at all, but rather a steppe climate. The moisture in this region, they point out, is generally sufficient to support a greater volume (though not necessarily variety) of shrubs, forbes, and grasses than is typically found in the drier reaches of land that lie to the south. And certainly this is true. Indeed, were it not for the fact that most of the moisture in this region falls here in the winter, when plants are dormant and can't take full advantage of it, much of this landscape would not resemble a desert at all, but rather a prairie rippling with grass.

With that in mind, many of the walks that follow do indeed stretch the formal definition of desert. I use the term loosely, primarily for the frame of mind it invokes. What I hope will surface when you visit the places that follow is a sense for the fabulous economy that occurs in an arid land, the luster that a place takes on when it is so completely driven by patience, by exactness. Most of us would probably agree with the old notion that nature doesn't do anything without a purpose. But nowhere does this purposefulness seem more evident than when you plant yourself in a dry, thirsty landscape, where the margins of life and death have been shaved to such clean, fine lines.

Oregon

SQUAW CREEK

Distance: 4 miles
Location: Ochoco National Forest. Head north out of Redmond on U.S. Highway 97 for just under 6 miles, and turn left (west) onto Lower Bridge Road. Follow this for 11 miles, at which point you'll reach an intersection; the road going straight (north) is dirt, but you'll want to turn left (west) onto Holmes Road, which is paved. Follow Holmes Road for 2.2 miles, and then turn right onto Forest Road 6360. In about 5.1 miles you'll come to a Y intersection; stay left. Go 1.5 miles farther, turn right onto Forest Road 6370. Follow this route for 1.6 miles, staying to the left at the one Y intersection. Park your vehicle when you reach the power line crossing the road. Our walk begins on the same road you drove in on. (Note: This route is not appropriate for low-clearance vehicles or those pulling trailers, or after heavy rains.)

While the walk along Squaw Creek is hardly the most accessible in this book, it's without question one of the most delightful. To drop out of the high desert on a hot summer day into a secret stream gorge riddled with the sweet chortle of bird song and the cool shade of ponderosa is an experience you'll not soon forget. Upon reaching the stream channel itself, you can lazily meander downstream as long or as little as you like. This is in every sense, as writer Paul Klee once put it, "a walk for a walk's sake."

From the power line where you parked your car, continue to walk along the road you drove in on, following it over the lip of the

223

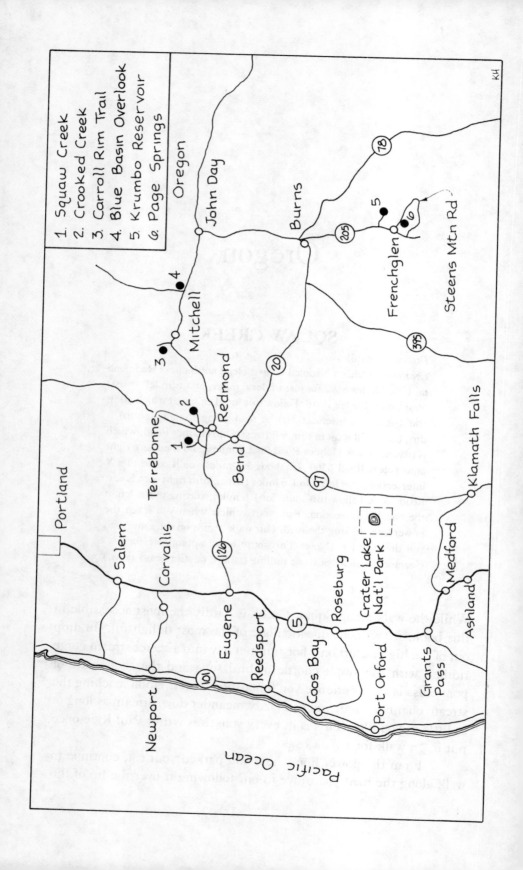

canyon rim and down the rocky flank that cradles the east side of Squaw Creek. Although at this point you'll be in the middle of a dry, pungent land filled with sage and juniper, 15 miles to the west you can see the high, rugged weave of snowcapped cinder cones and lava shields that make up the central Cascades. This is a portion of the peaks that is very effective at snagging the moist air running eastward from the coast—a catch that ultimately gives rise to thick, piney forests, and splendid rivers like the Metolius, Deschutes, and Squaw Creek.

Our road descends through rabbitbrush, sage, rice grass, and yarrow, and at 0.75 mile, passes through a lovely grove of mature junipers. The beautiful blue "berries" that you see growing on junipers are not really berries at all, but cones. These not only are used to make gin, but have been used around the world for a variety of food and drinks: with sauerkraut in Germany, as a coffee substitute in Sweden, and for certain kinds of beer in France. Juniper smoke, or incense, has long been used in sacred purification ceremonies by Indian peoples from the Puget Sound to the Great Plains. Noting that lightning never seemed to strike juniper trees, Cheyenne Indians once burned juniper branches as a protection against the fury of prairie storms. Though the list of medicinal applications for juniper is lengthy, one of the more intriguing ones comes by way of research at the National Cancer Institute, which is currently studying certain species of the tree to test their effectiveness in treating tumors.

At 0.8 mile the road comes to an end at an old campsite above Squaw Creek. From here you'll pick up a faint trail heading downstream. This quickly leads into a quiet mix of open glens spiked with buttercups, as well as woodlands of alder, ponderosa, red-osier dogwood, and willow. Incidentally, the name of this national forest, Ochoco, comes from a Paiute Indian word for willow. Like virtually every plant you see along this trail, the willow was of key importance to the native peoples who made their homes here.

Between 1 and 1.2 miles the willows are thick enough to make walking the trail difficult in spots, though if you stay with it, you'll soon find yourself in an open parkland filled with the hollylike leaves of Oregon grape. (Another, larger species of Oregon grape, *Berberis aquifolium*, is Oregon's state flower.) One of the alkaloids present in Oregon grape has been found to stimulate involuntary muscles, which may explain why the plant was used by some native peoples to ease the delivery of the placenta after childbirth. Today this drug is named berberine, after the plant's genus name, *Berberis*.

If you'd like to continue past this parkland, it will be much easier if you cross over to the west side of Squaw Creek and resume your walk downstream from there. At 1.8 miles on this western side, you'll come to one last area thick with alder and willow. If you plod through this, however, in fifty yards or so you'll find yourself in a vast open area. Here the west wall of the gorge has been pushed back 100 yards from the river channel, creating a sort of amphitheater. Much of Squaw Creek is lined with a lush tapestry of alder groves, many of them watered by several cool springs that issue from the base of the gorge.

Although this last open area is not the easiest of places to reach, those who make the effort to reach it will find it to be a perfect place to rest or lunch—or simply to contemplate the desert above them from the comfort of the cool, wet arms of an oasis.

CROOKED RIVER

Distance: 3 miles

Location: Smith Rock State Park. Head north out of Redmond, Oregon on U.S. Highway 97 for approximately 8 miles, to the village of Terrebone. Follow the signs eastward for 2 miles to Smith Rock State Park. Just after entering the park you'll see a Climber-Bivouac area and then a general parking area, both on the left. Continue past this second pullout for another 75 yards, to the next general parking area on the left. Our walk begins from here.

It must have been quite a sight. The air smelled of smoke and sulfur, and hot blizzards of red and gray ash poured down from the sky through the branches of alders, myrtles, and redwoods. Frightened oreodons—short-legged browsing animals with long, blunt faces— bolted through the forest and across the meadows until they could run no more, their lungs and nostrils thick with the debris that drifted through the air. Most of the ash that fell here was already cooled by the time it reached the ground, but occasionally there would come thick curtains of fallout that were still partially molten. When these hit the earth they would hiss and steam, and instantly solidify into solid rock. It was this latter kind of deposit, later sculpted by wind, ice, and water, that created much of the dramatic weave of colored cliffs and ramparts that now line the Crooked River in Smith Rock State Park.

There are several stories that identify the Smith behind Smith Rock, but the most widely accepted tale is not a particularly happy one. In 1863, a company of soldiers who had been sent out to show a little muscle to the local Indians were camped here along the Crooked River. One of them, a chap named Smith, decided to climb up a promontory for a look around. Unfortunately, no sooner had he reached the top than the boulder he was standing on gave way, and he fell to his death.

Today you're likely to spot a great number of better-equipped, more sure-footed climbers working their way up the sheer, hard face of not only Smith Rock but also the Monkey Face, the Dihedrals, Red Ryder Buttress, Picnic Lunch and Morning Glory walls, the Christian Brothers, the Monument, and Staender Ridge— in all, three splendid miles of rock face. A great many of the large number of climbers you'll see arriving here at dawn every summer morning will tell you this is the single best technical rock-climbing site in the state of Oregon.

Squaw Currant

While hanging hundreds of feet above the ground from a sheer slab of rhyolite may have its attractions, our trek through Smith Rock is designed to be a bit mellower. From the parking area you'll find a paved walkway leading northwestward across the canyon rim, past a fine cloak of juniper, yarrow, sagebrush, buttercups, and yellowbells. In 0.1 mile is an overlook that offers wonderful views of not only the rugged rock and riverscape lying far below you but off to the west, the snowcapped peaks of the mighty Cascades. Heading off from this overlook is a small dirt service road. Follow this sharply downward through juniper, ponderosa, and a smattering of red-osier dogwood, and almost before you know it, you'll find yourself in the arms of a beautiful river valley.

In moist, sandy areas along the trail look for clusters of horsetail—a spindly green plant with hollow, jointed stems and whorls of wiry branches. Like another kind of *equisetum*, the scouring rush, horsetail contains small amounts of abrasive silica, making it useful to native peoples and settlers alike as a cleaning and polishing agent. Folk medicine recognized horsetail as a diuretic, and as recently as a hundred years ago people were still using it to treat everything from kidney stones to dropsy. Interestingly, a Kootenai Indian legend tells us it was the trickster Coyote who gave horsetail its distinctive stripes. Having fallen into the river during one of his pranks, after a great deal of struggling Coyote finally managed to grab hold of a scouring rush growing along the river bank. Afraid that it would come out by its roots if he pulled too hard, he promised the plant that if it would just hold fast for him, he'd reward it with a handsome decoration. The horsetail held, and Coyote kept his promise. Using clay and charcoal, he painted strips up and down the stem, leaving the distinctive pattern you see today.

At 0.5 mile, after an enchanting walk beneath magnificent red, chocolate, and honey-colored spires and pinnacles, you'll reach a bridge over the Crooked River. Once on the other side, turn right, following the sign to Staender Ridge. From here we begin a lazy amble along the gentle sweep of the Crooked River, its channel cradled by banks thick with rabbitbrush, mullein, currants, wild asparagus, and wild onions. At 0.7 mile you'll reach the first of several beaver-gnawed trees, this particular one a hearty juniper measuring a good twelve inches in diameter. This location hardly fits our image of

Beaver

the beaver ideal: a remote, quiet pond surrounded by young deciduous trees such as willow, aspen, and cottonwood. Instead of being able to build their lodges out in open water, here the beaver must rely on tunnel-and-burrow systems dug into the softer spots along the riverbank. The gnawed bark of this old, gnarly juniper points to the beaver's remarkable ability to subsist on a wide variety of trees.

One hundred yards or so past this juniper is a beautiful old ponderosa with a bench underneath; as idyllic a daydreaming spot as you could hope to find. Ponderosas are among the most stately trees in all of western North America. Native peoples of this region didn't relish this tree as a food source the way they did some other conifers, but they did occasionally eat the seeds, as well as the sweet inner bark. In fact, you can still find ponderosas throughout central Oregon that bear deep, dark scars on the trunks where local peoples peeled the bark for food.

In 1.2 miles we reach our turnaround point, adjacent to a lush braid of meadow and marsh filled with cattails and horsetail. This is a good spot to see red-winged blackbirds and kingfishers, as well as golden eagles soaring along the edges of the canyon rim. Down-stream from where you now stand is a pair of nesting prairie falcons. These are among the swiftest of the great fliers, capable of reaching speeds of nearly 150 miles per hour when diving on prey or defending their nesting areas. The defense of the nest, incidentally, is something that most falcons take very seriously indeed, often fighting off golden eagles twice their size. Falcons do not build nests of their own, preferring instead to lay their eggs on protected ledges, or occasionally in the nests of other birds.

CARROLL RIM TRAIL

Distance: 1.5 miles
Location: John Day Fossil Beds National Monument, Painted Hills Unit. The turnoff for the Painted Hills Unit of the monument is located on the north side of U.S. Highway 26, 3.8 miles west of Mitchell. Once you make the turn, proceed along the entrance road for 7.1 miles, following signs for the Painted Hills Overlook. The Carroll Rim Trail is located just opposite of a turnout to the left that leads to the Painted Hills Overlook.

Those who manage to catch this trail on a sunny day at dusk or shortly after dawn are in for a real treat. At those times these gentle swells and hummocks of mineral-bearing clay seem to come alive with color—a volcanic rainbow of black, bronze, green, buff, and crimson. Wind and water have sculpted this sublime scene from the heart of the John Day Formation. This formation consists of layer upon layer of rhyolite ash, spewed over the land 30 million years ago from great volcanic eruptions in the southern Cascades. Within these stark layers of earth lie most of John Day's great fossil treasures, treasures that have captured the fancy of the world's greatest paleontologists for a hundred years. (Paleontology is the science that studies past geological periods by their fossil remains.)

If we could turn the clock back 30 million years or so, the scene in front of you would be very different indeed. The very wet rain forest of an even earlier time—a forest that received more than 100 inches of rain per year—slowly gave way to a more temperate climate, in large part due to the rise of the Cascade Range to the west. Could you have visited then you would have found a magnificent forest of alders, oaks, and dawn redwoods, as well as a variety of browsing animals, many of them unlike any creature you've ever seen. Today the fossil remains of this fanciful world—leaves and bones by the thousands—are found in abundance in the beautiful striated hills that lie before you. The John Day Formation is also, incidentally, the place where you'll find Oregon's state rock, the beautiful "thunderegg." Thundereggs were formed as circulating

Red-tailed Hawk

groundwater slowly filled small cavities in the compacted volcanic ash with silica. Often about the size and shape of a baseball, the inside of a thunderegg contains striking, colorful patchworks of quartz crystals and gray agate.

The vegetation along our trail to Carroll Rim is fairly sparse, though each species gives a little extra beauty to the dry skin of the desert landscape. Clumps of cheatgrass, foxtail brome, and wheatgrass soften the hills a bit, while blooms of prickly pear cactus, sage buttercup, salsify, yarrow, yellowbell, and sunflower lend splashes of color.

The trail rises steadily, and by 0.5 mile you'll be among rugged cliffs and rimrock comprised of a solidified volcanic ash known as ignimbrite. In another 0.25 mile is the wooden bench that marks the end of our walk. From this windswept overlook you'll be afforded magnificent views of the Painted Hills to the south, and farther off to the southwest, the juniper-laden Ochoco Mountains and the 17,000-acre Mill Creek Wilderness, located near the northern edge of the Ochoco National Forest. (The word Ochoco, by the way, was first given to a fine little creek that runs through Crook and Wheeler Counties. The most accepted definition of the word is that it means willow; even so, it may have first been borrowed from a Paiute Indian chief by that name who lived west of where you now stand.)

This high perch is also a fine place to look for red-tailed hawks. It's a treat to watch these striking birds of prey soaring on the hot summer winds, always on the lookout for small rodents on the ground below. In lightly forested areas red-tails will be found conducting their hunts in more leisurely fashion, scanning the ground while perched in the top of the tallest tree. Golden eagles, turkey vultures, and prairie falcons are also occasionally seen in the area, though none is as common as the red-tail.

BLUE BASIN OVERLOOK

Distance: 3 miles
Location: John Day Fossil Beds National Monument, Sheep
Rock Unit. From U.S. Highway 26, 33 miles east of Mitchell,
turn north on Oregon Highway 19. Approximately 2.3 miles from
this junction, on the east side of the road, is the primary information center for the monument, and one of the best places to get a
close-up look at fossils. Our trailhead is 3 miles farther north, also
on the east side of the road. (Note: Summer visitors should plan
this walk for the early morning or late evening hours. Carry
water.)

Simply mention John Day Fossil Beds National Monument, and
you're bound to light up the eyes of even the most jaded paleontolo-
gist. And for good reason. When it comes to the study of the
Cenozoic Era, which is roughly the 65 million years that stretch from
the end of the dinosaurs to the beginning of the last ice age, this
region holds what many scientists consider to be the most complete
fossil record in the world. Scattered throughout these warm, dry hills
are the fossils of saber-toothed cats and of ancient rhinoceroses.
There are the remains of the ancestors of our modern-day horse—
hardly bigger than a greyhound—as well as giant boars, elephants,
camels, horned gophers, tiny mouse-deer, and formidable-looking
"bear-dogs." Throw in the wide range of plant fossils located here,
including everything from avocados and palms to redwoods and
walnuts, and you can begin to sense the incredible richness of the
place.

But beyond stunning scientific value, there's also a striking
beauty to this monument. The Sheep Rock Unit is a sharp, austere
blend of blue sky and banded rock, split down the middle by the lazy
green twists and turns of the John Day River Valley. At the high point
of our walk, beneath the gnarled, pungent branches of an old juniper,
you'll find a log bench overlooking a wonderland of cliffs, spires, and
blue-green fossil beds. This is the perfect place from which to
consider the details of the 40-million-year-long climatic shift that
changed this country from a subtropical rain forest to the high,
windswept desert you see before you today.

Our trail to Blue Basin Overlook begins with a gentle meander through a garden of big sagebrush and snakeweed, spiked with bluebunch wheatgrass, cheatgrass, Idaho fescue, prairie stars, yellowbells, and sage buttercups. The gray-green tinge of big sagebrush is a very common sight across most of the dry country that stretches from central Oregon southward through the far reaches of the Great Basin Desert. The farmers who migrated into this region from the East in order to plant wheat or rye viewed big sage as nothing more than a nuisance—a tenacious hindrance to the progress of the plow—but early Indian peoples had no such prejudices against it. Many tribes made a tea from the leaves to ward off colds and stomachaches (just thinking of the horrible taste would cure me), while others routinely collected the seeds of the plants and ground them into flour. Many Indians still burn sage leaves to purify the air in their homes and sweat lodges.

Big sage sometimes lives to be 100 years old, and is extremely important to other plants and animals of the area. Beneath these branches various grasses and wildflowers are protected from trampling and grazing; Indian paintbrush often obtains the nutrients it needs to live by tapping into the roots of the sage. Western fence lizards and Nuttal's cottontails hide beneath the branches for both cooling and camouflage, while sage grouse can be found dining on the bitter leaves. Big sage is also a good place to look for sage sparrows—5-inch-long gray birds with small black spots on the middle of their breasts and a white ring around their eyes.

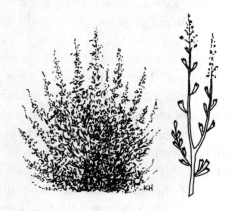

Big Sagebrush

Sage Buttercup

You may notice that many of the sagebrush plants along our trail have large balls clinging to their branches. Each year, various kinds of flies and wasps lay their eggs in the leaves and stems of big sagebrush. In much the same way that human skin responds to insect bites, the plants often react to this irritation by swelling, forming these curious growths, or galls. Once hatched, the insect larvae will feed on young plant tissue, eventually eating their way out of the gall.

The trail soon begins to ascend, rising slowly past a parade of highly eroded pinnacles, spires, and amphitheaters of rust-red, chocolate-cream, and honey-brown. Smatterings of junipers appear, especially in the bottoms of washes that are protected from the hot blast of the desert sun. At 1 mile you'll hit the first of several steep sections of trail, though none of these lasts for very long. There's a fine bench to rest on at 1.1 mile, and another waiting at the high point, just 0.25 mile farther down the path.

You'll have the option of either returning the way you came, or continuing around the high knoll to the right down a slightly longer, though no less beautiful pathway that eventually intersects the Islands in Time Nature Trail. At this junction, you'll turn left to get back to the parking lot. (Please note that some of this route is through private land; if it's to remain open to the public, hikers must stay on the designated trail.) Less than 0.25 mile after leaving the high overlook on this alternative route, you'll come to the edge of a small draw sporting a beautiful stand of ponderosa pine. This limited, but nonetheless stately little huddle of conifers has a wonderful way of taking the edge off the harshness of the surrounding terrain, especially if you happen to be here on a hot summer day. As you make your way down from here past the braid of gullies and ravines leading to the John Day River Valley, watch the ground for coyote and mule deer tracks. Also, stop and look up once in a while; sooner or later you're bound to see a red-tailed hawk or an American kestrel skimming the skies high overhead.

Mule Deer

236

KRUMBO RESERVOIR

Distance: 1.5 miles
Location: Malheur National Wildlife Refuge. From the town of
Burns, head south for approximately 50 miles on Oregon State
Highway 205, turning left (east) on a signed dirt road for Krumbo
Reservoir. Our walk is at the reservoir boat ramp, which is
reached 4.3 miles from State Highway 205.

Even though most of Malheur's sprawling 185,000 acres is closed to
the public for the protection of its wildlife, the few access points that
are available to visitors are wrapped in a weave of wild magic rivaling
that found on any bird sanctuary in the United States. In the wake of
melting ice in late February there begin the first movements of a
virtual symphony of birds—northern pintails kicking off the program, followed by tundra swans, Canada geese, lesser sandhill
cranes, and white-fronted geese. The waterfowl migration reaches its
crescendo in March, while migratory shorebirds such as willets, long-
billed curlews, and avocets claim center stage during the month of
April. By May we're well into yet another spectacle, this one featur-
ing literally hundreds of thousands of songbirds. In the past Malheur
has ranked among the top refuges in the continental United States
both for numbers of breeding waterfowl, upland game birds, fur-
bearers, and even big game. To date, more than 280 species of birds
have been observed on the refuge, along with nearly 60 species of
mammals.

The waters of Malheur are largely comprised of snowmelt,
carried here in the arms of the Blitzen and the Silvies Rivers (at least
in the years when agriculture doesn't suck the Silvies dry). Eight
thousand years ago glacial melt was running down the mountains at
full tilt, filling this entire basin with water. Today, however, the water
levels, and thus to some extent the number of birds, can vary from
year to year. Malheur's weave of marsh, meadow, and riparian zones,
nestled as it is in the middle of parched desert country, has been a
major stopover point and nesting area for thousands of years. Much of
the magic was severely threatened, though, when turn-of-the-
century plume hunters came here to kill swans, herons, grebes, and
egrets. The egrets were wiped out altogether. A storm of national

Sandhill Crane

publicity—a fair amount of it generated by the Oregon Audubon Society—helped push President Theodore Roosevelt into creating a new federal Wildlife Refuge System, of which Malheur was a part.

If you're up on your French, you might wonder how such a beautiful place like Malheur ended up with a name that translates literally into "bad hour." For that tale we need to go all the way back to 1826. In February of that year, Hudson's Bay Company trapper Peter Skene Ogden was camped north of here on what is known today as the Malheur River, having stopped to recover a cache of furs and other goods. "We camped on River au Malheur," he wrote in his journal on February 14, "so called on account of property and furs having been hid here formerly, discovered and stolen by the natives." (Thirty-three years later, at a point north of here near the narrows, a herd of cattle bolted on Captain H.D. Wallen of the Fourth Infantry, prompting him to name the water "Lake Stampede." Malheur, however, is the tag that stuck.)

From the boat ramp at Krumbo Reservoir head southeast on a faint path running along the shore. About the time this path begins to fade at 0.2 mile, look up to your right and you'll see a loose line of junipers on the slope above. Make your way up the slope, which makes a fine early-morning perch from which to survey the activity on the reservoir. What you'll actually see here on any given day, of course, depends entirely on what time of year you happen to be visiting. In spring you'll find excellent waterfowl populations, including pintails, mallards, gadwalls, green-winged and common teals,

Trumpeter Swan

239

Badger

western grebes, and coots. The beautiful tundra swan also passes through Krumbo in respectable numbers, and diving ducks like the redhead and canvasback often set up shop for the summer.

Krumbo is hardly less of a delight in the winter, primarily because it's one of the last places on the refuge to freeze. (If you've ever had the urge to go on an Audubon Society Christmas bird count, you could do no better than to find yourself at Krumbo.) On some days as many as 2,000 Canada geese can be seen here, as well as the beautiful trumpeter swan—a very large bird with snowy white plumage and a black bill. This open water is especially important to trumpeters because they don't migrate to warmer climates. In fact, there are times during winter when almost the entire Malheur population of trumpeters can be found right here on this reservoir. After teetering on the brink of total extinction, trumpeters were reintroduced to Malheur in the 1940s from a population at Red Rock Lakes.

If you're here in the summer things will not be as active as in other seasons. But if you watch the south end of the reservoir you're likely to see both redhead and canvasback ducks diving down to dig the starchy, nutritious tubers of sago pondweed out of the mud. Other ducks may flit in and out of the area, picking off insects that live among the leaves, as well as eating the "nutlets" that form as part of the plant's fruit.

When you're ready, continue walking on a faint trail that heads southeast along the bench. Once past the open water of the reservoir you can work your way down again to a path that follows along Krumbo Creek. (There may be nesting coots, redheads, and canvasbacks in the bulrushes and cattails, so give them as wide a berth as you can.) Our path continues eastward toward the Krumbo Creek Canyon, and you can basically turn around wherever you please. If birds are your primary concern, however, you'll probably want to spend most of your time under those junipers we passed earlier, where in the soft light of dawn you can look down on the comings and goings of some of the most beautiful creatures on earth.

PAGE SPRINGS

Distance: 1.8 miles
Location: Steens Mountain Recreation Lands. From the town of Frenchglen, located on Oregon State Road 205 approximately 61 miles south of Burns, head east on the Steens Mountain Road. In 3 miles you'll come to the turnoff for Page Springs Campground; turn in, and follow it to a gravel parking area at the far southern end of the campground. Our walk leaves from here on a path that runs along the river, marked by a "Desert Trail" sign.

If so far you've been reluctant to embrace the notion that deserts can be fabulous places, this is the walk to change your mind. Here the canyons of parched, ragged rimrock and the vast swells of sage have been softened by the magic of a beautiful river—a long, winding ribbon of green flushed with bird song and wildflowers. (Of course it's that wonderful, dry tumble of desert knocking at the door that actually defines the oasis; that makes it such a celebration of plenty.)

The river responsible for all this is the Donner und Blitzen—and no, it did not get that name because it's the secret winter pasture for Santa's reindeer. The truth is that one night during the Snake Indian War of 1864, troops under the command of Colonel George B.

Currey were camped along the banks of this river in a terrific rain-storm. Someone was struck with the very appropriate notion of chris-tening the watercourse with the German words for thunder and lightning, and the rest is history.

This beautiful area, and indeed the entire western flank of Steens Mountain, was once part of a sprawling cattle empire financed by Hugh Glenn and ultimately controlled by his son-in-law, Peter French. (Hence the name of the nearby village, Frenchglen.) Glenn was a wealthy farmer who controlled more than 50,000 acres of wheat land in California's Sacramento Valley, which in the middle-1800s made him one of the biggest wheat barons on the continent. One year Glenn got the notion to get into the cattle business. So in 1872 he bankrolled Peter French and sent him north into the Malheur country with 1,200 head of cattle and six Mexican cowboys. Over the next seventeen years French would create—some say by illegal land swindles—a cattle empire of 45,000 animals running on nearly 200,000 acres of land.

With lumber taken from the Blue Mountains 150 miles to the north, French built his outbuildings and corrals, as well as a stunning mansion for his wife. However, her definition of "for better or worse" apparently did not include living on a ranch in the middle of no-where. Before long French's wife divorced him and headed back to California, leaving him to his bovine dreams. Though at 5 feet, 5 inches tall and 130 pounds, Peter French was hardly an intimidating sight, more than a few people in Oregon felt the sting of his ruthless-ness. On the day after Christmas in 1897, one of French's neighbors decided he'd had quite enough of this little cattle king's habit of fencing off land that wasn't his, and shot him to death.

Our walk basically follows the lazy meanders of the Donner und Blitzen River, the broad ribbon of grass, shrubs, and western juniper gradually narrowing as you make your way farther upstream into the river canyon. As for shrubs and grasses, you'll see willow, thinleaf alder, Nebraska sedge, Kentucky bluegrass, scouring rush, reed canary grass, and red-osier dogwood. You'll see flowers as well: look for lots of beautiful monkeyflower, as well as lupine, salsify, and teasel. Two of these common flowers, both of them European intro-ductions, have rather interesting backgrounds. The first is teasel. It's especially easy to spot teasel at about 0.4 mile—a coarse, "weedy" plant four or five feet high sporting spikes of light purple flowers. In late summer large burrs form on the tops of the plants, which often persist until the following year. Settlers found that when dried, the long, curving spines of these burrs were perfect for carding or "teasing" wool, hence its common name. (Its genus name *dipsacus*, on the other hand, comes from a Greek word meaning "thirst"; this is thought to be a reference to the water that accumulates in the cups formed by the base of the leaves.)

The other plant, another rather "weedy" fellow, is salsify, a flower with thick stems that bear bright yellow, dandelionlike flowers about two inches across. New England colonists brought salsify over with them from Europe, where the roots had been used for centuries as a food source. The easiest way to describe the flavor of salsify root is to call it a blend of artichoke, parsnip, and oyster, the latter taste having led to another common name for salsify, oysterplant. (To make things more confusing, in the East salsify is sometimes called noonflower, because the flowers tend to close up about that time of day.) Over time a great many American Indian peoples also adopted salsify as a food source; some also used it to treat heartburn.

Continue up the canyon, past some fine music provided by house finches, meadowlarks, bluebirds, robins, rock and house wrens, horned larks, and various types of sparrows. If you're lucky, you might also spot a dipper bobbing in and out of the Donner und

Dipper

Blitzen River. These rather plain birds—some of John Muir's favorites—hunt for insects on the bottoms of streams, sometimes walking partially submerged along the gravelly bottoms with wings held out at half-mast for balance. Dippers are a cheery bunch, singing merrily even in the middle of wind and rain and thunder. The English know dippers as water ouzels.

At 0.75 mile the trail makes a swing to the east. For about 0.1 mile it follows a canyon wall lined with the mud nests of swallows, who make quite a nice living here feeding off the large insect populations found along the river. Just past the point where the river turns south again you'll cross a small stream that in most years you can jump over, and then another, which you cannot. We're going to turn around at this second stream. If you haven't had enough, however, by all means carry on! The trail continues its riverside meander for many more miles, offering you plenty of places to soak up the magic of this place—in a thick run of chest-high grass, by the cool quiet of a spring-fed pool, or beneath the thick, gnarled arms of a western juniper.

This beautiful walk along the Desert Trail was made possible by the tireless work of many people, including members of a national conservation and recreation group known as the Desert Trail Association. The Desert Trail is not limited to just the Oregon Desert; in

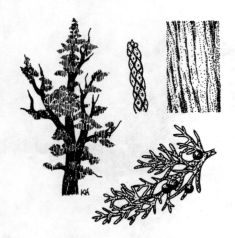

Western Juniper

fact, when completed it will stretch from Canada to Mexico, winding through what are arguably some of the most beautiful slices of desert in North America. Given the abuse and neglect of America's deserts in the past, the accomplishments of this group are a refreshing bit of progress in the long battle to preserve these precious ecosystems.

Deer Mouse

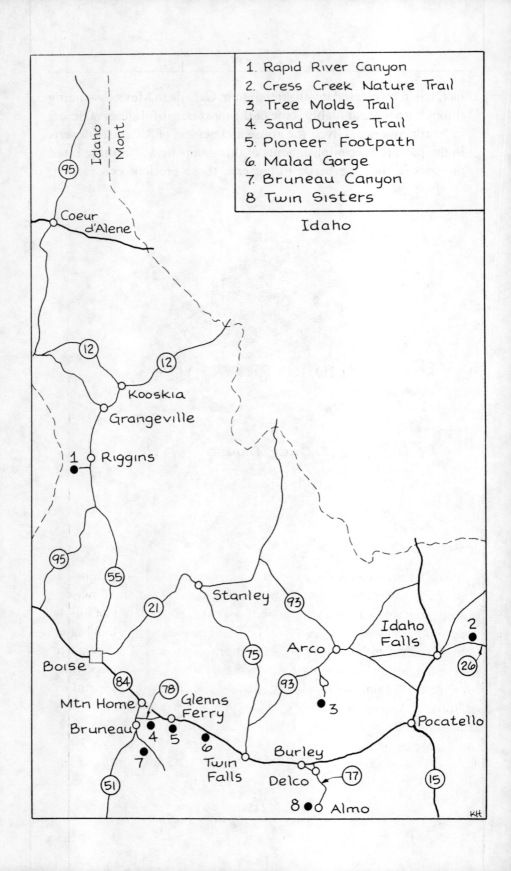

1. Rapid River Canyon
2. Cress Creek Nature Trail
3. Tree Molds Trail
4. Sand Dunes Trail
5. Pioneer Footpath
6. Malad Gorge
7. Bruneau Canyon
8. Twin Sisters

Idaho

Idaho

RAPID RIVER CANYON

Distance: 2 miles
Location: Nez Percé National Forest. From the town of Riggins,
Idaho, head south on U.S. Highway 95 for about 4 miles. Turn
right onto Forest Road 2114, following the signs for the Rapid
River Fish Hatchery. Our trail takes off from the fish hatchery, up
a rutted dirt road climbing to the southwest. (Please be sure not
to block any gates or hatchery thoroughfares.)

To call Rapid River a high-desert walk may be stretching things a
bit. Standing on the bottom of one of this canyon's serpentine twists,
you'll often find yourself surrounded by a thick green weave of life—
one you perhaps never would have believed possible when looking at
the dry, grassy hills visible from U.S. Highway 95. Lying out of reach
of the hot fingers of the sun, in a bottomland where precious moisture
is channeled from the surrounding landscape, this canyon is full of
surprises. Appropriately, Rapid River has been classified as a National Wild River, so that its singular beauty will be here to enjoy for a
long time to come.

Park your car near the fish hatchery, and walk up the steep
two-track that climbs to the southwest. In fifty yards or so the road

will end and the trail will take off, clinging to a bench high above the roar of the river down below. The kinds of plants you'll see along any given stretch of this walk will, of course, depend to some extent on the time of year. Spring and early summer visitors will find themselves shuffling through a pleasant mat of salsify, filaree, rice grass, bluegrass, and balsamroot. Notice how the north slope, on the other side of Rapid River, is cloaked with thicker robes of ponderosa, maple, and various deciduous shrubs than is the south side, which is much more thoroughly wrung dry by the rays of the sun. Each time you round one of these hills, watch how the vegetation changes. Serviceberry will show up in one ravine, its lovely cream-colored blossoms flying from the ends of its branches, while on some dry, rocky outcrop you will find little but greasewood—a plant as thoroughly accustomed to desert living as any you'll find.

When it comes to tracing how the Rapid River Canyon came to be, we have to reach back very far indeed. One hundred million years ago, the edge of the continent ran roughly along the line where the Salmon River courses today. Lying offshore of this ancient coast was a series of volcanic and sedimentary "island arcs," which eventually collided against the edge of the westward-moving continent. The metamorphosed sedimentary rock you'll be passing on this walk was actually a part of such an island arc. To add even more color—or confusion, depending on your point of view—Rapid River traces almost exactly a major thrust fault (a horizontal line where one sliver of the earth's crust was thrust over another). Indeed, the very location of Rapid River may have been controlled by this fault.

Much later this entire portion of Idaho, which was rather flat at the time, experienced a rather sudden uplift. As it occurred, rivers and streams that were once fairly flat and gentle-flowing began moving faster and faster, cutting through the rock like a knife pulled through a tub of butter, creating extraordinary gorges like Rapid River Canyon, as well as Salmon River Canyon to the northeast and Hells Canyon to the west. The lilting, rolling terrain you see at the tops of these canyons is the remnant of this old erosional surface.

At 0.5 mile you'll come upon the first of a long line of curl-leaf mountain mahogany, a small, twisted tree capable of living for more than 300 years. The curl-leaf mountain mahogany gets the first part

Wallflower

of its name from the fact that the smooth edges of the thick, leathery leaves curl under slightly. As for the "mountain mahogany" part, the only resemblance that this tree has to the mahogany of the tropics is both sport wood that is dark and heavy—so heavy, in fact, that it won't float. Curl-leaf mountain mahogany is found growing in some of the driest, harshest conditions in the West, from the sandstone canyons of Arizona to the dry eastern flanks of the Sierra Nevada; from the blistering Mojave to the high deserts east of the Cascades. One ingenious adaptation members of this genus have developed in response to trying climatic conditions is their long, straight, feathery seed. Once this plumelike seed falls from the tree and begins to dry, it twists like a corkscrew, actually drilling itself right into the ground!

Soon the trail leaves this dry slice of landscape, with its sporadic clusters of paintbrush, arrowleaf balsamroot, and wallflower, to join the thick green belt of vegetation that frames the river. By 0.75 mile you'll be rubbing elbows with ocean-spray, hawthorn, ninebark, and serviceberry, as well as a host of other plants that grow nowhere else in this canyon but here.

At a mile into the walk you'll see the number 1 painted on a rock outcropping. Continue just past this point, climbing to a small promontory that will afford you splendid views both up and down Rapid River. This blend of dry, soft-shouldered hills cut by a cool twist of water is pure Idaho. To me it seems one of the more light-hearted landscapes—a bright, yet spartan collage that brings together the very best of desert, mountain, and prairie.

CRESS CREEK NATURE TRAIL

Distance: 1.1 miles
Location: From the town of Idaho Falls, head east on U.S. Highway 26. About 10 miles out of town, turn left (north), following the signs for Heise Hot Springs and Cress Creek Nature Trail. (This turn is 0.3 mile past mile marker 352.) Follow this road north for 2 miles, turn right (east) for 1.4 miles, and then left (north) for 1.2 miles to the trailhead.

This wonderful little nature trail will take you along the shady banks of Cress Creek, as well as high above the lazy green meanders of the Snake River, steeping you in that magical mix that occurs when arid lands and riparian zones meet. Here are the hot, spicy smell of sage and the cool yellow blooms of monkeyflower, the hiss of wind, and the gurgle of water. The Bureau of Land Management has produced an interpretive brochure keyed to numbered posts along the trail; it's an especially fine publication for introducing you to many of the more common plants found throughout the area.

After a short, steep scramble up a dry slope peppered with juniper and tufts of crested wheatgrass, you'll come to the lush banks of Cress Creek. This is a perfect place to look for watercress, the perennial aquatic plant that provided the name for this delightful little stream. Watercress was actually introduced from Europe, brought here by early settlers who knew that its high content of vitamin C was an excellent preventative against scurvy. The plant

250

Golden Eagle

also contains significant levels of vitamins A, B, B$_2$, D, and E, and was once a very popular ingredient in spring herbal tonics.

From here you'll continue climbing through a dry, pungent mix of rabbitbrush, bitterbrush, squawbush, juniper, and sage, with stalks of cheatgrass, buckwheat, paintbrush, and bluebunch wheatgrass rounding out the vegetation mat. As you climb, scan the sky for glimpses of golden eagles, which are frequently sighted here. Much of a golden eagle's diet consists of large rodents, especially rabbits. This is why when the sagebrush community that rabbits make their homes in is cleared for agriculture, eagle populations may suffer. Though the shape of a golden eagle in flight is very similar to that of certain hawks, the easiest way to distinguish between the two is by

Turkey Vulture

the adult eagle's wing span, which is much larger—typically from six to seven feet across. Another large bird you may see here that can soar with the best of them is the turkey vulture. While mature golden eagles have an overall dark brown look, the turkey vulture sports a band of dark gray flight feathers capped by a black wing lining.

The views along the high line of this pathway are wonderful, the finale coming in 0.5 mile at marker post 20, high above the beautiful meanders of the mighty Snake River. Beginning in Yellowstone Park along the Continental Divide (a short distance to the northeast from where you now stand), the Snake traces a rugged route from the mountains to the high deserts before finally joining the Columbia more than 1,000 miles from where it began. A very old river, the Snake has had to do battle with hundreds of miles of volcanic rock in order to make its way across southern Idaho, and then cut northward through basalt, diorite, granite, limestone, gneiss, and schist to carve Hells Canyon—the deepest gorge in America.

Though you may not have heard very much about the history of the Snake River and its tributaries, it played a very important part in the development of the American West. Unable to divvy up the Northwest in an equitable manner, Great Britain and the United States agreed to occupy the area jointly for a period of ten years. Immediately after this agreement was reached, the British stepped up their fur trapping efforts in this area to a fevered pitch. Many historians feel their intention was utterly to deplete the supply of beaver, thus forcing the Americans to stay on the east side of the Rockies or in the Southwest. The southern and eastern borders of Idaho—the Snake River and its tributaries—proved to be center stage for this all-out fur trade war. By the late 1820s it had become painfully apparent that the British plan was working; most of Idaho's easy-to-get beaver had been trapped out, and the Americans had to settle for better opportunities on the other side of the Tetons. All this is not to suggest that it was only the British who were ruthless when it came to trapping. The Americans thought nothing of taking every beaver they could get their traps on, never giving a thought to sustaining the resource for the years ahead. While it may have been a change of fashion that decimated the value of beaver pelts, it was the trapping companies themselves that decimated the supply.

At 0.9 mile you'll find yourself back at the point where you got your first good look at Cress Creek. Soak up the lush weave of vegetation and the chorus of bird song one last time, and make your way down the dusty trail back to the parking lot.

TREE MOLDS TRAIL

Distance: 2.2 miles

Location: Craters of the Moon National Monument. From the town of Arco, Idaho, head west on U.S. Highway 20/26/93 for approximately 18 miles, where you'll see the monument entrance road on the south side of the road. This is the beginning of the Craters of the Moon Loop Road, a 7-mile tour road complete with several trailheads, interpretive exhibits, and a nature trail. Our walk takes off from the southern-most reach of the drive, at the parking area for the Tree Molds Trail and Craters of the Moon Wilderness. (A good introduction to this volcanic wonderland can be had at the Visitor Center, which will be on your left just after making the turn into the monument.)

One does not come to appreciate this strange landscape of volcanism by whizzing through it in a car. Indeed, the literally hundreds of square miles of basalt flows you see while driving along the Arco Highway can be more than a little intimidating—especially during the sizzling days of midsummer. This is the one place where even grandmas in their '64 Impalas just can't seem to help but put the pedal to the metal in a mad dash to the shady streets of Carey. Yet when you stop the car and start walking through these buckles and spatter cones and lava caves, you find a world that is not without its own special brand of enchantment. This is especially true in spring, when the monument is peppered with dwarf monkeyflower, bitterroot, arrowleaf balsamroot, mock orange, dusty maiden, eriogonum, and larkspur. There are, in fact, more than 200 species of native plants growing within the borders of this monument.

As you begin your walk, to your left will be Broken Top, while farther ahead and also on the left is Big Cinder Butte—at 6,515 feet, the highest cinder cone in Craters of the Moon. Rather than consisting of the lava from one giant volcano, the region before you is part of something geologists commonly refer to as the Great Rift—a fifty-mile-long band of vents and fissures running to the southeast. Covering more than 600 square miles, this is one of the largest volcanic regions in the world. Things really started hopping along the Great

Rift about 15,000 years ago, and so far the zone has managed to cough up at least eight major eruptions. The last of these was only about 2,200 years ago, making this the most recent active volcanic site of anywhere along the 400-mile-long Snake River Plains. (Given the history of these eruptions, it would not be stretching things to say that another eruption may not be far off.)

At about 0.2 mile into the walk you'll pass a small crater on the right side of the trail. To understand why this crater is here, we need to take a closer look at stages of a volcanic eruption. At some point in time, when this was all a flat volcanic plain, lava from deep within a magma chamber started throwing debris into the air not out of a hole, but out of a long crack, or fissure, in the earth. These initial eruptions formed lines of hot volcanic debris—sometimes called "curtains of fire"—that spewed hundreds of feet into the air. As the eruption continued, part of the fissure line was to be sealed off as the ejected lava began to cool over the top of it. After a time, the continuous line of eruption (that curtain of fire mentioned earlier) was replaced by several isolated vents. More and more of those cracks were sealed off, until finally all of the lava was coming out of a single large vent.

Lava blowing out of that one remaining vent was charged with tremendous quantities of gas. The pressure of the gas sent a single

Limber Pine

column of very frothy lava spewing out of the ground high into the air. When it reached its apex it began to fall, in what can best be described as a rainstorm of cinders that slowly began to build up around the vent, creating a cinder cone. The size of a cinder cone, incidentally, depends both on how long the eruption lasts and how much lava is blown out. Whether or not the cone ends up with a crater in it—as the one beside you did—depends on how quickly the eruption ceases. If that column of erupting lava stops quickly, then the material surrounding the vent will tend to fall in on itself, forming a crater. If, on the other hand, the eruption dies out slowly, then the vent will fill itself in, and no crater will be seen. Also, if it's very windy at the time of the eruption you may end up with an elliptical crater, since the wind tends to blow the cinders away from the vent opening.

A short distance after passing this crater, you'll find yourself walking in the company of some fine limber pines. No matter where you happen to see it growing, limber pine is a rather small, twisted tree with rough brown bark. It sports five needles in each bundle, those bundles growing from branches that are often so limber that they can be tied in a knot without breaking! (Please don't try this, however, as it doesn't always work.) This flexibility comes in especially handy at high altitudes, when high winds can rip through the tree's branches with brutal force, and heavy snows weigh them down for months at a time. Speaking of wind, as you pass these hearty fellows, stop for a moment and listen to the sharp rush made by the fingers of the wind running through the short needles. It's a wonderful strain, and it goes a long way in easing the harshness that seems to rise from the stark fields of lava stretching off to the west.

The mountains you see slightly behind you and off to your right are the Pioneers, Idaho's second highest mountain range. Lying just east of Ketchum-Sun Valley, these are spectacular mountains, highly glaciated and thick with alpine meadows, cirque lakes, and cool green huddles of subalpine fir. Quite literally, they are a world away from where you are now.

In 1.1 miles you'll reach our turnaround point, at a cluster of tree molds. As the sign near the trailhead explained, these are not molds of the kind found growing on your shower curtain, but rather castings of ancient trees made when they were overrun with rivers of lava flowing at 2,000 degrees Fahrenheit. As the trees burned they released steam, which cooled the surface of the lava enough that an impression of the tree trunk was permanently cast. There are both horizontal as well as vertical tree molds.

As you walk back, notice that some of the lava flow next to the trail has a bluish cast. This is part of what's referred to as the Blue Dragon flow. The colors result from the glassy surface of the flow, which contains thousands of tiny crystals that reflect blue light back to the viewer. Like the tree molds and the wildflowers that seem to shout out colors from the cracks in the rock, the hue of the Blue Dragon is just one more delight that waits for you in these miles and miles of hot black basalt.

SAND DUNES TRAIL

Distance: 5 miles
Location: Bruneau Dunes State Park. Leave Interstate 84 at either exit 90 or 99, following Business Route I-84 toward Mountain Home. When you reach Idaho State Highway 51, head south for approximately 16 miles, and turn left (east) onto Idaho State Highway 78. The entrance to Bruneau Dunes State Park is 1.7 miles east of this junction, on the south side of the road. Follow this entrance road for just over a mile to the park Visitor Center. Our trail takes off from here. (Note: Always fairly strenuous, this route can be very hot during the summer; if you plan to hike during this season, start your trip early in the morning and carry plenty of water. Trail brochures can be obtained in the Visitor Center, and are strongly recommended for this walk.)

The Sand Dunes Trail at Bruneau Dunes State Park is one of those wonderful walks that slaps the twentieth century right out of you. To wander along from wooden post to wooden post across a vast slice of trackless high desert, mats of rippling cheatgrass underfoot and the

Black-tailed Jackrabbit

burn of a hot blue sky overhead, is to find the antidote for a troubled modern mind. If after a couple miles the sheer vastness of this place doesn't get to you, then the slink of a coyote or the flash of a black-tailed jackrabbit probably will. Admittedly, this is a fairly strenuous walk, especially if you climb the crest of the dunes instead of walking around the base. But if you let your foot off the gas a little, if you waltz across this place instead of plod, you'll discover a mix of sights, sounds, and smells that are amazing indeed.

If we're to understand the dynamics of the dunes themselves, which are among the largest on the continent, we'll have to turn the clock back a long way. To begin with, the sheltered pocket of rock that holds the sands of Bruneau Dunes, a place called Eagle Cove, is simply the result of a river meander, cut by the Snake 2.5 to 3 million years ago. Wind blowing across the sand-laden plains carried particles of dark-colored basalt and light quartz into the cove, a process that continues to this day. About 15,000 years ago, however, the north shore of a huge, 600-cubic-mile glacial lake broke and caused massive flooding throughout southern Idaho. Most geologists seem certain that such floodwaters—flowing 600 feet deep in places—would

258

have washed away any sand lying in Eagle Cove; thus, the dunes you see here are thought to have taken shape since that time.

As mentioned above, much of the Sand Dunes walk follows not a path per se, but rather a series of wooden posts erected in the desert. (The section of the walk back toward the visitor center section can be rather tricky for first-time visitors, since the posts blend in rather well with the background. This seems especially true during evening hours.) At 1.8 miles you'll gain your first glimpse of the lake lying at the feet of the Bruneau Dunes. This cool water shimmering in the desert is certainly beautiful, and also provides excellent habitat for a variety of waterfowl and marsh birds. The surprising part is it got here by accident. Irrigation dams built along the Snake River caused the water table to rise, creating in 1950 the lake and marsh areas you see before you. Today the park sustains these areas through pumping. Perhaps the most notable consequence of this watering is that because it allows the growth of many plants that would not otherwise be here, what were once very dynamic, changing dune fields are slowly being fixed in place.

From this point, you have a choice of routes. You can climb the 470 feet to the crest of this 600-acre dune complex, pass the large crater at the top and then drop down to the east side of the lake, or simply work your way along the south shore of the water, keeping the dunes above you. Yet another option is to cut across the strip of land between the ponds and the west side of the lake—an area thick with tamarisk, scouring rush, Russian olive, and bulrush—and rejoin the Sand Dunes loop near the picnic grounds. (This latter route will cut about a half-mile off of your walk.) No matter what route you choose, spend as much time as you can spare around the lake and ponds. Depending on the time of year you visit you may see great blue herons, avocets, terns, coots, and northern harriers. This latter bird, formerly called a marsh hawk, is especially fun to watch, since it will often let loose with an amazing free-form display of rolls, dips, and loops. Some people refer to these antics as "sky dancing"—a term that seems wonderfully appropriate. Northern harriers hunt by both day and night, flying low along the edges of these marshes, eyes peeled for an unsuspecting mouse, vole, or kangaroo rat.

Bruneau Dunes is the kind of place that continues to grow on you. Listening to the autumn clatter of waterfowl on the lake, watching soft yellow moonlight pour onto the ripples of the dunes, or catching sand lily, primrose, bee plant, and pentstemon blooms spilling colors across this landscape are experiences not soon forgotten. What at first seemed a harsh, even overwhelming place now begins to show its soft side; begins to point to mysteries that, in all the world, only deserts can reveal.

PIONEER FOOTPATH

Distance: 0.8 mile
Location: Three Island Crossing State Park. From Interstate 84 head to the town of Glenns Ferry via either exit 120 or exit 121. There you'll find a signed road that runs south for about two miles to Three Island Crossing State Park. Once inside the park, continue past the information center and campground to an outdoor interpretive area with a covered wagon display. Our trail takes off from here.

August 9
This day we traveled five or six miles to the river, where we remained all day. Made several attempts to swim our cattle, but without success.

August 10
This morning we finally abandoned the idea of crossing the river; gathered up our cattle, hitched up our teams and took the sand and sage for it.

—PIONEER CORNELIA A. SHARP, writing of
the Oregon Trail at Three Island Crossing, 1852.

Of all the grand adventures undertaken by everyday Americans in the settling of this country, it would be hard to imagine any more dramatic than making the seven-month journey along 2,000 miles of Oregon Trail from the Missouri River to the green, fertile valley of the Willamette. The migration along the route started modestly enough in the early 1840s, but by 1847 nearly 4,000 emigrants took to the dusty trail; in the twenty years between 1840 and 1860 more than

50,000 people had landed in Oregon via the Oregon Trail. Thousands of others came west via ship, on a six-month journey around South America's Cape Horn.

The reasons people had for enduring such a journey to start anew in the far West were of course varied. A financial panic in 1837 had pushed a great many Midwestern farmers into serious debt; indeed, poor farmers from the Mississippi River region made up a great portion of those who migrated to Oregon throughout the 1840s. What's more, several seasons of terrible flooding occurred in this region from 1836 to 1849, giving rise to severe outbreaks of malaria. The West, which had gained the reputation of having a "healthful climate," became increasingly attractive. (Not that the trail was free from disease. A cholera outbreak in St. Louis in 1849 spread rapidly westward, leaving a long line of graves along the route.)

Taking the dream of Oregon and turning it into a reality was hardly a simple process. A good wagon made of hardwood, a cover, and a team of eight oxen would set you back about $400; if you preferred a six-mule team, you could expect the bill to run $400 higher. (One of the many absurd myths perpetuated by Hollywood is that Oregon-bound immigrants pulled their wagons with horses. Oxen were not only cheaper, but they didn't stampede easily, and could cover distances far better than any horse.) Of course, once you had your team, wagon, and canvas cover, then you had to outfit yourself and your family with supplies, a process that could easily run you another $200 to $300. There were food staples to buy, including flour, sugar, coffee, dried fruit, bacon, rice, and lard, and also equipment, such as a tent, cooking utensils, tools, candles, and soap.

When you packed all this into a four-foot-by-ten-foot wagon box, and then squeezed in whatever farm implements you could manage, there was hardly any room for the deluxe furnishings and late-night in-wagon confabs featured in episodes of "Wagon Train." In fact, in most cases space was so tight that unless you were very sick or very young, you walked the Oregon Trail instead of riding in a seat in the front of the wagon.

The typical wagon train left the Missouri River Valley in April, timing the journey not only to get to the coast before bad weather set in, but also to catch good grass on the Great Plains. (One reason for the many changes in the original Oregon Trail route was to access better grass and water.) While it's true that settlers did worry about attacks from Indians, in fact this proved to be far less of a danger than you might think. In fact, over the entire history of the Oregon Trail only 400 people died because of hostile encounters with Indians. Far more of a problem were the profound challenges offered by the land itself.

In that regard, perhaps no portion of the Oregon Trail was more dangerous than the section right here in southern Idaho. Having already endured nearly 1,300 miles of trail—typically in ten-to fifteen-mile chunks per day—the settlers reached these dry, vast sagebrush flats in July, when temperatures usually hovered over the 100-degree mark. Yes, the cool water of Snake River was here, but the canyons it flowed through were often so precipitous as to make it impossible to reach. Also not helping matters in southern Idaho were the sharp volcanic rocks, which routinely cut the feet of oxen and mules.

Our walk is a more simple journey. At 0.2 mile down the trail, when the path begins to double back to the interpretive area, continue straight, following a small dirt road that leads down to a riverside parking area. From here you can wander up and down the river bank, enjoying not only fine flushes of Canada geese, terns, herons, and ducks but also the strange, haunting daydreams that rise from these waters: of a long line of wagons snaking down the bench across the river; of precious mule teams suddenly caught by these strong currents and pulled under and drowned; of men and women kneeling on this bank giving thanks for having been delivered one giant step closer to a new life in the far West.

MALAD GORGE

Distance: 2 miles
Location: Malad Gorge State Park. From Interstate 84 west of
Twin Falls, Idaho, take exit 147 and follow the signs to Malad
Gorge State Park. Our trail takes off beside a large outdoor
interpretive area.

Located not even a good hop and skip from Interstate 84, at first
glance Malad Gorge doesn't exactly appear to be a pocket of tran-
quility. But thanks to the roar of the Malad River making a sixty-foot
plunge over a lip of basalt into the Devil's Washbowl, it doesn't take
many steps before you almost forget the long line of civilization lying
just to the north. Besides being a good cure for the 500-miles-a-day
driving blues, this walk is a great introduction to the complex workings of water both on and beneath the Snake River Plains. (The
Snake River Plains aquifer is one of the largest in the world: The
springs here in Malad Gorge alone produce 1 million acre-feet of
water every year.)

Springs occur in this region because both the Malad and the
Snake rivers have cut down below the water table. Still, the height of
the springs is such that you'll see more of them along the canyon walls
during winter, when the river is low, than you will during the high
runoff of spring and early summer. During spring runoff the Malad
River comes thundering into the north end of the gorge full of mud
and silt; it's amazing to watch how fast the clean water of the incoming
springs turns it clear again. The near-constant 58-degree temperature of this spring water produces a striking flush of plant life, lining
the inflow areas with lush rings of green. Because they tend to seek
out weak zones in the rock, these springs are actually helping to
excavate this and other nearby gorges.

Once across the bridge, make a left turn and follow the path
out onto what is really a pie-shaped peninsula of land. At the trail
junction in 0.8 mile stay to the left, following this peninsula clock-
wise around the point. When you reach a place where you can look
into the rugged drainage just to the west, you'll see a clear, spring-
fed pool, the edges stitched with bulrush, coyote willow, and gold-

enrod. (Unfortunately, only a portion of the water's beautiful green color is natural; algae is flourishing here in part because of chemical fertilizers entering in the spring.) This drainage, by the way, was carved by the backward-cutting of the Malad River, as was the one to the east, where Devil's Washbowl lies. In fact, the Malad River tried various routes to reach the Snake, always working along the weakest, most yielding rock.

Almost no one traveling on the Oregon Trail in the early years was inspired to unhitch his wagon and settle on these vast, arid plains. But little did most of them know how rich some of the pockets of this landscape could be. The Shoshone Indians, on the other hand, were living here on a permanent basis more than 7,000 years ago, fishing for salmon, collecting wild plants, and hunting big game. It's a shame that so many of us are coming to appreciate the special riches held in the arms of Idaho's high deserts, just as development is pushing them forever out of reach.

BRUNEAU CANYON

Distance: 2 miles
Location: Leave Interstate 84 at either exit 90 or 99, following Business Route I-84 toward Mountain Home. When you reach Idaho State Highway 51, head south for approximately 21 miles, to the town of Bruneau. Turn left (south) here onto Hot Springs Road. In 16 miles you'll see the entrance road to Bruneau Canyon overlook on the right; turn here, and follow the road for 3.2 miles to the viewpoint.

You will no doubt question my sanity at suggesting a walk in a region where you're greeted with the following sign:

WARNING

THIS ROAD CROSSES A U.S. AIR FORCE
BOMBING RANGE FOR THE NEXT 12 MILES
OBJECTS MAY DROP FROM AIRCRAFT

Mountain Lion

The truth is that the future of this entire magnificent river system, slicing through 800 feet of ancient Pliocene volcanic basalt and in places barely 40 feet wide, does not look good. Indeed, *American Rivers* has listed both the Bruneau and the nearby Jarbridge Rivers as among the most threatened watercourses in the country. The problem is the Air Force wants to expand its already huge 100,000-acre Saylor Creek bombing range to include these rivers and adjacent areas. More than 1 million acres of wilderness-quality public lands would be withdrawn and dedicated to low-level, supersonic bombing, including live ordinance air-to-ground missiles. Recreation potential aside, such a move would almost certainly wreak havoc with the mountain lions, bobcats, bighorn sheep, and golden eagles that now call this desert home.

This is one of those marvelous, little-known gems of the American West that offers visitors what can only be described as a sense of personal discovery, of finding a splendid place that at least for a few hours seems all your own. Curiously, it's precisely these kinds of areas that seem to be regularly commandeered for bombing ranges, nuclear waste sites, and other projects that generally abuse the desert ecosystem. My advice to you is to visit the canyon as early as possible. And if you can, do it early in the morning or else late on a summer evening, when the drone of jets will have died away, and the air will be filled with nothing but the roar of the Bruneau River rapids far below.

Besides the sheer splendor of Bruneau Canyon, this gorge has a fascinating tale to tell about the geological history of the country commonly referred to as the Snake River Plains. The walls of this canyon are actually the interior of the mighty Bruneau-Jarbridge volcano—a caldera that was spewing ash over hundreds of square miles perhaps 15 million years ago. The reason you don't see the caldera today is it was eventually filled in with ash, and later, thick flows of basalt lava. Some geologists consider this to be the beginning of the great Yellowstone eruptions that created a vast plain of rock, belched from the earth and later sculpted by the Snake River into the long line of enchanted canyons and rich riparian areas you see today.

One of the things that can make the canyons and riparian areas of the Snake so striking is their contrast to the parched, dry country that lies on either side. But looks are deceiving. Within this complex web of fractured volcanic rock, covered with its thin green skin of sage, is a tremendous underground aquifer. The amount of water you see pouring from the high banks at Thousand Springs fifty miles to the east is greater than what flows in the river itself further upstream. Contrary to the opinion held by the Los Angeles County Board of Supervisors, however, which is regularly overcome by grand illusions of diverting Snake River water to Los Angeles, there is really little surplus water to be had here. Indeed, many consider the Snake River and its aquifers to be already grossly overutilized.

It would appear on first glance that the remote, rocky folds and sheer cliffs of this area would make it a perfect place for nesting raptors, and indeed, prairie falcons, kestrels, golden eagles, and red-tailed and ferruginous hawks do sometimes nest here. But they are not as common as in the Snake River Birds of Prey Area to the northwest, which supports one of the largest concentrations of nesting raptors in the world. One reason is this area lacks a good mix of the native shrubs and grasses that provide homes for mice, ground squirrels, voles, and rabbits, all of which are regular entrées in the diets of raptors. (Managers at Snake River Birds of Prey have even begun to sow sagebrush seeds in an effort to bring back dwindling jackrabbit populations; this decline is thought to be a major factor in the current low populations of nesting eagles.)

This walk is a completely free-form amble along the rim of Bruneau Canyon. You can stroll for several miles in either direction, often without seeing another person. (If you wish, you can make your return trip along a dirt road that runs fairly close to the rim.) Access into the canyon is very limited, the only trail in the area—and a rugged one at that—being about three miles upstream from the overlook. You'll be glad you made this trip even if you do nothing but sit on the rim of the canyon and gaze into the wild reaches far below. This is a special place. And because right now it is teetering on the brink of destruction, it could use all the friends it can get.

Bobcat

TWIN SISTERS

Distance: 3 miles
Location: Silent City of Rocks. From Interstate 84 in southern
Idaho, take exit 208 and head south on Idaho State Road 27 to
Burley. From Burley, head east on State Road 81 for 8 miles to
Delco, and turn right (south) onto State Route 77. Follow Route
77 for 20 miles to the village of Conner, and then bear right onto a
road to Elba and Almo. Just south of the town of Almo is a road
taking off to the right (west) leading to Silent City of Rocks.
About 4.2 miles from this right turn is a major junction of two dirt
roads; bear left here, and in 2.5 miles you'll come to the Twin
Sisters Picnic Area, on the right side of the road. Our walk takes
off 0.1 mile past this picnic area on the right, along a small dirt
road running west through the high desert.

The stark, bold beauty held in the granite domes and towers of Silent
City of Rocks has been a surprise to visitors ever since the days when
California-bound pioneers on the Oregon Trail first rolled through
here in their covered wagons. "We were so spellbound with the
beauty and strangeness of it all, that no thought of Indians entered
our heads," wrote one pioneer in 1849. "A most wild and romantic
scenery presents to the eye. Rocks upon rocks, naked and piled high
in the most fantastic shapes," wrote another, three years later. The
California Trail and the Lander Cut-Off—both wagon routes that left
the Oregon Trail and headed for California—came together near
here, making this a busy place indeed. Some historians have estimated that more than 200,000 pioneers passed by this geological
fantasy land. Many of their names, as well as messages for friends
who would follow later, can still be seen either etched in the rocks or
painted in axle grease. (Modern-day rock climbers take note: given
the astonishing location of some of these names, it's evident that the
writers must have been hanging from ropes off the cliffs.)

   The formations you see here are granite. They were formed
inside of the earth from molten rock only about 3 million years ago,
long after the Rocky Mountains had been created. Most of the
formation, known as the Almo Pluton, intruded upward through a

much older field of granite known as the Green Creek Complex. Over two billion years old, the Green Creek Complex is some of the oldest granitic rock in the continental United States. At Twin Sisters, which will be on your right as you begin this walk, the southern pinnacle is comprised of the older Green Creek granite, while the northern spire is of younger Almo Pluton.

The fantastic shapes you see in the Silent City of Rocks, which is probably as great a mix of granite sculpturing as you'll find anywhere in America, are due not so much to the way the rocks were formed, but to how they were eroded. While still lying underneath the ground, this granite broke down into soil not evenly but along distinct fracture lines. The rock that lay sandwiched between the fracture lines was left basically intact. Then something happened to the plants growing overhead—perhaps they were burned—opening the way to massive erosion of the topsoil, a process that eventually left the intact rock between the fracture lines standing above the ground. Today weathering continues, water ever-seeping into cracks, and splitting off squared corners to reveal the smooth, rounded shoulders that lie beneath.

While it's true that much of this route can be driven, only by walking it will the fullness of this vast, quiet beauty come through. Especially on the return trip, it takes very little imagination to gaze off to the southeast and imagine a long line of covered wagons rolling toward the fabled riches of the California gold fields. Also good for setting the imagination spinning is the tale of the great stage robbery of 1878. As the story goes, two bandits held up a stagecoach on a run from Kelton to Boise, getting away with gold worth an astounding $90,000. One of the robbers was killed soon afterward, while the second was sent to prison. From his jail house deathbed, this second bandit supposedly confessed to having buried the treasure among five junipers in the Silent City of Rocks. Near the turn of the century someone did find a cluster of five junipers. In no more time than it took to round up a team of friends and some sharp shovels the digging began. Alas, no treasure was ever found.

When you come to a fork in the road at 0.8 mile, bear to the right. From here the road continues steadily upward across the sage flats, and at about 1.3 miles, fades into a trail that climbs through an open stand of juniper and piñon pine. The piñon produces a delectable nut—long a staple food of many southwestern Indian peoples, and for years a main offering on the streets of New York, where vendors sold them to people who longed for the pistachios and pine nuts of their homelands. If you're surprised to see the lovely piñon this far from the Southwest, you should be; this arid slice of southern Idaho is the northern-most limit of the tree's range.

The trail may become faint in places, but continues to climb up the main drainage (past a fence at 1.4 miles) until it tops a rise on the north side of Twin Sisters. This is our turnaround point, and from here you'll have a lovely, sweeping view northward into the granitic hoodoos and spires of "downtown" Silent City of Rocks. As if that were not grand enough, when you turn around to head back down the trail you'll have a fabulous look southward into the empty, windswept high deserts of northern Nevada. Such lonely vistas are an increasingly rare delight these days—an affirmation that at least in a few areas of the West, there is yet a wild, untrammeled landscape shining on to the far horizon.

Sage Grouse